September 1939: Hitler reviewing victorious German troops in Warsaw. (RG 200, Gift Collection; National Archives, no. 200(S)-M-77-49.)

WORLD WAR II

An Account of
Its Documents

This Special Edition
published by Howard University Press for the
National Archives Trust Fund Board
National Archives and Records Service
General Services Administration
Washington, D.C.

WORLD WAR II

AN ACCOUNT OF ITS DOCUMENTS

edited by

JAMES E. O'NEILL

and

ROBERT W. KRAUSKOPF

HOWARD UNIVERSITY PRESS

WASHINGTON, D.C. 1976

NOTICE: Contributions by the following persons are in the public domain and are not covered by the copyright to this volume: Jack Eckerd, James B. Rhoads, James E. O'Neill, Robert W. Krauskopf, Benedict K. Zobrist, Stetson Conn, Rudolph A. Winnacker, Meyer H. Fishbein, and Joseph Howerton.

Printed in the United States of America

Library of Congress Cataloging in Publication Data

Conference on Research on the Second World War, Washington, D. C., 1971.
  World War II : an account of its documents.

  (National Archives conferences; v. 8)
  Bibliography: p.
  Includes index.
  1. World War, 1939-1945—Historiography—Congresses. I. O'Neill, James E., 1929-
ed. II. Krauskopf, Robert W., ed. III. United States. National Archives and Records Service. IV. American Committee on the History of the Second World War. V. Title. Vi. Series: United States. National Archives and Records Service. National Archives conferences; v. 8.
D743.42.C66 1971   940.53′07′2   74-34112
ISBN 0-88258-053-1

Foreword

Since 1967, the National Archives and Records Service has held a series of conferences for the exchange of ideas and information between archivists and researchers. These conferences are designed to inform scholars about the wealth of useful research materials available in the National Archives and Records Service, as well as to provide an opportunity for researchers to suggest ways in which their use of these records could be facilitated.

The National Archives and Records Service, a part of the General Services Administration, administers the permanently valuable, noncurrent records of the federal government. These archival holdings date from the days of the Continental Congresses to the present.

Among the nine hundred thousand cubic feet of records now constituting the National Archives of the United States are hallowed documents such as the Declaration of Independence, the Constitution, and the Bill of Rights. However, most of the archives, whether in the National Archives Building, the federal records centers, or the presidential libraries, are less dramatic. They are preserved because of their continuing practical utility for the ordinary processes of government, for the establishment and protection of individual rights, and for casting light on our nation's history when subjected to the scrutiny of the diligent scholar.

One goal of the National Archives staff is to explore and make more widely known these historical records. It is hoped that these conferences will be a positive act in that direction. The papers of each conference are published in the belief that this lively exchange of ideas and information should be preserved and made available in printed form.

JACK ECKERD
Administrator of General Services

NATIONAL ARCHIVES

CONFERENCES

VOLUME 8

Papers and Proceedings of the Conference on Research on the Second World War

June 14-15, 1971/The National Archives Building/Washington, D.C.

Preface

In this volume can be found the papers prepared for and presented at the Conference on Research on the Second World War held on June 14 and 15, 1971, at the National Archives. This was the eighth of the series of National Archives conferences inaugurated in 1967 to reinforce the close relationship between archivists and scholarly researchers and to make the rich resources for research in the custody of the National Archives and Records Service even better known and more frequently used.

The Second World War seemed an eminently suitable subject for a conference in 1971. That war had generated a very large volume of records, most of which had come to rest in the National Archives. While some were still security classified, most had become available for research and many had, indeed, been used by scholars in writing books, articles, and dissertations that had increasingly swelled the bibliographies of the war. Finally, the year 1971 marked the thirtieth anniversary of what Winston Churchill aptly called the "Grand Alliance": the German attack on Russia in the summer of 1941 and the Japanese attack at Pearl Harbor near the end of that year had brought the Soviet Union and the United States fully into the war. The lapse of that much time meant that the first generation of students of the war was giving way to the second. The new generation of younger historians was already beginning to reappraise and reinterpret the war from their own perspective, the perspective of non-participants. For them the written record—the documents on the shelves of the National Archives—was, necessarily, all-important.

This conference differed from its predecessors in two ways. First, it took on the nature of an international conference, largely because of the work of the conference cosponsor, the American Committee on the History of the Second World War. Second, the conference involved for the first time the presidential libraries operated by the National Archives and Records Service. The international character of the conference was symbolized by the presence of participants from fourteen different nations and can be seen in the papers by General Zhilin, Henri Michel, and Noble Frankland in the pages that follow. The involvement of the presidential libraries was particularly appropriate: the Roosevelt, Truman, and Eisenhower libraries—which were all represented on the program—contain material of exceptional value for research on the Second World War.

The codirectors of this conference (and coeditors of this volume) were James E. O'Neill, who was in 1971 the director of the Franklin D. Roosevelt Library and who is now the deputy archivist of the United States, and Robert W. Krauskopf, chief of the Old Military Branch in the Office of the National Archives. The success of their careful planning will be manifest to all who read this book.

JAMES B. RHOADS
Archivist of the United States

Contents

III
UNFINISHED BUSINESS OF WARTIME DIPLOMACY

IV
MILITARY BIOGRAPHY

V
MAJOR RESOURCES OF THE NATIONAL ARCHIVES AND RECORDS
SERVICE FOR RESEARCH ON THE SECOND WORLD WAR

VI
ACCESSIBILITY OF SOURCES FOR THE HISTORY
OF THE SECOND WORLD WAR

VII
SCIENCE AND TECHNOLOGY IN THE SECOND WORLD WAR

VIII
WARTIME EMERGENCY AGENCIES

IX
RESEARCH FOR OFFICIAL SECOND WORLD WAR
HISTORICAL PROGRAMS

Illustrations

Introduction

In the early morning hours of September 1, 1939, German troops crossed the Polish frontier, and the Second World War began. Six years and one day later—and nearly half a world away—the war ended when representatives of Japan signed the formal instrument of surrender on the deck of the U.S.S. *Missouri* in Toyko Bay. As its beginning and end suggest, it was a "world" war to a degree that no earlier war, including that of 1914–18, had ever been. Moreover, it was fought on a scale and with a sophistication of weapons and techniques that earlier generations would have found impossible to imagine: by its end more than seventy million men and women had borne arms, and such devices as radar, missiles, and the first nuclear bomb had transformed the character of warfare. Finally, the Second World War was a "total" war, in which the mobilization of economies and ideas became as important as the mobilization of men and weapons, and the distinction between civilian and combatant became so blurred as to lose meaning.

A struggle so vast and complex produced comparably vast and complex documentation. Literally tons of official records were accumulated by each of the major participants. Complemented by the personal papers of leaders, they constitute a large and rich body of sources for the history of the war. Yet, even after nearly a generation of research and publication, their potential had not been fully exploited. Their very bulk was intimidating—both to archivists and to historians—and only slowly were they transferred to permanent archives and brought under the kind of archival control that could make them usable. In addition, most official records, including many of civilian agencies, remained under the bar of security classification for some years. By 1971, however, enough control had been established and enough records opened for research that a National Archives conference seemed appropriate.

Like all conferences in this series that on the Second World War was designed to effect a dialogue between archivists and historians, the custodians of the records and their principal users. In this instance an extra dimension was added by the cosponsorship of the American Committee on the History of the Second World War. Through their work the conference was broadened to embrace a significant number of participants from outside the United States, including the president and vice president of the Comité International d'Histoire de la deuxième guerre mondiale, M. Michel and General Zhilin, respectively. The addition of Dr. Frankland from the United Kingdom provided a symbolic reconstitution of four of the five principal Allied powers that had waged and won the war a quarter century earlier.

The papers in this volume are, with a few modifications made necessary or desirable by the passage of time, those which were delivered in the theater of the National Archives Building on June 14 and 15, 1971. They appear in the order in which they were originally presented. In many cases the papers were followed by comments or questions from other conference participants; these have been summarized in the Discussion Summaries. In addition a Bibliography has been appended to indicate the various guides, inventories, and other finding aids to the records and papers relating to the Second World War in the National Archives and the several presidential libraries.

Organizing a conference such as this (and transforming it into a published volume) would not have been possible without the assistance of a great many people. High on the list of those to whom we are indebted are the members of the American Committee on the History of the Second World War, especially Forrest C. Pogue, the committee's chairman, Arthur L. Funk, its secretary, and Louis Morton, all of whom agreed to appear on the program and who provided frank and valuable counsel on sessions and speakers. To the chairmen of the sessions, too—Robert Wolfe, John E. Wickman, Dean C. Allard, Paul Ward, Nathan Reingold, Stanley Falk, and Herbert E. Angel—we are likewise grateful.

Various members of the staff of the National Archives and Records Service, in addition to those already mentioned, also contributed their time and talents in making the conference a success. Mayfield S. Bray and William T. Murphy of the Audiovisual Division and Patrick D. McLaughlin of the Cartographic Division produced papers for the conference participants on the World War II holdings of their respective units. Frank G. Burke, Steven Lee Carson, and Rose Gabel of the Educational Programs Staff handled the thousand little logistical crises so deftly we did not know there were any problems. Our secretaries, Annette G. Baltimore, Johanna

W. Wagner and Jennie K. Lasko, together with those of the archivist and deputy archivist, Patricia E. Carr and Frances E. Brooks, kept the lines of communication open, typed the letters and manuscripts, and cheerfully stepped in to handle the inevitable last-minute emergencies. Betty A. Cooks of the Publications Division prepared the copy for publication and patiently tolerated our editorial idiosyncrasies.

Finally to the Archivist of the United States, James B. Rhoads, we owe a special debt of gratitude. He selected us as directors, asked us to produce the best conference we could, and gave us all the support, financial and otherwise, that we asked for. We hope the results justify that confidence.

JAMES E. O'NEILL
ROBERT W. KRAUSKOPF
Conference Directors

WORLD WAR II
An Account of
Its Documents

I

Historical Research and Writing on the Second World War

The first session of the conference was held on the morning of June 14. After welcoming the participants on behalf of both the administrator of General Services (who was unable to be present) and the National Archives and Records Service, the archivist of the United States introduced Forrest C. Pogue, chairman of the cosponsoring American Committee on the History of the Second World War, who served as chairman of the session. Pogue described the work of the American Committee and drew attention to the large number of conference participants from outside the United States. He then introduced Louis Morton, who presented the opening paper.

A captured Japanese photograph of the Pearl Harbor attack. (U.S. Navy; National Archives, no. 80-G-30554.)

LOUIS MORTON

Prologue to Pearl Harbor: Changing Patterns of Historical Interpretation

A knowledge of the causes of the Second World War is essential to an understanding of the world today and, unquestionably, constitutes one of the major concerns of historians of the twentieth century. It is altogether appropriate, therefore, that the opening paper of this volume should probe the problem of origins—in this case, of the relationship between the United States and Japan during the years 1937–41 and of the historian's perception of that relationship.

Specifically, this paper is concerned with the changing patterns of historical interpretations that have been put forward to explain the sequence of events that led from the Marco Polo Bridge to Pearl Harbor and to America's entry into the war. During the war and for the first decade and a half after its close, most accounts of American policy before the war fell into two groups, categorized by Prof. Wayne Cole, largely with reference to Europe, as internationalist and isolationist—terms that link the postwar interpretations to the prewar debate over foreign policy.[1] In part, these historical accounts were the product of the political controversy over the wisdom of the policies the United States had pursued during the prewar years; political considerations undoubtedly played a part in the interpretation of these events. To brand the foreign policies of the Roosevelt administration as shortsighted, or to assert that a Democratic president deliberately maneuvered the nation into the war, was not without benefit to a Republican opposition seeking to gain power.

As new generations of American historians entered the field, the old molds of debate were cast aside. The opening of new official and private records and the opportunity to search the documents of both the victors and the vanquished brought a more careful examination not only of the diplomatic background of the war but also of the political, economic, and

This is a shortened and somewhat different version of a longer paper that was prepared for the A.H.A.-Ford Foundation Committee on American-East Asian Relations. Its longer version was published in Ernest R. May and James C. Thomson, Jr., eds., *American-East Asian Relations: A Survey*, Harvard Studies in American-East Asian Relations, vol. 1 (Cambridge, Mass.: Harvard University Press, 1972). Copyright 1972 by the president and fellows of Harvard College.

social forces that had led to the conflict. The base of research was broadened, the scope of inquiry deepened. And with the passage of time came perspective and better understanding of Japan's needs and political behavior in the years before the war. The entrance of Japanese scholars into the field also brought changes in interpretation. First they amplified and later complemented the work of American historians. Then on the basis of new materials, they extended the search for the causes of their country's conflict with the United States into new areas, often with gratifying results.

Events since 1945 in China, Korea, and Southeast Asia have also undoubtedly contributed to the changing interpretations of America's prewar Far Eastern policy. The urgency of a better understanding of the nations in that part of the world and of the relationship of the United States to these nations has become once more as it was in 1941 the center of a passionate political debate. As new concepts of American involvement are sought and the limits of national interest in that area are painfully reconsidered by the nation, the search for the historical origins of our present dilemma assumes ever greater importance.

To understand these changing interpretations of American policy in the Far East, it is necessary to define first the internationalist and isolationist positions.[2] The former, represented by the works of Langer and Gleason, Bemis, Dexter Perkins, Herbert Feis, and others may be summarized as follows: President Roosevelt and many of his principal advisors viewed Japanese expansion as a threat to world order, to the territorial integrity of China and to America's interest in the Far East, but they were forced to proceed cautiously because of strong isolationist sentiment and America's military unpreparedness in the face of a growing crisis in Europe. Moderation failing, the United States adopted a stronger policy, moving from diplomatic protest to open aid to China and finally to economic sanctions in the hope that firmness might prevail where persuasion had not. In its negotiations with Tokyo and conversations with the Japanese emissaries in 1941, the State Department and the president, it is said, acted in good faith, making every effort to preserve the peace. These efforts failed, according to the traditionalists, because of Japanese obduracy and insistence on continuing the war in China and expanding into Southeast Asia. The sudden and unexpected attack on Pearl Harbor that brought negotiations to a close was therefore in the traditional view an unprovoked act of treachery by Japan.

The isolationist historians or revisionists of that period (a group that included originally Charles Beard, Harry Elmer Barnes, and Charles Tansill) found much to criticize in the policies of the Roosevelt administration.[3] In general, they argued that American participation in the war had been avoidable and had been brought about through either blundering or sinister intention by a policy that deceived the American public and provoked Japan. Roosevelt had erred in his support of China and by imposing on Japan intolerable economic pressure. During the negotiations with Japan, the revisionists argued, Roosevelt and the State Department had made unreasonable demands and had rejected reasonable proposals for a settlement. Hull's reply in November 1941 to the last Japanese proposal they termed an ultimatum. Deliberately or unintentionally, Roosevelt had invited the attack at Pearl Harbor by a series of moves that left Japan little choice but war. The revisionists characterized America's prewar policy as shortsighted at best and disastrous at worse. It had unnecessarily involved the United States in a long and costly war on two fronts, cut off a lucrative trade with Japan, and committed the United States to a decadent and corrupt regime in China and to the defense of colonial interests in Southeast Asia.

More recently, a new generation of American scholars, many using original Japanese sources, had begun to dispute the traditional interpretation. In a sense, these historians were revisionists. But the arguments of the early revisionist writers like Beard and Tansill held little appeal for them. Instead of picturing Japan as a country under a totalitarian regime dominated by a conspiratorial military clique pursuing an aggressive program of expansion, they saw Japanese policy as an effort to achieve and maintain security and economic self-sufficiency. For a country as poor as Japan, the only way to achieve this goal was through control of strategic areas necessary for the defense of the homeland and of territories capable of supplying the resources required to maintain its military forces in peace and war—in short, a program of expansion. Thus Japanese policy was, in the view of these new revisionists, not the result of a military conspiracy but a pursuit of legitimate national aims by the leaders of Japan, civilian as well as military. Representing the basic aims of the nation for survival and economic well-being, this policy could be neither compromised nor negotiated.

David J. Lu was one of the first to review Japanese policy in the light of Japanese as well as Western material.[4] Lu argues that the immediate cause of the war was Japan's unwillingness to withdraw its troops from China and America's uncompromising stand on the freezing order and oil embargo. He asserts also that the Japanese army, which pressed for an expansionist policy, totalitarian control, and a planned economy, was largely to blame for the conflict. To the army, he claimed, China represented a power base that made possible its control of the nation. And like others who have studied Japanese policy, Lu finds that the machinery for decision making in Japan was inflexible and cumbersome, failing to provide the means for reconciling contradictory views. But he does not blame the military alone for prewar Japanese policy. The conservative wing of the business community, he says, willingly supported the aggressive policies of the military, as did other elements of the ruling class.

Unlike most other students of the period, Lu argues that the Tripartite Pact was really directed against the Soviet Union, not the United States, and was used by the American policy makers simply to identify Japan with Hitler and the hated Nazis. It was, he says, never really an issue and was only made so by Roosevelt and Hull to manipulate American public opinion. With respect to the effect of economic sanctions on Japan's decision for war, Lu agrees that these sanctions were of first importance but believes that their imposition was unfortunate and the timing wrong. Had the embargo been imposed on Japan in July 1937, he writes, "the result might have been entirely different."[5]

Robert Butow's study of Tojo, published in the same year as Lu's volume, focuses on the responsibility of the military for the Japanese decision to go to war. Skillfully blending history and biography, Butow, who had earlier written perhaps the best analysis of Japan's decision to surrender, traces the role of the Japanese army in the events leading to war through the career of General Tojo. While not denying the importance of senior military men, Butow argues that figures of lesser rank, the middle echelon officers in the general staff and war ministry, working behind the scenes, often played a decisive role in the unfolding drama.

Alvin D. Coox, in his study of the Japanese military, comes to virtually the same conclusion. Hostilities in China, he asserts, resulted from a corrosion of discipline within the army which opened the way for subordinate officers to wield considerable influence.[6]

James B. Crowley deals with the Japanese military also, but in a broader context than either Butow or Coox. His work is concerned primarily with the roots of Japanese foreign policy from 1930 to 1938, with policy making as well as with policy. Boldly, Crowley challenges two of the hallowed generalizations of the traditional interpretation of the origins of the Pacific War—first, that the basic cause of the war was Japan's aggressive foreign policy after 1931; and second, that this policy was the work of a military clique that seized political power after 1931 through a program of terror, political assassination, and conspiracies. The Japanese quest for *hegemony* in East Asia was not a conspiracy, he says, but a pursuit of security and economic strength. It was the pursuit of these valid national aims that led Japan ultimately, he argues, to the war in China.[7]

The most comprehensive reassessment of American Far East policy is Dorothy Borg's study of the years 1933 to 1938.[8] Borg views the Marco Polo Bridge incident in July of 1937 as a turning point, not so much because U.S. policy altered sharply at that time, but because Japan by this move created a new situation that challenged world peace. She rejects the traditional idea that President Roosevelt wanted to take strong action but was prevented from doing so by isolationist sentiment. Although the United States failed to take a firm stand against Japanese aggression in 1937, Secretary Hull condemned the move in strong moral terms, stressing the sanctity of treaties and the necessity of abstaining from force. Linking the Japanese move to world peace, he had invited other nations to take a similar position, but he avoided collective action. By the end of the year 1938, the aims of U.S. policy had changed significantly, according to Borg. The Japanese attack on China was now regarded as involving larger issues than the dispute between China and Japan, issues, Borg writes, which were intimately connected with the welfare of all nations and might precipitate a concerted effort on the part of the Axis powers to overwhelm the European democracies.[9]

One of the most perceptive and broad-ranging analyses of the prewar period is Akira Iriye's *Across the Pacific*.[10] The distinguishing characteristic of Iriye's work is his treatment of the subject as a four-way relationship involving the domestic and foreign policies of the major powers in the Far East—China, Japan, Russia, and the United States—based upon a knowledge of the sources and languages of these countries. The result of this kind of comparative history is revealing and suggestive. American concern, says Iriye, was less with China than with Japanese aggression and its global implications in which the United States coupled moral globalism with political universalism. The Japanese, he says, recognized the possibility of a war with the United States, but did not believe their actions in China would precipitate hostilities. The Chinese, for their part, he says, looked to a Japanese-American war as a solution to their difficulties and maintained this belief even when American aid was not forthcoming. Unlike the traditionalist historians, Iriye denies that Japanese aggression in China was the root cause of the Pacific War. Rather it was Japan's decision to move southward in 1938 that brought the United States and Japan into sharp conflict. There was a connection, of course, between Japan's policy in China and in Southeast Asia. Japan required the resources of Southeast Asia to carry the war in China to a successful conclusion, which once accomplished would release additional forces for expansion to the south. Japan's leaders, said Iriye, recognized that the southern advance posed real risks but felt they were necessary to secure the resources needed for such a conflict. And after 1939, with the outbreak of war in Europe, the risks seemed less. German victories in Europe and Britain's struggle for survival thus opened the way for the southward advance.

Japanese historical writing on the origins of the Pacific War in the immediate postwar period tended to follow the American lead, translating or paraphrasing those studies that held greatest appeal.[11] Most Japanese historians accepted the dominant American view that war with the United States had come as a result of Japanese aggression in China. Others found the work of the revisionists more attractive and took solace in studies that were critical of American policies in general.[12] But both groups displayed a preoccupation with the role of the military and naval officers in Japanese politics and their influence in leading the nation into war. More recently a group of young Japanese scholars, on the basis of fresh and hitherto unused materials, have begun to reexamine Japanese policy during the 1930s. The result has been reinterpretation of many of the accepted views of the immediate postwar years. The most complete Japanese account of the entire period is the eight-volume *Road to the Pacific War* prepared by a group of scholars working under the aegis of the Japanese International Relations Association.[13] Based on the records of the former military agencies, archives of the foreign office and other government offices, unpublished private papers, and interviews with many Japanese leaders, these volumes cover Japanese foreign policy from Manchuria to Pearl Harbor. Altogether fourteen authors, among whom were some of the ablest diplomatic historians in Japan, participated in the project. Throughout there is an emphasis on military matters and a concern with the role of the military in decision making, one of the major problems that confronts a student of prewar Japanese policy. Among the contributors to this series was Chihiro Hosoya, author of an earlier important study on the Siberian expedition.

In a paper read at the 1966 meeting of the American Historical Association, Hosoya identified two factions in the American government involved in the making of policy in the period before the war: a "hard-line" group consisting of Hornbeck, Stimson, Morgenthau, and others, and a "soft-line" group among whom he placed Hull and Sumner Welles.[14] The hard-line faction, he stated, argued for forceful measures against Japan and the imposition of economic sanctions to deter Japan from aggression, a policy that eventually triumphed over the soft-line faction. Hosoya's analysis was not exactly original, but his point that the policy urged by the hard-line faction had the opposite effect from that intended was important. Instead of deterring the Japanese, the hard-line policy only stiffened them in their determination to move south. Believing they had no choice but submission or war, they opted for war. Thus the Americans, because of a mistaken policy, had forced Japan into war. Hosoya recognized the Japanese decision was irrational and attributed it in large part to the influence of the middle echelon officers, who were less responsible than their superiors, and to the weakness of the decision-making process. Hosoya's argument was deliberately framed in contemporary cold war terms. His characterization of American policy makers as hard-liners and soft-liners carried unmistakable connotations to his audience of hawks and doves. Even more interesting was his description of American policy as a policy of deterrence. For Hosoya the lesson of 1941 was plain—the hawks had failed. Instead of deterring the Japanese, the hard-line policy had escalated the conflict and led finally to war.

This analogy between 1941 and the postwar period is not an unreasonable one. Others have noted it and drawn a similar lesson. Nobutaka Ike also described American policy in the prewar period as a policy of deterrence. That it failed to deter the Japanese in 1941 seemed to him to demonstrate that there are definite limits to the effectiveness of threats as a deterrent against one nation by another, and he thought the experience of 1941 cast serious doubts on the validity of the theory of deterrence developed during the 1950s.[15] Russian and Chinese historiography, as well as much Japanese historical writing on the 1930s, is, as one would expect, Marxist in character, although Marxist interpretations of the period are by no means limited to the historians of those countries. In Marxist works the United States is pictured as one of a number of capitalist nations, albeit the most powerful, exploiting China for its own ends. Inevitably, the capitalist countries struggled for supremacy in China and during the 1930s, according to the Marxist view, this struggle narrowed to a contest between Japan and the United States. Some Marxist historians assert that the United States encouraged Chiang Kai-shek to submit to Japan so that the two could divide China between them. Others, that the United States encouraged Chinese resistance to Japan to gain the Chinese market for itself. Another view is that the United States opposed Japan's advance to the south because it wanted the Japanese to move north against the Soviet Union.[16]

An example of Marxist interpretation is D. J. Goldberg's study of Japan's foreign policy published in Moscow in 1959.[17] The driving force behind Japanese aggression, says Goldberg, was pressure from the monopoly bourgeoisie whose aspirations were fueled by concessions made by Western powers, usually at the expense of China and of the Soviet Union. When these concessions were no longer forthcoming, Japanese capitalists pushed for a program that would give them what they wanted even at the risk of war. The United States, he says, hoped to profit from a long war between China and Japan that would weaken the latter and give American capitalism a monopoly of the Chinese market, the real aim of American policy in China. In one respect, the inevitability of the clash between American policy in China and Japanese imperialism, this interpretation was not very different from that of some American writers. Criticism of American prewar policy in the Far East has come also from the New Left. Non-Marxist in nature, this Leftist interpretation places heavy reliance on American economic interest in the Far East. Illustrative of this point of view is Noam Chomsky's essays in his book *American Power and the New Mandarins*.[18] In expanding her influence on the continent, Chomsky asserts, Japan was merely following the traditional imperialist policies of the Western powers. When this policy challenged America's position in Asia, the Roosevelt administration took even more stringent measures to protect American economic and political hegemony in China. Opposed at every turn by the Americans, the Japanese turned to Germany and Italy, and when denied the materials they needed, turned southward. During the conversations with Japan's emissaries in 1941 the United States, he says, made the Tripartite Pact a major issue when in fact it was not. American terms for a settlement were such that Japan would have had to abandon its legitimate interests and aims in Asia and become "a mere subcontractor in the emerging American world system."[19] Aware that it could not win, but hoping for a negotiated peace, Japan chose war rather than accept second-power status and American domination.

Though not himself a historian, Chomsky based his work on a wide reading of the historical literature on the subject, with heavy reliance on Paul Schroeder's scholarly study of the Axis alliance and its effect on relations between the United States and Japan. Sharply critical of Hull's legalistic and moralistic approach to Japan, Schroeder argues that a more conciliatory attitude, especially on the China question, could have produced a settlement and avoided war.[20] The evidence he and others present for their criticism of American Far East policy provides Chomsky with a scholarly basis for his study. More representative of the New Left historical scholarship is the work of Lloyd Gardner, Barton Bernstein, Gar Alperowitz, or Gabriel Kolko. Intellectual godfather of this school of historical thought is William A. Williams who taught for many years at Wisconsin. In a series of original and thought-provoking volumes, Williams offers a view of American society and foreign policy that has had a profound effect on the New Left historians.[21] It is the view of a small agrarian nation expanding first to its continental limits and then, after 1890 when the frontier was closed and the nation industrialized, moving outward beyond the seas in search of raw materials in markets—in short, the Turner thesis industrialized and globalized. A mark of Williams's work and that of many of his students is an emphasis on economic factors and on the relationship between the domestic issues of an industrial society and its foreign policy.

Illustrative of this approach is Lloyd Gardner's *Economic Aspects of New Deal Diplomacy*. Like other New Left writers, Gardner is unwilling to accept at face value the liberals' view of the war as a crusade against the evil forces of fascism, and finds in the concern for overseas trade in the event of a Nazi victory and other economic factors an important basis for American foreign policy. Having decided "that the country could not achieve its destiny in a closed world dominated by the Axis," he writes, "the Roosevelt Administration had to accept political commitments to restore an open-world society."[22] But Gardner does not charge Roosevelt, as some others have, with going to war in order to redeem the failures of the New Deal. Though the New Left historians have not fully explored the origins of the war or the wartime strategy, they have focused attention on the relationship between domestic problems, foreign policy, and military strategy and, in that sense, have performed a valuable service indeed.

It would seem that with so voluminous and diverse a literature for so brief a period there would be little left for the historian to do. But there are many questions for which we have no answers and many areas that need to be explored further. For example, we know comparatively little about the relationship of events in Europe and elsewhere to American and Japanese policy, both before and during the war. There are several excellent studies of German policy in the Far East, but there is certainly room for more work in this field.[23]

Nicholas Clifford has recently published a study of British policy in the Far East, and there may be a rich harvest for enterprising students in the recently opened British archives for the period.[24] As one of the major powers in the Far East, Soviet policy has been studied extensively, but the effect of its policies on American relations in the area remains obscure.[25] As for France and other European nations, there is little available.[26] China is a special problem. There has been some excellent work on U.S. policy in China, notably the recent study of Stilwell by Barbara Tuchman, but most of this work is based on Western sources.[27] Chinese sources are difficult to obtain, the language is particularly difficult for Western scholars, and the victory of the Chinese Communists in 1949 has made difficult any historical writing on China that does not conform to a Marxist-Leninist interpretation.[28]

The role of the military in Japan has been extensively researched,[29] but not that of the American military, apparently on the assumption that the military in the United States played only a subordinate role in policy formulation. Was this actually the case? Thanks to the historical program of the services, we have a number of excellent studies of prewar planning,[30] but little except indirect evidence to indicate to what extent they were able to influence executive and congressional decisions. During the 1920s and 1930s the military planners complained frequently that they lacked policy guidance on which to base their plans, and they offered schemes from time to time to remedy this lack.[31] After 1935 such complaints were rarely heard, and by 1939 they had virtually ceased. Were there other ways in which the military influenced policy? What policies did they favor, and why? Were there internal struggles in the services over policy? Were there cliques with different views on strategy that competed for influence? What was the role of the middle echelon officers? How about interservice competition? To what extent did strategic plans reflect a particular view of the world or a particular policy? Were strategic plans formulated and supported as much with an eye to congressional appropriations or the needs of the services as to political and strategic requirements?[32] We know something—not nearly enough—about the role of the navy in the Pacific for the early period, but very little for the years immediately preceding the Pearl Harbor attack, and less about the army's role.[33]

Despite the great amount of research in the United States and Japan, there still remain a number of important areas of disagreement among scholars in the field, disagreements that may never be resolved. These disagreements reflect the differences in interpretation that appeared in the immediate postwar period between those who had supported President Roosevelt's foreign policy, Far East policy, and those who had opposed it; between an internationalist or a traditional interpretation and a revisionist interpretation. But these terms have begun to lose their meaning. A new generation of historians in Japan and the United States viewing these events with more detachment and from a different perspective from their elders have produced fresh and challenging interpretations of the period. These historians may not settle the outstanding controversies, or answer the questions that have not been answered, but there is every reason to believe that we can look forward to continued vigorous research and new insights on the events that led to Pearl Harbor.

Notes

1. Wayne S. Cole, "American Entry into World War II: A Historiographical Appraisal," *Mississippi Valley Historical Review* 48 (March 1957): 596–617. See also Louis Morton, "Pearl Harbor in Perspective, A Bibliographical Survey," U.S. Naval Institute, *Proceedings* 81 (April 1955): 461–68; Robert Ferrell, "Pearl Harbor and the Revisionists," *Historian* 1955, pp. 215–33.
2. William L. Langer and S. Everett Gleason, *The Challenge to Isolation, 1937–1940* (New York: Harper & Row, 1952); *The Undeclared War, 1940–1941* (New York: Harper & Row, 1953); Walter Millis, *This Is Pearl* (New York: William Morrow & Co., 1947); Basil Rauch, *Roosevelt, From Munich to Pearl Harbor* (New York: Creative Age Press, 1950); Ernest K. Lindley, *How War Came* (New York: Simon and Schuster, 1942); S. F. Bemis, "First Gun of a Revisionist: Historiography for the Second World War," *Journal of Modern History* 19 (March 1947): 55–59; S. E. Morison, *The Rising Sun in the Pacific* (Boston: Little, Brown & Co., 1948) and "Did Roosevelt Start the War? History Through a Beard," *Atlantic Monthly* 182 (August 1948): 91–97; Herbert Feis, *The Road to Pearl Harbor* (Princeton: Princeton University Press, 1950) and "War Came at Pearl Harbor: Suspicions Considered," *Yale Review* 45 (March 1956): 378–90; Dexter Perkins, "Was Roosevelt Wrong?" *Virginia Quarterly Review* 30 (Summer 1954): 355–72.
3. The major revisionist works of this period are Charles A. Beard, *American Foreign Policy in the Making, 1932–1940* (New Haven, Yale University Press, 1946) and *President Roosevelt and the Coming of War, 1941* (New Haven: Yale University Press, 1948); George Morgenstern, *Pearl Harbor: The Story of the Secret War* (New York: Devin-Adair Co., 1947); Charles C. Tansill, *Back Door to War: The Roosevelt Foreign Policies, 1937–1941* (Chicago: H. Regnery Co., 1952); William Henry Chamberlin, *America's Second Crusade* (Chicago: H. Regnery Co., 1950); Frederick R. Sanborn, *Design for War: A Study of Secret Power Politics, 1937–1941* (New York: Devin-Adair Co., 1951); Harry Elmer Barnes, *Perpetual War for Perpetual Peace* (Caldwall, Idaho: Caxton Printers, 1953); Richard N. Current, *Secretary Stimson: A Study in Statecraft* (New Brunswick, N.J.: Rutgers University Press, 1954) and most recently T. R. Fehrenbach, *F. D. R.'s Undeclared War* (New York: David McKay Co., 1967).
4. David J. Lu, *From the Marco Polo Bridge to Pearl Harbor: Japan's Entry into World War II* (New York: Public Affairs Press, 1961), p. 238.
5. Ibid., p. 245.
6. Butow, *Tojo and the Coming of the War* (Princeton: Stanford University Press, 1961); Alvin D. Coox, *Year of the Tiger* (Tokyo: Orient West, 1964).
7. James B. Crowley, *Japan's Quest for Autonomy: National Security and Foreign Policy, 1930–1938* (Princeton, N.J.: Princeton University Press, 1966); idem, "A Reconsideration of the Marco Polo Bridge Incident," *Journal of Asian Studies* 22 (May 1963): 227–91.
8. *The United States and the Far Eastern Crisis of 1933–1938* (Cambridge, Mass.: Harvard University Press, 1964).
9. Ibid., p. 543.

10. Iriye, *Across the Pacific: An Inner History of American-East Asian Relations* (New York: Harcourt, Brace & Co., 1967).

11. This survey of Japanese historical writing is based on Akira Iriye's admirable essay "Far Eastern Scholarship on United States Far Eastern Policy," in Borg, *Historians and American Far Eastern Policy*, pp. 22–31, and the papers prepared by a number of Japanese historians for the Conference on Japanese-American Relations, 1931–1941, held at Hakone, Japan, July 14–18, 1969. Among the Japanese papers used by the author were Seiichi Imai, "Cabinet, Emperor, and Senior Statesmen"; Katsumi Usui, "The Role of the Foreign Ministry"; Taichiro Mitani, "Contemporary Japanese Studies of Japan's Foreign Policy with Special Reference to China"; Sadao Asada, "The Japanese Navy and the United States."

12. See, for example, William A. Williams, *The Tragedy of American Foreign Policy* (Cleveland: World Publishing Co., 1959); Beard, *President Roosevelt and the Coming of the War;* Tansill, *Back Door to War;* Lloyd C. Gardner, *Economic Aspects of New Deal Diplomacy* (Madison: University of Wisconsin Press, 1964); William L. Neumann, *America Encounters Japan* (Baltimore: Johns Hopkins University Press, 1963).

13. Nihon Kokusai Seiji Gakkai, *Taiheiyo Senso e no Michi,* 8 vols. (Asuhi, Tokyo, 1962–1963). This discussion is based on Akira Iriye's "Japanese Imperialism and Aggression: Reconsiderations, II," *The Journal of Asian Studies* 23 (November 1963): 103–13. The separate volumes are as follows:
    Eve of the Manchurian Incident
    Manchurian Incident
    Sino-Japanese War, pt. 1
    Sino-Japanese War, pt. 2
    Tripartite Alliance; Soviet Japanese Neutrality Pact
    The Southward Advance
    The Outbreak of War between Japan and the U.S.
    Documents

14. The paper was published under the title "Miscalculations in Deterrent Policy: Japanese-United States Relations, 1938–1941," *Journal of Peace Research,* 1968, no. 2, pp. 97–115. The present author was chairman of the session and has based this discussion of the paper on papers in his personal possession.

15. Nobutaka Ike, *Japan's Decision for War* (Stanford: Stanford University Press, 1967), p. 26.

16. Taichiro Mitani, "Contemporary Japanese Studies of Japanese Foreign Policy with Special Reference to China, 1931–1941," Conference on Japanese-American Relations, 1931–1941, pp. 26–33; Iriye, "Far Eastern Scholarship on United States Far Eastern Policy," in Borg, *Historians.*

17. The discussion of Goldberg's book is drawn from Paul E. Sanger's review in *Journal of Asian Studies* 22 (1963): 107–8. See also the review of another Soviet history in ibid., p. 201.

18. "The Revolutionary Pacifism of A. J. Muste," in *American Power and the New Mandarins* (New York: Pantheon Books, 1969), pp. 159–220; Lionel Abel, "The Position of Noam Chomsky," *Commentary* (May 1969) and the exchange between Chomsky and Abel in ibid., (October 1969), pp. 12–43.

19. Chomsky, *American Power,* p. 204.

20. Schroeder, *The Axis Alliance and Japanese-American Relations, 1941* (Ithaca: Cornell University Press, 1958).
21. Williams, *The Tragedy of American Diplomacy* (New York: Rinehart, 1962); *The Contours of American History* (Cleveland: World Publishing Co., 1961); idem, *American-Russian Relations, 1781–1947* (New York: Rinehart, 1952).
22. Gardner, *New Deal Diplomacy*, p. 174.
23. In addition to Schroeder's study cited above, there is Ernst L. Presseisen, *Germany and Japan* (The Hague: M. Nijhoff, 1958); Frank W. Iklé, *German-Japanese Relations, 1936–1940* (New York: Bookman Associates, 1956); Johanna Menzill Meskill, *Hitler and Japan: The Hollow Alliance* (New York: Aeherton Press, 1966); Hans L. Trefousse, *Germany and American Neutrality, 1939–1941* (New York: Bookman Associates, 1951) and "Gemany and Pearl Harbor," *Far Eastern Quarterly* 11 (November 1951): 35–50; James T. C. Liu, "German Mediation in the Sino-Japanese War, 1937–1938," *Far Eastern Quarterly* 8, no. 4 (1949): 157–71.
24. Clifford, *Retreat from China* (Seattle: University of Washington Press, 1967); also, Irving S. Friedman, *British Relations with China, 1931–1939* (New York: Institute of Pacific Relations, 1943). The British ambassador in Japan, Sir Robert Craigie, has written his memoirs, *Behind the Japanese Mask* (London: Hutchinson, 1946).
25. Harriet L. Moore, *Soviet Far Eastern Policy, 1935–1945* (Princeton: Princeton University Press, 1945); Pauline Tompkins, *American-Russian Relations in the Far East* (New York: Macmillan Co., 1949); Henry Wei, *China and Soviet Russia* (Princeton: Princeton University Press, 1956); David J. Dallin, *Soviet Russia and the Far East* (New Haven: Yale University Press, 1948).
26. Roger Levy, *French Interest and Policies in the Far East* (New York: Institute of Pacific Relations, 1941); Hubertus J. van Mook, *The Netherlands, East Indies and Japan: Battle on Paper, 1940–1941* (New York: W.W. Norton & Co., 1944); Frank M. Tamagna, *Italy's Interests and Policies in the Far East* (New York: Institute of Pacific Relations, 1941).
27. Barbara W. Tuchman, *Stilwell and the American Experience in China, 1911–1945* (New York: Macmillan Co., 1971); William L. Neumann, *America Encounters Japan* (Baltimore: Johns Hopkins University Press, 1963); Tang Tsou, *America's Failure in China, 1941–1950* (Chicago: University of Chicago Press, 1963); Herbert Feis, *The China Tangle* (Princeton: Princeton University Press, 1953).
28. See Iriye, "Far Eastern Scholarship on United States Far Eastern Policy," in Borg, *Far Eastern Crisis;* Warren I. Cohen, "The Study of Sino-American Relations" (Paper read at the National Archives, June 17, 1969). Leopold, "American Policy and China," *Conflict Resolution* 8 (December 1964): 505–6; Taichiro Mitani, "Contemporary Japanese Studies . . . with Special Reference to China," Conference on Japanese-American Relations.
29. See Hugh Byas, *Government by Assassination* (New York: A. A. Knopf, 1942); E. E. N. Causton, *Militarism and Foreign Policy in Japan* (London: G. Allen E. Unwin Limited, 1936); Mark Gayn, *Japan Diary* (New York: Sloan Associates, 1948); Kenneth W. Colgrove, *Militarism in Japan* (Boston: World Peace Foundation, 1936); John Maki, *Japanese Militarism* (New York: A. A. Knopf, 1945). The transcript of Session IV (July 15, 1969) of the Conference

on Japanese-American Relations contains an interesting discussion comparing the Japanese and American military. In addition to the Japanese studies already cited, see Shigenori Togo, *The Cause of Japan* (New York: Simon and Schuster, 1956); idem, *The Yoshida Memoirs: The Story of Japan in Crisis* (Boston: Houghton Mifflin Co., 1962); Leonard Mosley, *Hirohito, Emperor of Japan* (Englewood Cliffs, N.J.: Prentice-Hall, 1966); Frederick Moore, *With Japan's Leaders* (New York: Scribner, 1942); Mamoru Shigemitsu, *Japan and Her Destiny* (New York: E.P. Dutton & Co., 1958); Toshikasu Kaze, *Journey to the Missouri* (New Haven: Yale University Press, 1950).

30. Louis Morton, "War Plan Orange: Evolution of a Strategy," *World Politics* 11 (January 1959): 221–50. Reports of the military attaches during this period are summarized by Russell F. Weigley, "The Role of the War Department and the Army" in a paper prepared for the Conference on Japanese-American Relations, 1931–1941, Hakone, Japan, July 14–18, 1969. See also, Louis Morton, *The War in the Pacific: Strategy and Command* (Washington, D.C., 1961); Mark S. Watson, *Chief of Staff: Prewar Plans and Preparations* (Washington, D.C.: U.S. Department of the Army, 1950); Maurice Matloff and Edwin M. Snell, *Strategic Planning for Coalition Warfare, 1941–1942* (Washington, D.C.: U.S. Department of the Army, 1953); Ray S. Cline, *Washington Command Post: The Operations Division* (Washington, D.C.: U.S. Department of the Army, 1951).

31. See Louis Morton, "Interservice Cooperation and Political-Military Collaboration," in *Total War and Cold War*, Harry L. Coles, ed., (Columbus: Ohio State University Press, 1962); Ernest R. May, "Development of Political-Military Consultation in the United States," *Political Science Quarterly* 70 (June 1955).

32. See Waldo Heinrich, "The Role of the U.S. Navy" read at the conference held in Japan (Summer 1969), as well as the paper read at the National Archives Conference, June 17, 1969. Not much has been done on the question of fortification of the Japanese (or American) islands, or the relationship between possession of the Pacific Islands and policy. See Earl S. Pomeroy, "American Diplomacy Respecting the Marshalls, Carolines, and Marianas, 1898–1941," *Pacific Historical Review* 17 (February 1948), and his *Pacific Outpost* (Stanford: Stanford University Press, 1951).

33. O. J. Clinard, *Japan's Influence on American Naval Power, 1897–1917* (Berkeley: University of California Press, 1947); Gerald E. Wheeler, *Prelude to Pearl Harbor: The United States Navy and the Far East, 1921–1931* (Columbia: University of Missouri Press, 1963); Armin Rappaport, *The Navy League of the United States* (Detroit: Wayne State University Press, 1962); William R. Braisted, *The United States Navy in the Pacific, 1897–1909* (Austin: University of Texas Press, 1958), and *The United States Navy in the Pacific, 1909–1922* (Austin: University of Texas Press, 1971).

II

Research Abroad on the Second World War

Arthur L. Funk served as chairman for the second session of the conference, which emphasized the connection with the International Committee on the History of the Second World War. At the request of the author, Funk read Henri Michel's paper in English. General Zhilin's opening remarks, emphasizing the need for research on the origins of the war, were delivered in Russian and translated by his aide Col. Oleg A. Rzheshevski. His paper was presented in English by Rzheshevski.

HENRI MICHEL

Archives of the French Resistance
Methods of Collection and Results

I will try to provide some information on the work we are doing in France to collect, collate, and analyze all the different records concerning the opposition of the French people to the German occupying forces between June 1940 and February 1945.

By its very nature, the Resistance Movement inside our national territory was an underground activity which produced as few papers as possible and which was supposed to destroy all documents afterwards for obvious security reasons. The problem seemed at first insoluble—how to preserve records that did not exist?

In fact, the underground resistance movement had been in touch with another resistance movement outside the territory, which, at the call of General de Gaulle, had been built up first of all in London and later in Algiers. In addition, a double authority had gradually been set up on parallel lines in the sense that outside France a government had founded its own administration, of which the most important section was the department responsible for establishing and maintaining relations with occupied France. The underground resistance movement, for its part, had formed its own institutions, the top section being constituted by the "National Resistance Committee" (Conseil National de la Résistance). Between these two powers, the necessary links had been ensured by various agents. There had been reports, accounts of different actions, and directives circulating from one section to another affirming that many valuable documents had been destroyed.

On the other hand, the resistance movements, both internal and external, were virtually compelled to rely on the Allies for the necessary money, arms, and material means. A whole interdependence was built up in this way, the French and Allied services being closely linked. It must be added that the British, and later the Americans, anxious to take fully direct action in France, had set up and staffed their own information and action networks; and, when the time of the landing came near, they had sent their own groups to France to cooperate with the French Resistance Movement. In short, there existed British and American records concerning the French Resistance, but they were the property of foreign governments.

19

A poster publicizing anti-German resistance efforts. (Office of Government Reports; National Archives, no. 44-PF-35.)

The German authorities in France had been able gradually to get informed about the organization and the men of the Resistance. But the German papers had often been destroyed, and sometimes they had been seized by the Allied armies. To a lesser degree, the situation was the same for the records of the Italian army of occupation.

The records of the Vichy régime also had files on the Resistance Movement. First of all, certain departments had undertaken actions hostile to the occupying forces in violation of the armistice agreement. Moreover, when a resistance movement was born, which was, at the same time, anti-German, anti-Italian, and anti-Vichy, the police and newly formed departments, such as the Board of Anti-national Activities (Bureau des Menées anti-nationales) had often discovered this underground activity. There existed, in the administrative departments of the Vichy régime, numerous documents concerning the Resistance. But the major part of this documentation had been destroyed at the moment when the Germans entered the southern zone in November 1942. A certain number of documents had also been destroyed intentionally, for the leaders of the Vichy régime, upon learning that they would have to face a trial, had taken the precaution of getting rid of all compromising papers. But self-harm had not always been able to destroy such evidence completely. Records existed, then, in which the action of the Resistance could be traced. The task was to find them again, to collect, and to preserve them.

After the war, the members of the Resistance Movement had drawn up personal records with accounts of their activity and occasionally some documents of the period. For their part, group leaders had been invited to compile a history of their group with lists of members and an account of the operations in which they had taken part. On the other hand, the enemies of the Resistance, the informers, enemy agents, and others had been summoned before special courts of justice. The documents thus produced had, of course, to be read very critically, but were often useful in filling in gaps or clearing up obscure points in the original documents.

Last, but by no means least, even when the members of the Resistance had neither written nor kept any documents, they nevertheless could still remember. Because of the arrest and disappearance of a great number of documents, the recollections of the survivors became an invaluable aid for the historian. It was essential, then, to collect such reminiscences by inviting those members to speak of their actions.

An enormous documentation, however uneven in quality, had existed, and still existed. But it was widely scattered, always fragmentary, and sometimes difficult to decipher and to use because of the pseudonyms and codes that had to be broken.

Nothing in the immense documentation concerning the Resistance must be neglected by the historian because of the fundamental character of the action of the French Resistance—an action that was rarely coordinated and was not directed until the final stages of the occupation. Most of the time it consisted of small operations accomplished by individuals or small groups. The great number of men involved and the small scale of their actions make it difficult to reconstitute the whole picture, but this only makes such a reconstitution all the more necessary. The strength of the Resistance lay, in fact, in the repetition of small-scale operations to harass the enemy—acts of sabotage, distribution of tracts, work stoppages, attacks directed against individuals, and refusals to obey. Thus, it was essential to omit none of the constituent elements of the movement, however small. It meant that we had to attempt to retrace, to collect, and to analyze all the documents in which the history of the Resistance was related piecemeal.

It was obvious that if immediate and large-scale actions were not undertaken, using new methods, the bulk of the documentation concerning the Resistance would be destroyed by the effects of time and lost forever, taking with it all hope of compiling a history of the Resistance. It was clear, moreover, that it would be difficult for the historians of the future to understand the Resistance Movement, owing to its novelty as a historical phenomenon and because of the obstacles placed in the path of any research, which we have already alluded to, unless men who had experienced and had often taken part in the Resistance were enabled to give their version of events first.

For this reason, a Commission for the History of the Resistance (*Commission d'Histoire de la Résistance*) was set up within the framework of the "Committee for the History of the Second World War" (*Comité d'Histoire de la 2° guerre mondiale*), which is a body unique in the annals of French historiography and having no equivalent abroad up to now. It was placed, first of all, under the authority of the *Président du Conseil* and is now under that of the prime minister. It receives a subsidy from the National Research Center (*Centre National de la Recherche Scientifique*). This commission comprises not only delegates from all the organizations concerned with the Resistance but also representatives of the main associations of former members of the Resistance. In addition, it has a number of investigators at its disposal, both in Paris and in the provinces.

As far as records are concerned, one can sum up the activity of the Commission for the History of the Resistance in four words: it has preserved, collected, created, and elucidated a huge and varied mass of documents.[1]

For example, the reports made by the gendarmerie were normally destroyed every five years. Those of 1940 were therefore due to disappear in 1945, and those of 1944, in 1949. The committee was able to have these police reports kept, corresponding to the period of the war. The reports of the gendarmerie are extremely valuable for the information they give on the daily life under the occupation. The gendarme was led to make investigations into all attacks or acts of sabotage. He is a reliable witness who describes exactly what he has seen or what he has found out. In this way, the circumstances, place, and time of the action performed by a Resistance group can easily be ascertained. Of course, the names of the men responsible remain unknown.

The same is true of the records of the National Railroad Corporation (*Société Nationale des Chemins de Fer—S.N.C.F.*), which were also preserved and collected by the corporation itself. In this way, the exact place and the extent of all the acts of sabotage performed on railway lines have been revealed with a wealth of precise details by the technician whose job was to repair and therefore to assess accurately the damage done.

The commission was responsible for the decision to place in the National Records Office (*Archives Nationales*) the majority of the files from the Central Office for Information and Action (*Bureau Central de Renseignements et d'Action—B.C.R.A.*), which was the Free French organization responsible for arming and equipping the internal resistance movement.[2] These files contain, in particular, accounts of parachute drops drawn up by the pilots, reports by members of the underground resistance movement concerning the operations in which they had taken part, information on the enemy provided by the networks, and surveys of the underground organization.

The underground press had developed considerably in France. Thanks to a considerable effort of research, a very valuable catalogue has been drawn up, comprising 1,106 titles.

The occupying forces often informed the population of their decisions by means of posters that record threats, sanctions, arrests, and firing squads taking hostages. These posters enable us to follow the evolution of the police repression and, later on, the activity of the underground resistance movement.

If it is certain that the Resistance Movement ran extra dangers through keeping papers, it is also true that systematic destruction of such documents would have constituted a serious handicap for any action. Moreover, as the Resistance Movement became diversified simultaneously with its growing unity and as its activity and numbers increased, a real administration was set up and the directives were multiplied. Many members of the Resistance have thus kept documents, which are always fragmentary, it is certain, but often extremely valuable. Great efforts have been made to persuade the owners of these documents to make a gift of them or to lend them to be reproduced.

It is obvious that the photographs of the underground period have a still more exceptional character. However, the soldiers in the army of occupation often indulged in keeping "souvenirs" of their repressive acts—firing squads and burning of farms. On the other hand, some "*maquisards*" (underground fighters) occasionally took their cameras with them to the forests and the mountains where they lived in hiding. In short, several thousands of photographs have been found and identified, thanks to a patient effort of investigation and collection. Occasionally, even films were shot, such as those showing the temporary liberation of Oyonnax in the Jura mountains on November 11, 1943, the escape of a group of American airmen with the help of the "Burgundy Network" (*Réseau Bourgogne*), the underground movement in the Vercors massif (*le maquis*), and the liberation of Paris.

This whole collection is and will remain incomplete by its very nature. On the other hand, many documents, photographs, and objects are difficult to identify, even to authenticate, for want of precise indication of names, dates, and places, or because such details are in codes. To be able to use such records, it was necessary to question members of the Resistance. The latter had, at all events, memories to relate which, in many actions, were the indispensable complements of the text and the image, when they were not the sole source of information.

Up to date, nearly two thousand witnesses have been interviewed. There could be no question of interviewing all the members of the Resistance, but only of selecting a cross section from which to build up a picture representing a microcosm of the Resistance, including all the political parties, different resistance movements, networks, regions, and religious denominations.

The most logical method in appearance was to ask the leaders of movements and networks for reports. This was done, and many answered the appeal for such cooperation. But this method soon proved insufficient. Indeed, the present-day leaders or the liquidators of movements were only rarely the leaders of the underground action. They do not know everything about their own movement and they tend generally to exaggerate their own role, to the detriment of their predecessors, another regrettable tendency being to inflate the number of members. Often they have become politicians, and their present positions are very far removed from the views they held during the underground period, so that they may not care to be reminded of them.

In short, we had to interview not only the generals but also the troops, the printers and distributors of tracts, the liaison agents, the sabotage teams, the parachutist sections, the collectors of information, the radio operators, the document forgers, and the soldiers in the maquis.

A good many refused to answer our questions because of various reasons—some secret agents had sworn not to divulge anything, some hired gunmen had performed actions they were afraid of having revealed, some Communists had received the order to say nothing, some questionable members of the Resistance had done things they preferred to keep to themselves, and honest citizens often simply considered that the parts they had played were over and done with.

In short, many people refused, but fortunately, even more people accepted such investigations. The commission drew up questionnaires with great care, only to discover very quickly that they were of little use, for, if questionnaires have the merit of fixing ideas and attracting the witnesses' attention to the points that one would like to see developed, on the other hand, they suffer from the defect of limiting the field of the investigation. A questionnaire can therefore only be useful for establishing a first contact.

Another lazy method would have consisted in waiting for a report that was drawn up by those who had taken part in an action, but most of them never found the time to write it, and the word-spinners could boast to their heart's content. With the best will in the world, the witness might also omit the most interesting points without mentioning them.

In short, only one method proved efficient: direct conversations between the witnesses and the specially trained, experienced investigators. The essential was to begin with a well-informed and trustworthy witness, who would indicate in his interview the names of other witnesses, whom the investigator could then question, knowing he was on the right track. In this way, by means of a constantly renewed conversation, it was possible for the facts to be established and the truth to be discovered little by little.

The stumbling block in this approach is that the investigator may color the declaration made to him with his own personal tone. This danger has sometimes been obviated by having the same witness interviewed by two investigators in turn. This obviously means that we thus have as our basic material, not first-hand documents, but something more in the nature of a rewrite. All things considered, the results are no worse than memoirs written several years after the event. The presence of the investigator even presented the advantage of limiting the element of self-advocacy, with the additional gain of it being possible to ask embarrassing questions.

What are the results obtained? It is clear that their value and interest diminish as time passes. Twenty years after the events, it is hopeless to expect a witness to be able to give an accurate and complete account of an experience which was doubtless exalting, but also often trying, and one which he subsequently tries to forget. For this reason, the investigations are being brought to an end and are now only undertaken either for very specialized research into a particular aspect of the problem or for a precise period or region during the Resistance.

The testimonies collected in this way present an interest which is not always equal, varying with the witness, the time, or the investigator. Some are summary and fill only a few pages. Others are book-length documents, which the member of the Resistance would never have written of his own free will. Certain testimonies show grievances, but many of them are marked by serenity and objectivity.[3] As a whole, however, they describe a mood, an atmosphere, and an organization rather than a precise fact.

If a cursory reading of the records of the Resistance presents problems, the historian attempting to make a critical analysis of them is often faced with something like a positive jigsaw puzzle. The documents are seldom dated, the facts are not localized, and those engaged in the action seldom appear under their real names. The Resistance had created its own sections and organization; these are generally referred to by abbreviations. This documentation had first of all to be "elucidated," for any use to be made of it.

For instance, as regards the underground press, it was necessary to find out the real names of the authors of the articles, the names and addresses of the printers, and the exact dates of the appearance of the papers, which was sometimes later than indicated.

Lists of code names of the Resistance groups have been drawn up[4], and organigrams have been worked out on a national and regional scale. The same groups, it must be said, often had a succession of different leaders, the hierarchy of responsibilities was not always clear, certain movements merged, whereas others split, and sometimes the same group depended on several authorities.

The viva voce investigations could only be carried out by a daily card-indexing of the persons interviewed and the persons still to be questioned. For an understanding of most of the documents, it was necessary to know the real names of the Resistance members, who had used pseudonyms in the underground movement. A double system of card-indexing was thus essential: one gave all the patronyms followed by all the pseudonyms used by the same person, while the other listed the pseudonyms followed by the patronyms, thus providing a cross-check. Indeed, if it was common for two members of the Resistance with the same name to have adopted different pseudonyms, it was fairly frequent also for two or several persons with different names to have chosen the same pseudonym.

With the help of correspondents in the provinces, we have undertaken a considerable collective task, aiming at working out a complete chronology of the Resistance Movement. It is a huge task, for the Resistance consisted essentially of a multiplicity of small-scale, scattered operations. Our aim was to retrace all these actions: the printing and distribution of tracts, acts of sabotage, attacks on individuals, parachute drops, escapes, arrests, strikes and demonstrations, armed clashes, and transmission of information. I will confine myself to saying that six working groups and 750 correspondents in the provinces are cooperating as a team to compile a chronological card-index. According to a method worked out in common, each team member uses standardized cards to note interesting facts on the Resistance Movement. It will suffice to add that all the records have to be analyzed, for no scrap of information must be neglected, and that 55,000 cards have already been filed in Paris and about the same number in the provinces. Once complete, the chronological card-index, which is centered in Paris, will comprise approximately two hundred thousand cards. It will be a simple matter, then, to extract from them precise and detailed statistics concerning not only the periods and regions but also the types of actions.

Already this chronology has enabled maps of the Resistance to be drawn up, on which all the actions of the underground movements can be plotted at a given moment in any given district (*département*).

The edifice would not be complete if it were not crowned by some publications. Indeed, this period is so exceptional and so difficult to study that it would be unthinkable if those who lived through it were not given the opportunity—even the duty—of recounting their version of the facts —the first version.

It is for this reason that the *History Review of the Second World War* (*Revue d'Histoire de la 2° guerre mondiale*), in addition to the current bibliography and the book reviews which are brought out regularly, has produced several special editions, dealing with the Resistance and written by the specialized teams that have been formed.

The commission coordinates and helps to the best of its ability an ever-increasing number of university research projects, such as theses at different levels of the doctorate (*thèses de doctorat d'État ou de troisième cycle, diplômes d'études supérieures*).

Finally, I should mention that, without being directly responsible, the commission has sponsored a collection entitled "Spirit of the Resistance" (*Esprit de la Résistance*).

Thus, in patient, successive stages—growing more accurate all the time—the history of the French Resistance Movement is gradually taking shape. Not the least originality of the work is that, occasionally, the synthesis has to precede the collection of the records necessary for the survey to be written up. Another novel feature is the necessity of teamwork extending over the whole country. Last, in a more traditional way, the cooperation between historian and archivist—sometimes leading to the historian being transformed into an archivist—is closer than ever.

Such is the group of tasks undertaken in France concerning, in the widest sense of the word, the records of the Resistance.

Notes

1. For a general survey of the work of the *Comité d'Histoire de la 2° guerre mondiale,* see the article by H. Michel, "Les centres de recherche historique." See also, "Le Comité d'Histoire de la 2° guerre mondiale," in *Revue historique* (January 1965), pp. 127–38.
2. Cf. H. Michel, *Histoire de la France libre,* Paris 1963, p. 128; C. Passy, *Souvenirs,* 3 vols., Paris, pp. 237, 387, 439.
3. The witnesses were given the promise—and this promise has been kept—that their statements would be neither published nor communicated, but such testimonies have occasionally been examined by the Committee for the History of the Second World War for research purposes, always with the authorization of the witnesses.
4. Cf. particularly vol. 1 of the *History Review of the Second World War (Revue d'Histoire de la deuxième guerre mondiale),* November 1950.

PAVEL A. ZHILIN

Research on the History
of the Second World War
in the Soviet Union

It would be no exaggeration to state that historiography on the Second World War, in the number of publications and their scale, occupies one of the most prominent places in contemporary literature. This is natural and understandable. The Second World War has become a colossal event. It embraced the greater part of the globe and its population. Thus there are full grounds for regarding the Second World War as a landmark in human history.

Almost everyone would agree that the geography of historiography is not yet well studied. But it is quite evident that a most voluminous literature has been built up in the USSR, Yugoslavia, Poland, the USA, Britain, France, and other countries that suffered from Hitlerite aggression.

The International Committee on the History of the Second World War is taking steps to study the geography and classification of the historiography of World War II. A special conference on historiography took place in Hungary, and that conference was devoted to the same problem.

The Second World War achieved a total, universal character. It involved an aggregate population of hundreds of millions. The popular masses participated in the Second World War in various ways, of which the three main ways were: involvement directly in the armed struggle, resistance movements and the partisan struggle, and labor activity in the production of all the material means needed for the conduct of the war.

The study of trends of historiography reveals that the majority of historical books, documents, and memoirs deal with armed struggle, resistance and the partisan movement, while the minority examine the role played by the popular masses in the war years.

A chronological examination of the historiography of the Second World War reveals that historians concentrate their main efforts on discovering political, economic, and military processes that directly accompanied the course of war. They are studied more thoroughly than other events. The prewar period, results of the war, and its lessons and social consequences are probed with significantly lesser detail. For the time being there are few fundamental books concerned with the problem of the causality of war and its world-wide historical consequences.

However, these problems are of great importance. V. I. Lenin pointed out that every war should be examined in a concrete historical situation. While examining any war, one should first determine its political and class content, probe its origins, and accurately study its prewar policy, the policy that for a long period of time in prewar years had been conducted by a certain state and by a certain class within this state. "If you did not show the links . . . of war with the preceding policy," V. I. Lenin said, "you understood nothing in this war!" To demonstrate on the basis of scientific methodology these links—often hidden due to objective and subjective factors from view of a superficial observer—is an essential historical task.

We cannot avoid pointing out that authors of some studies evade revealing the causality of the war and do not want to brand the forces of reaction and militarism the only perpetrators of world tragedy. Moreover, some people are exerting efforts to rehabilitate Hitlerism and to relieve it of responsibility for its human victims and destruction.

Of similar importance is the study of the outcome, the lessons, and the consequences of war. Some authors, however, show their disinterest in investigating these problems. That is probably the result of the fact that the war caused stormy revolutionary processes, creation of a world socialist community, and destruction of the colonial system. The major lesson of the war lies in the fact that the people who prepared and unleashed the war took a gigantic step toward their own destruction, but those who really struggled against warmongers proved to be victorious.

The history of the Second World War is widely represented in Soviet historiography. In the postwar period and in recent years, particularly, publications on the Second World War and, what is quite natural, on the Soviet-German front or as we used to say, on the Great Patriotic War, took a very important place in Soviet military-historical literature. Public interest in these publications is becoming ever greater.

Everybody knows that the Second World War involved many countries, but the Soviet people bore the brunt of the struggle against the Fascist bloc. For the Soviet Union, this war was a particularly bitter experience; it demanded great losses. The war affected the life of almost every Soviet family and every Soviet citizen.

Although the war was a tragedy, many heroic pages of the history of our people are linked with it. Soviet people are proud of their country's outstanding, decisive contribution towards the defeat of Nazi Germany and her accomplices in aggression. We hope that many scholars will agree with the opinion of Prof. Louis Morton, a prominent American historian, who discussed the Soviet-German front in one of his publications issued in 1970. He called it the biggest and most decisive theater of the Second World War.

The past war and its major component, the Great Patriotic War, are studied at many research institutions. Most of this research is concentrated at the institutes of history of the Academies of Sciences of the USSR, the Union republics, and the Institute of Marxism-Leninism and its branches. The armed struggle is studied at the Research Department of the General Staff and, since 1967, at the Institute on Military History of the Ministry for Defense. The Institute deals now with the problems of the Second World War.

Moreover, problems linked chiefly with the USSR's participation in the war are studied at many universities and other institutions of higher learning. These institutions not only conduct research under coordinated plans but also help historians working in other institutions.

During the past quarter century, a voluminous scientific literature on the Second World War has been built up in the Soviet Union. This literature may be divided into three groups: documentary publications, scientific research, and war memoirs.

We have given first place to documentary publications because documents are the foundation of any serious research. Most of the documents concerning the past war are to be found in specialized military history archives. The largest of these is the Archive of the Ministry for Defense of the USSR. Its repositories contain several million documents tracing the entire activity of the Soviet Armed Forces during the war years, from the top leadership to individual units. There is also a large collection of documents at the Naval Archives.

Documents relating to the activity of Party and local government bodies during the war years are kept at the Central Archives of the Institute of Marxism-Leninism and its branches and also in the archives of the All-Union Central Council of Trade Unions and the Young Communist League, and the Central State Archives of the October Revolution.

Altogether in the Soviet Union there are more than ten central state archives, four hundred thirty-two republican, territorial and regional archives, and over three thousand local archives. These have accumulated an enormous number of documents showing the Soviet people's heroic struggle against the Nazi invaders and their allies. Archives have become the centers of scientific work. Many thousands of scientific workers visit their reading halls.

The publication of collections of documents was started by the Soviet archival organizations during the war, and this work is being continued to this day. Altogether about four hundred seventy volumes of archival documents have been published in the USSR, not taking into consideration the documents published by the Soviet press.

Of the recent documentary publications, the following may be named: The most recent is a volume of documents and materials under the title *The USSR in the Struggle for Peace on the Eve of the Second World War*, which deals with Soviet foreign policy and international relations on the eve of the war. It contains many documents that are being published for the first time. We are presenting a copy of this volume to the organizers of the conference.

In the USSR we have published the war correspondence of Franklin D. Roosevelt, Joseph Stalin, Winston S. Churchill and Harry S. Truman, and a documentary volume, entitled *Teheran-Yalta-Potsdam*, devoted to the wartime conferences of the heads of governments of the three Great Powers. A collection of documents under the title *The Communist Party in the Great Patriotic War* (published in 1970) deals with the leadership of the war and the organization of the Soviet people's struggle against the invaders.

Much has been added to the documentary literature on the partisan movement on Soviet territory and in European countries. An extremely informative work has been published under the title *People's Partisan Movement in Byelorussia during the Great Patriotic War (July 1941–July 1944)*, documents and materials in three volumes, of which the first volume is published.

An interesting volume of documents on Soviet frontier guards has been published under the title of *Frontier Troops during the Great Patriotic War of 1941–1945* (Moscow, 1968).

Currently being prepared for publication is a volume of documents on the basic aspects of the Soviet people's armed struggle against the Nazi invaders.

Important documents on the history of the Second World War have been concentrated at 1,200 museums of our country. There are large establishments among them. The Central Museum of the Soviet Armed Forces contains, for example, up to five hundred thousand exhibits, the majority of which refer to the history of the Second World War. The Museum on the History of Artillery, the Museum of Engineers, the Central Navy Museum, and museums of military districts and fleets also have large exhibits. Documents and military relics are preserved and exhibited at museums of the armed forces in rooms named after combat glory.

Events of the past war have been widely reflected in memorials and monuments. More than one hundred thousand monuments have been erected in our country. There are world-known memorial complexes in Volgograd on Mamayev Hill, in Leningrad, in Khotyn (Byelorussia), and in other places immortalizing the feat of the Soviet people and the Soviet Armed Forces.

The collection of documents and relics of the past war is being continued in our country up to the present. The general public, including war veterans, scientists, writers, journalists, and various public organizations, take an active part in this activity. Marches of young people to the places of combat glory have become a tradition. Participants in these marches reveal new documents, names of heroes, and unknown pages of the struggle against Fascist aggressors.

On the basis of documents and materials, the Soviet scientific literature depicts prewar history, causes of the war, the march of war events, and the results of the war. The works relating to these problems are the result of extensive and painstaking research.

From 1961 to 1966, the Institute of Marxism-Leninism completed its work on *History of the Great Patriotic War of 1941-1945* in six volumes. Recently, the first book of the fifth volume of a multi-volume publication *History of the Communist Party of the Soviet Union* was published. The book depicts the activity of the party in the war years. The Institute of Economy has published a book entitled *The Soviet Economy in the Great Patriotic War.*

A voluminous research literature on the history of the Great Patriotic War has been written in Union republics, particularly in those which had been under Nazi occupation. Institutes of Union republics' Academies of Sciences and other local research establishments published a number of fundamental works. The Ukraine put out a three-volume book, *The Ukrainian SSR in the Years of the Great Patriotic War of the Soviet Union, 1941-1945* (published in 1968–1969). The Byelorussian contribution is *Byelorussia at War.* Scholars of Latvia, Lithuania, Estonia, Moldavia, Kazakhstan, Central Asian, and Transcaucasian republics have prepared some detailed works.

Much work is being done by departments of institutions of higher learning, individual authors, and competitors for candidate and doctor degrees. The scale of this research may be seen from the fact that the Second World War is the subject of four hundred sixty published monographs, nearly six hundred fifty dissertations for the scientific degrees of doctor and candidate, and some four thousand popular works.

Major military developments and operations that decided the outcome of the war are dealt with in works devoted to the battles of Moscow, Stalingrad and Kursk, the battle for the Caucasus, the battle for Leningrad, the Byelorussian strategic operation, the battle for Berlin, and the defeat of the Japanese army in the Far East. The teams of authors of these works were headed by outstanding Soviet military leaders: I. K. Bagramyan, A. M. Vasilevsky, A. A. Grechko, M. V. Zakharov, K. K. Rokossovsky, V. D. Sokolovsky, and others. Nearly two hundred works have been written only on the initial period of the war and on the Battle for Moscow; over fifty books have been written about the Stalingrad operation.

Along with previously mentioned works dealing with the history of combat operations on the entire Soviet-German front, our historians have worked out and published some four hundred fifty generalizing books in which separate periods, campaigns, and battles of the Great Patriotic War are analyzed.

Soviet historians have published some seventy books on the defeat of Nazi Germany dealt by the Soviet Armed Forces in the final period of the war and more than thirty works depicting the defeat of militarist Japan.

Soviet military historians have extensively studied the experience of the various arms of the Soviet Armed Forces during the past war. Many books deal with the development and battle experience of the fighting services, the organization and operations of armored and mechanized troops, artillery, engineer troops, and the combat experience of the Soviet navy and air force.

Soviet historians study many problems linked with other theaters of the Second World War. These problems are dealt with in more than seventy books, which examine the developments in Europe in 1939–1941 and the operations conducted by our Allies in Europe, Asia, and Africa. We have published a three-volume work entitled *The Second World War,* which contains the materials of the International Scientific Conference held in Moscow and reports of Soviet and foreign historians.

The reminiscences of veterans are an important source of the history of the war. As early as during the war, the Academies of Sciences of the USSR and the Union republics set up commissions which, in addition to amassing materials related to the war, did much to build up a fund of manuscripts of reminiscences by war veterans. These eyewitness accounts written on the heels of developments are of immense value for research because they recreate many facts and circumstances that are not sufficiently dealt with in documents. But in recent years many memoirs have been published in which personal impressions of the war are backed with documents. They combine research with reminiscences. A particularly valuable contribution to Soviet military-historical literature is

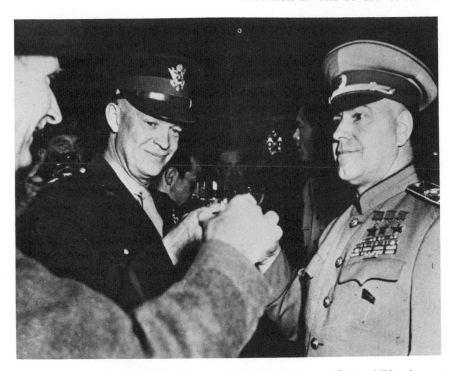

Allied victory toast, June 1945: Field Marshal Montgomery, General Eisenhower, and Marshal Zhukov. (Dwight D. Eisenhower Library, no. 66-990-3.)

made by the memoirs of Soviet senior officers who, during the Great Patriotic War, were in leading posts in the central apparatus or in command of fronts, armies, corps or divisions. *Recollections and Reflections* by G. K. Zhukov, *The Year 1945* by I. S. Konev, *The Soviet General Staff at War* by S. M. Shtemenko, *In the Service of the People* by A. K. Meretskov, *On the Eve* and *Action Stations in the Fleets* by N. G. Kuznetsov, *Tested by Fire* by M. K. Kalashnik, *Moscow-Stalingrad-Berlin-Prague* by D. D. Lelyushenko and many other war memoirs have won a wide audience.

More than one thousand war memoirs and collections of reminiscences have been published in the Soviet Union since the war. They help a great deal in depicting facts that lack documental materials.

Foreign, including American and British, works on the history of the Second World War are being translated into Russian and published in the Soviet Union. These include *The Supreme Command* by F. C. Pogue, *Command Decisions* from the series *U.S. Army in World War II*, a number of books by S. E. Morison about the United States Navy, and the multi-volume British work *Grand Strategy*. Mention must also be made of publications like the *Halder Diary* in three volumes, the works on the history of the Second World War by J. F. C. Fuller and K. Tippelskirch, and the memoirs of de Gaulle, O. Bradley, M. Ridgway, and U. Cavallero.

In the postwar period we have published several hundred such books. They help us to compare various viewpoints about the developments of the Second World War. Naturally, in some cases, we cannot agree with the interpretations by foreign authors of the fundamental problems and openly criticize them. However, to further the interests of science, we publish these works in the Soviet Union.

Regrettably, very few Soviet works on the Second World War are translated in the West, and in some cases where these books are published, it is done for unseemly purposes. This is in contradiction with the fact that in recent years there has been a growing interest in the West in the study of developments on the Soviet-German front.

What are the subjects and chief developments of the Soviet historiography of the Second World War at the present time?

Great attention is directed to the research and interpretation of prewar history, causes of the war, and all circumstances connected with the unleashing of the conflict. This is one of the major concerns of Soviet historians. I may frankly say, hoping that our foreign colleagues understand us, that problems of the foreign policy of the Soviet Union in the prewar years are treated by some of the Western historians in a nonobjective way.

One of the essential problems that invariably attracts the attention of Soviet historians is the participation of the popular masses in the war. We mean books dealing with efforts of the working class, peasantry, and intellectuals in the war years as well as with the nation-wide partisan movement behind the Nazi lines.

Going on with a painstaking study of the complicated processes that took place during the Second World War in various countries, Soviet historians once again turn their attention to the theme: the war and the people. Pursuing their aims, Soviet scholars are examining efforts of the popular masses in the war years and the forms and methods of mobilization of these efforts. The historical and scientific importance of the problem is quite evident, as it is impossible to give a true picture of the entire war and analyze its results without a thorough study of the participation of broad popular masses in the armed struggle at the firing lines and in the production of material means for the front. Certainly, the knowledge accumulated by historical science in every country considerably eases the solving of this problem.

When considering the problem of the war and the people as a whole, the Soviet scientists are always aware of a fundamental tenet of the Marxist theory about the decisive role of the popular masses in history and in war as well. On the basis of concrete and objective analysis of the course and outcome of the Second World War, they consider the popular masses of the anti-Fascist coalition the principal force that secured victory over Fascist Germany and imperialist Japan.

The Second World War demanded the mobilization of huge manpower and material resources and in many countries affected all spheres of the life of peoples.

For the Soviet Union the war was a people's patriotic struggle against Nazi invaders. The Soviet people participated in the war in various forms. The principal ones were the armed struggle against the enemy conducted by the Soviet army, the partisan movement in occupied territories, and labour activity of the Soviet people in the rear. These are the key themes in the research of Soviet historians.

One of the important problems for our historians is the activity of the Soviet rear, the reorganization of the national economy on a wartime footing in particular, and the creation of a developed war economy capable of satisfying all the material requirements of the front.

At the same time, the Soviet historiography of the Second World War concentrates its main efforts on the armed struggle, and first of all, on the operations conducted at the Soviet-German front as it objectively was the principal theater of hostilities, and all major turning moments were closely connected with that front.

One of the trends in the development of Soviet historiography of the Second World War is further research of the problems which are waiting for solution. The second trend, closely linked with the first, consists in building up fundamental works taking up the war as a whole.

At present the leading Soviet historical institutes are engaged in compiling a multi-volume scientific work entitled *History of the Second World War*. The main task of this work is to give a true, well-documented picture of the beginning and development of the Second World War, to reveal its causes and explore the political, economic, military, and ideological factors that determined its course and outcome.

Great attention is given in this work to specific political and military events, to the scale and character of hostilities in all theaters of the Second World War, and to illustrating the efforts of countries of the anti-

Hitlerite coalition and all progressive forces in gaining victory over Fascist Germany and militarist Japan. The principal lessons of the Second World War, theoretical conclusions drawn from its history, and processes caused and accelerated by it in the postwar world will be considered in this work.

In producing this scientific work, as well as other publications on the Second World War, Soviet historians have as their aim not only to explore more deeply and to throw light on one of the most tragic events of the twentieth century but also to contribute to the struggle for averting the danger of a new world military conflict.

Such are the main and most important trends of research on the history of the Second World War and its nearest perspectives.

In conclusion, permit me to express the confidence that the Conference on Research on the Second World War will promote a more attentive attitude toward archives and help to improve the source base for the study of the Second World War. Soviet historians favor a further strengthening of cooperation between scientists within the framework of the International Committee for the History of the Second World War and consider that, in this sense, an exchange of views will be both useful and mutually interesting.

Discussion Summary

Most of the discussion following these two papers was devoted to the issue of access to archival materials. Diane S. Clemens (M.I.T.) described her inability to use records in Soviet archival repositories, and Julius Epstein (Hoover Institution) commented upon the paucity of Russian published sources concerning various aspects of the War, including the German-Russian Pact of 1939. In response, Zhilin (through his translator) noted the extensive documentary publication program undertaken by the Soviet Union which had already produced some five hundred volumes of documents on the Second World War. Foreign scholars had been given access to documents in Moscow, and Zhilin invited his questioner to revisit his country if further material were needed. Replying to Epstein, Zhilin noted that the issue of Russian relations with Germany, Japan, Britain, and France in 1939 was a complicated one which could not be dealt with through questions and answers. The Soviet Union did the most they could to prevent German aggression, but Britain and France were unwilling to join with them.

Speaking in French, Michel expressed the view that the question of access to records was fundamental, not only with regard to research in Russia but with regard to research in other countries as well. Most countries had restrictions upon access to their records. He added his hope that the conference itself might lead to the opening of archives not just to official historians but to all researchers.

III

Unfinished Business of

Wartime Diplomacy

The third session of the conference, on the afternoon of June 14, was under the chairmanship of Robert Wolfe, specialist for Modern European History in the National Archives. The session dealt with two areas of the world which represented minor problems during the Second World War but which had become the most serious problems twenty years later, namely, Palestine and Vietnam.

SELIG ADLER

American Policy vis-à-vis
Palestine in the
Second World War

As the European phase of World War II neared its end, the American Zionists split sharply over credence in Franklin Roosevelt's pledges on Palestine. The majority, following the lead of the lantern-jawed Stephen S. Wise, proclaimed its faith in the president's recent campaign promise to implement the creation of a Jewish commonwealth. A minority, whose spokesman was the Lincolnesque Rabbi Abba Hillel Silver, acknowledged the president's benevolent intentions. The Cleveland Rabbi insisted, however, that Roosevelt had purposely dragged his heels on the issue, papering over with high-sounding rhetoric the grim fact that hundreds of thousands of the doomed had been allowed to perish while the British, with American contrivance, kept the door to the Holy Land all but shut.[1] It is the purpose of this paper to evaluate these antithetical assessments of FDR's Palestine policy in the light of the archival evidence.

A few examples will suffice to prove that Dr. Silver's suspicions were well founded. On March 9, 1944, the president stated that a Jewish national home was, in the face of the manifest Nazi genocide, more urgent than ever and that he would, in proper time, implement this goal. Yet that very same day FDR congratulated Speaker Sam Rayburn for holding the House in line against a resolution calling for a Jewish commonwealth. Following this action, six Arab states were once more assured that no decision would be made on Palestine without full consultation with both parties, another way of saying that nothing would be done.[2]

In that election year of 1944, both parties vied with each other in promising the eventual creation of a Jewish state, the Democratic platform repeating almost verbatim the Zionist demand for a commonwealth. The president specifically endorsed this plank on October 15 and promised, if reelected, to carry it out. On the very morrow of this commitment the State Department, with White House approval, dispatched new guar-

This article was published in *Judaism* 21, no. 3 (Summer 1972): 265–76. Copyright 1972 by the American Jewish Congress.

antees to the Arabs. Two months later another pro-Zionist resolution was killed in Congress as a result of presidential orders.[3] Moreover, on three separate occasions Roosevelt approved a projected joint Anglo-American statement freezing, for the duration, the status quo in the Holy Land. The purported objective of this declaration was to silence Zionist agitation at a time when general postwar planning was already under way. For a complex of reasons the joint statement was never issued, but Roosevelt's consent to it is revealing.[4]

Zionist intelligence had uncovered the imminence of this joint statement and the broad outlines of other projected administration measures harmful to the Jewish cause. With the notable exception of the forthright Silver faction, however, American Jewish leaders pinned the blame for the thwarting of Jewish hopes upon a covey of anti-Zionist State Department underlings who would, in due time, receive their comeuppance from the White House. A few weeks before Roosevelt's death, this grass roots Jewish confidence in the president was severely shaken by a series of happenings widely broadcast by the media. These electric events involved the meeting between FDR and the king of Saudi Arabia on the president's return from the historic Yalta Conference. Knowing that another summit meeting of the Big Three was in the making, noted Jewish leaders, including even Albert Einstein, petitioned the president to find a place for Palestine on the Yalta agenda.[5]

Meanwhile, the State Department strongly urged FDR to meet Ibn Saud and to reach an accord with him in order to tighten the king's agreements with the American oil companies whose concessions on his soil were now producing in gusher proportions. Secretary Stettinius also highlighted the fact that we were in serious need of landing rights on Saudi Arabian soil to refuel military aircraft en route to the Japanese front. It is obvious from this correspondence that Washington wished to keep the desert kingdom from returning to its prewar status as a British fief. Correctly suspecting that his chief might try to make a deal with Ibn Saud on Zionism, Stettinius reminded Roosevelt that any attempt to renege on our "solemn commitments" to the Arab world on Palestine would jeopardize our cherished economic and strategic interests in Saudi Arabia.[6]

Despite these admonitions, FDR clung tenaciously to his pragmatic belief that the grizzled king might, in return for American technical aid, agree to champion the Jewish cause. The president must have recalled two acid letters from Ibn Saud about the "vagrant Jews" who betrayed Mohammed and his uncivil remarks about Zionism in a published interview in *Life* magazine.[7] Further, Roosevelt certainly knew of the dramatic failure of a wartime effort to enlist the Bedouin king, the religious leader of a fanatic Moslem sect, on behalf of the Jews. The gist of this scheme, as arranged by a longtime British confidant of Saud and approved by Churchill and Roosevelt, was to make the king the "boss of bosses" in the Middle East and to give him £20 million, the money to be provided by world Jewry. In return, the king was to persuade other Arab nations to abandon Western Palestine to the Jews in exchange for complete independence. When FDR sent an emissary to sound out the king on the matter, Saud's anger reportedly knew no bounds.[8]

In face of these stubborn facts, the president, against the advice of all whom he consulted, tried for a long shot. In one fell swoop he attempted to bring Saudi Arabia into the American orbit and to find an Arab spokesman for a Jewish national home. Possibly FDR took the gamble because he was genuinely convinced of the workability of the Zionist blueprint. Or, more likely, the president was leaping in the dark. On occasion, he was given to such deviations from his ordinary caution in diplomatic matters when opportunity arose to capitalize upon his own impenetrable charm and considerable powers of persuasion.

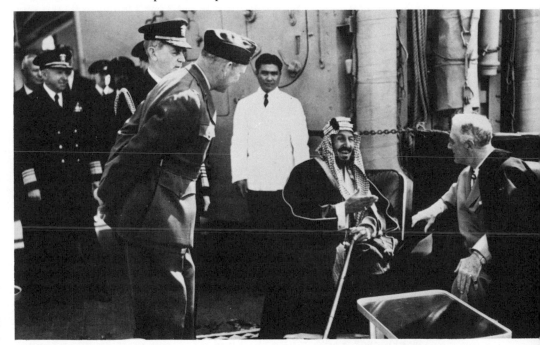

King Ibn Saud and President Roosevelt on the U.S.S. *Quincy* at the Great Bitter Lake, February 1945. At the left are Adms. Ross T. McIntire and William D. Leahy along with Marine Col. William A. Eddy, the United States minister to Saudi Arabia. (Franklin D. Roosevelt Library, no. 48-22-3659 /94/.)

The king and the president met on a sunny February day aboard the *Quincy*, lying at anchor in Suez waters. After Roosevelt carefully explained the tragic plight of tens of thousands of homeless Jews, Saud said the solution was simple—just follow an old Arab custom and hand over defeated Germany to the Jews. The conversation became stalemated, but not before the king made it clear that he wanted no Western benefits of any kind if they were tied to cooperation with the Zionists. Moreover, he warned that any expansion of the Allied commitment to the Zionists would lead to certain bloodshed in the Middle East. Taken aback, FDR promised his royal guest that he would take no steps hostile to the Arab cause; which meant, of course, that the endless deadlock over Palestine would continue.[9] Jewish leaders surmised the negative results of this colloquy at Bitter Lake, but their doubts about the president multiplied when Roosevelt ad-libbed some unfortunate remarks about the meeting with Saud in the course of a personal report to Congress on the results of the Yalta Conference. Then, to quiet the Zionist uproar, FDR publicly assured Rabbi Wise that he still stood by his campaign pledge to support a Jewish commonwealth. Subsequently, harried by a letter from the king which equated Zionism with fascism, the president replied that his promises to Saud remained "unchanged," and these guarantees were repeated by the State Department to two other Arab states. By this time the president's health was failing rapidly and he was preparing to entrain for his fateful journey to Warm Springs.[10]

This sorry record fully confirms Secretary Hull's verdict that the president "talked both ways to Zionists and Arabs, besieged as he was by each camp." Moreover, in one of the very few cases in which FDR committed anything to writing on the Palestinian hot potato, he advised Hull to take no sides on the issue since "if we pat either side on the back, we automatically stir up trouble."[11] This note, penned during the darkest days of the war, mirrored the president's conviction that all attention must be focused on a knockout victory over the Axis by placing a moratorium on the discussion of all postwar territorial settlements. Political considerations in 1944 broke the president's resolve for a blackout on the issue for the duration. Confronted by the press with the contradiction between his promises to the Zionists and White House opposition to the pending congressional pro-Zionist resolution, Roosevelt differentiated between a wartime policy dictated by military factors and a future situation "when other considerations can guide us."[12]

The evidence is so confusing that it is impossible to determine just what solution, if any, Roosevelt had in mind for the problem of Jewish homelessness. The president was given to telling different stories to different men about the same subject. Moreover, when faced with a vexing question for which he had no answer, he characteristically tried shotgun therapy, flitting from one plan to another.

Thus, FDR told Dr. Chaim Weizmann that he was entirely convinced of the economic potentialities of Palestine, dismissing Arab objections to large-scale Jewish settlement there as impediments which could be silenced with a "little baksheesh." To Sen. Robert F. Wagner, staunch friend of Zionism, the president envisaged World War II as a splendid opportunity "to put an end once and for all to the homelessness of the Jewish people." Yet, at another time, he wrote the New York senator that the trouble with Palestine was that while 500,000 uprooted Jews wanted to go there, the land was surrounded by many millions of Arabs waiting "to cut their throats the day they land."[13] Nor is it possible to uncover any single plan for the solution of the Jewish territorial problem that the president thought really viable. Publicly on record for a Jewish commonwealth to be established in the Holy Land, Roosevelt privately expressed serious doubts as to whether Palestine could domicile the survivors of the holocaust without taxing world Jewry with more economic assistance than the traffic would bear. Hence, he often turned to alternate arrangements designed to meet the mounting refugee problem. He toyed with the idea of a "world budget" among the free nations to accept the expellees, but despite strong encouragement from Churchill, he dropped the idea because he feared the political risk of securing liberalized immigration quotas from Congress.[14]

True to his fashion, Roosevelt kept a number of balls in the air at the same time. Ever since 1938 he had been flirting with the founding of a Jewish haven in some faraway corner of the earth, a project that intrigued him in his capacity as an amateur geographer. At one time or another he played with the idea of Northern Rhodesia, Cyrenaica, Tanganyika, Kenya, the seething Orinoco valley, and a score of other possible havens. All of these plans came to naught save an inconsequential settlement at Sousa in Santo Domingo, the brainchild of the tyrant, Trujillo. The simple fact remained, that even if an out-of-the-way refuge could be found with a climate suitable for a westernized urban-oriented folk, such a region would take time to develop. In contrast, Palestine, where the wayfarers would receive a cheering welcome, would offer an immediate asylum. But the British stood in the way of this feasible solution and Roosevelt was convinced that it would be harmful to the war effort to force London's hand.[15] So the president tried once more to solve the Palestinian puzzlement. Musing aloud one day in 1943 he asked, "Why not make Palestine a genuine Holy Land, to be administered by trustees representing the world's three major faiths?'' This was only a typical Rooseveltian trial balloon, but whatever chance the scheme had of implementation was killed by a State Department underling who seized the opportunity to come up with a plan for administering the trusteeship so patently anti-Zionist as to render the plan ludicrous.[16]

As the pendulum on Palestine oscillated to and fro, one scheme recurred so repeatedly in FDR's thoughts that it is safe to assume that it represented his innermost convictions. This plan would create a semiautonomous Jewish Palestine, to be melded into a political federation which would include Syria, Lebanon, and Transjordan. A bundle of coincidental factors gave the scheme logic. A faction of Palestinian Jewry had formed the *Ihud* (or Union) party which called for rapprochement with the Arabs along binational lines, albeit this group was thinking primarily of Palestinian self-government rather than federation in a greater Syria. Many non-Zionist American Jewish voices, including the prestigious *New York Times*, championed *Ihud*. At the same time, Roosevelt's idea paralleled a movement among the Arab states for closer union. The president argued that a Jewish state, to be included in a larger political body, would accelerate Middle Eastern economic and social development. But prior to his 1945 confrontation with Ibn Saud, FDR failed to grasp that an inflamed Arab nationalism would not allow sufficient concessions to the Jews to make either political federation or binationalism in Palestine acceptable to the Zionists.[17]

In the waning months of his life, Roosevelt was talking of ''some formula, not yet discovered'' for the solution of his Palestinian dilemma. Evidently he had begun to doubt his notion that the Arabs would accept a Jewish Palestine in exchange for massive technological assistance from the West. Twice he stated to separate observers that the soon-to-be-born United Nations would have to create a Jewish commonwealth which, in turn, would have to be defended, for the time being, by Anglo-American arms.[18] We will never know if this was just another one of FDR's will-o'-the-wisp suggestions or whether, at long last, he was ready to substitute deeds for words.

Roosevelt's Palestinian diplomacy can only be rated a failure. It did not make adequate preparation before the war for the major tragedy that was forseeable; it did not make sufficient use of Palestine during the conflict as the most available haven of refuge, and no meaningful steps were taken to solve the Arab-Jewish problem at a time when the fires of war had rendered the international situation fluid. Moreover, the president's public statements on the issue did violence to the facts.[19]

For these blunders and misrepresentations FDR must bear ultimate responsibility, but historical justice demands an exploration of the circumstances which made his problem peculiarly difficult. The aging president stood at the head of the biggest war effort in all history and sheer necessity forced him to delegate decision making on secondary matters. Responsibility for the Middle East thus devolved upon the military chieftains and the State Department, with both groups sending up to the White House for approval anti-Zionist decisions. The army, understandably enough, wanted arrow-swift victory with a minimum loss of men. This strategy required that the supply route to the Soviet Union be kept open so that the Russians could reverse the German big push eastward, thus buying time for the Anglo-American powers to prepare for the massive invasion of France. Inasmuch as the northern passage to the Soviet Union was impeded by ice and Nazi U-boats, the bulk of war materiel to Russia passed (after November 1942) through the Persian Gulf Command route to Iran. The lands adjoining this vital supply artery to the Soviet Union were studded with American bases manned by noncombatant personnel. The War Department argued that, unless the restive Arabs who surrounded this Allied lifeline were appeased, a Palestinian uprising might endanger American lives in the region, pin down for garrison duty Allied troops needed elsewhere, and deprive the Russians of the Arabian oil which fueled the Soviet war machine.[20]

Roosevelt, in routine manner, referred all Middle Eastern correspondence to the State Department. Here, Secretary Hull and his successor, Stettinius, insisted that we take no position in the Arab-Jewish rift, a dispute which they reasoned lay within the jurisdiction of our wartime ally, England.[21] In actuality it was not Hull, but rather Wallace Murray, veteran chief of the Division of Near Eastern Affairs, who came up with most of the suggestions on Palestinian matters. Murray, whose animus against Zionism had long been most emphatic, repeatedly warned his superiors that if we forced Britain's hand on easing entry into Palestine, the United States would in the event of disorder, be duty bound to help Britain police the mandate.[22] Similar thinking also percolated upward to the White House from our legations in the Middle East. Cairo, Baghdad, and Jerusalem sent repeated admonitions that the United States could not fight in the name of democracy if, in the process, its government denied self-government to the Arab majority in the Holy Land.[23]

Roosevelt, in the fashion of all modern presidents, often bypassed State Department channels in order to try his hand at personal diplomacy. The information he garnered from these sources also damaged the Zionist cause. Sumner Welles was undersecretary of state from 1937 to 1943, but as a protégé and social intimate of the president, he carried more than ordinary influence at the White House. Despite the feeling of his Jewish contemporaries that Welles leaned toward the Zionist position, archival evidence reveals that he shared the general anxiety that large-scale immigration to the Holy Land would delay the defeat of the Axis.[24] Staunch Zionist though he was, Justice Felix Frankfurter only on the rarest of occasions mentioned the Palestine issue in his chatty notes to the president.[25] If Frankfurter leaned backwards on the issue, other White House intimates proved far less restrained. Adm. William D. Leahy, close to the seat of power as FDR's wartime military adviser, made no attempt to disguise his hostility to the notion of a Jewish state.[26] James V. Forrestal who, in 1944, became secretary of the navy, was to become in time pathologically anti-Zionist. This wiry, pugnacious man enjoyed close relations with the American oil magnates, first as president of a Wall Street firm which floated many of their securities and later as undersecretary of the navy where he supervised fuel purchases. Convinced that the projected United Nations would fail to maintain global order, he argued incessantly that the United States must maintain full naval strength after victory in order to meet the Russian threat that would surely follow the end of our wartime marriage of convenience with the Soviets.

Forrestal accepted at full value mistaken estimates that our domestic reserves were nearing exhaustion, and he, therefore, reasoned that Middle Eastern oil was absolutely essential for our future security. A corollary to this proposition read that Uncle Sam must consciously woo the Arabs who controlled this incomparable strategic and commercial prize.[27]

Because FDR so seldom committed his reasoning to writing, it is hazardous to analyze his motivations. It is an educated guess, however, that he was thinking not only of preventing an Arab uprising during the war, but also of future strategic and commercial assets to the United States. These factors were brought home to Roosevelt by two personal observers whom he dispatched to the Middle East. In 1943 Patrick J. Hurley, lawyer and lobbyist for Harry F. Sinclair, pointed out the allurements of an American substitute for a weakened Britain as guardian of the Middle East and its priceless oil. Harold B. Hoskins, an American born in Beirut, was even more emphatically pro-Arab in the reports he submitted to the White House following two separate missions to the Moslem world.[28]

In sum, if the Zionists had a single champion in FDR's inner circle, he has covered his tracks beyond recognition. The conclusion is inescapable that, owing to domestic political considerations, the president merely sparred in his frequent White House meetings with Zionist bigwigs, invariably failing to put his oral reassurances and light-hearted promises into the executive pipeline.

We do not know if Roosevelt felt any pangs of conscience as he helped bar the doors of Palestine to Hitler's innocent victims who could find no other shelter. Any remorse that the president may have felt was, possibly, assuaged by the thought that the grim facts of war permitted him no option. Unquestionably, the Soviet factor weighed heavily in his decisions. Persistent reports from the American embassy in Moscow pointed out the unremitting hostility of Communist theology to Zionism, plus reminders of the age-old Russian territorial ambitions in the Middle East. Hence, it was not difficult for Ambassador W. Averell Harriman to predict that the Soviets would soon openly side with the fifty million Arabs against the half million Jews. From all parts of the globe, warnings poured into Washington, many of them presumably reaching the president, of the dangerous long-run implications of an American pro-Zionist stance.[29]

Quite possibly, FDR was less disturbed by the peril of future complications in Western Asia than by fear of making a permanent American-Soviet deténte impossible. The president viewed such an understanding as indispensable for the proper functioning of collective security in the postwar world. The State Department advised that any agreement on Palestine should be subject to Soviet consent.[30] If Roosevelt followed this choice, then no arrangement on the Holy Land could be made that would carry out his 1944 campaign pledges. Caught in this vise, he stood still on the issue until death tossed the prickly problem into his successor's lap.

One of the great "ifs" of the Palestine story remains: What would have happened had FDR lived and Churchill remained in power when the war ended? While the prime minister had proclaimed himself "the heir of Lord Balfour" and "the architect of the Jewish future," he had frequently kept his American partner from giving the Zionist cause any meaningful aid. Churchill went along with the Colonial and Foreign Offices and the British High Command, all of whom insisted that any wartime showdown on Palestine would impede victory. Long after the tide of war had turned, Roosevelt was repeatedly told by the British that any positive action on behalf of the Jewish cause involved an unjustifiable military risk. In truth, the prime minister was as ambivalent as Roosevelt on Zionism. A theoretical friend of the movement since 1917, Churchill naturally placed British interests first, and Foreign Minister Anthony Eden convinced him that the active promotion of Arab unity would preserve at least a fraction of England's once predominant influence in the Middle East. These interests seemed vital at the time, for in addition to oil concessions, imperial needs made it necessary to maintain the security of the Suez linchpin. Some world Zionist leaders suspected the sincerity of Churchill's promises for the future, but the prime minister did lessen the intensity of Jewish pressure upon the Allies by convincing the Weizmann wing of the organization, less militant than the Palestinian faction headed by Ben-Gurion, of his sincerity.[31] Chaim Weizmann in England and Stephen Wise in the United States put their faith in the promises of the president and the prime minister that patience in war would be rewarded in peace by a joint Anglo-American effort to build a Jewish state on the banks of the Jordan. Did they intend to make good their promises? One cannot say for certain since when the time came to redeem the note, one guarantor of the obligation had been laid to rest at Hyde Park while the other had been relegated to political exile at Chartwell. The overwhelming probability, however, is that they did not intend to keep their promises, barring drastic changes in the circumstances of Middle Eastern politics.

Notes

1. Unpublished notes, intended as memoirs by Dr. Abba Hillel Silver but never completed before his death in 1963, Abba Hillel Silver Papers, The Temple, Cleveland, Ohio.
2. Typescript of statement made by Roosevelt at the White House to Rabbis A. H. Silver and Stephen S. Wise, 9 March 1944, Zionist Archives and Library, New York, N.Y.; FDR to Sam Rayburn, 9 March 1944, Official File 700: Palestine, Roosevelt Papers, Franklin D. Roosevelt Library, Hyde Park, N.Y., hereafter cited as FDRL; *Papers Relating to the Foreign Relations of the United States, 1944,* vol. 5, pp. 589–90; Bartley C. Crum, *Behind the Silken Curtain* (New York: Simon and Schuster, 1947), pp. 39–40.
3. The Palestine platform planks of the major parties are capsulized in George Kirk, *The Middle East in the War* (London: Frederick A. Praeger, 1953), p. 318. FDR's message to the Forty-Seventh Annual Convention of the Zionist Organization of America, transmitted by Sen. Robert F. Wagner, 15 October 1944, is in the Robert F. Wagner Papers, Georgetown University, Washington, D.C.; Wallace Murray to Edward R. Stettinius, 27 October 1944, *Foreign Relations, 1944,* vol. 5, pp. 624–26; FDR to Stettinius, 9 December 1944, ibid., p. 645; Jacon C. Hurewitz, *The Struggle for Palestine* (New York: W. W. Norton & Co., 1950), p. 214; Joseph B. Schechtman, "Roosevelt and the Jews," *Jewish World* 1 (February 1955): 7–10 and (March 1955): 11–13.
   For proof that the president himself approved of killing the second set of resolutions, FDR to Stettinius, 8 December 1944, Official File 700: Palestine, Roosevelt Papers, FDRL.
   For fresh assurances to the Arabs, Cordell Hull to the American Delegation at New Delhi, 29 April 1944, File 867N.01/2317, General Records of the State Department, Record Group 59, National Archives, hereafter cited as State Department Records, RG 59, NA.

4. The Zionist leaders had an exaggerated fear that the issue of this joint Anglo-American declaration would crystallize Allied policy in pro-Arab form. A. H. Silver to Arthur H. Sulzberger, 9 November 1943, Silver Papers.
   The proposed statement had a long history both before it was almost issued in August 1943, and for some time thereafter, *Foreign Relations, 1943*, vol. 4, p. 763. Information as to why it was not issued, owing to a leak by Drew Pearson, *Washington Post*, 9 August 1943, and the intervention of Representative Emanuel Celler of New York, who threatened the president with a congressional inquiry, can be found in Richard P. Stevens, *American Zionism and United States Foreign Policy, 1942–1947* (New York: Pageant Press, 1962), p. 77. Proof that the president approved the proposed declaration on several occasions is based on Murray to Hull, 16 August 1943 and 17 August 1943; Murray to Long, 25 October 1944, File 867N.01/1908$\frac{1}{2}$, 867N.01/10–2544, State Department Records, RG 59, NA.

5. Silver to FDR, 29 January 1945, Silver Papers; Wagner to FDR, 15 January 1945, Wagner Papers.

6. Hull to FDR, 3 April 1944, *Foreign Relations, 1944*, vol. 5, pp. 679–80; Stettinius to FDR, 13 December 1944 and 22 December 1944, pp. 648–49, 757–58; Stimson to Hull, 27 October 1944, James V. Forrestal Papers, Princeton University, Princeton, N.J.
   FDR wrote to James Landis, American director of Economic Operations in the Middle East on 11 January 1945, asking for a memorandum that might help in bringing about a rapprochement between Ibn Saud and the Zionist leaders, Stevens, *American Zionism*, p. 87.

7. Ibn Saud to FDR, 30 April 1943, FDR to Ibn Saud, 20 May 1943, *Foreign Relations, 1943*, vol. 4, pp. 773–75, 786–87. In the latter letter, following closely a statement by Lord Cranborne in the House of Commons on 6 May 1942, the president pledged "that no decision altering the basic situation of Palestine should be reached without full consultation with both Arabs and Jews." FDR, the next month, urged upon Saud as "highly desirable" a bilateral understanding between Jews and Arabs prior to the termination of hostilities. Samuel Halperin and Irvin Oder, "The United States in Search of a Policy: Franklin D. Roosevelt and Palestine," *Review of Politics* 24 (July 1962): 320–41.
   For FDR's belief that it was possible to enlist Ibn Saud's help in behalf of the Jews, see Joseph B. Schechtman, *The United States and the Jewish State Movement* (New York: Herzl Press, 1966), pp. 51–52, 103–4, 109–10. The interview with Saud is in *Life*, 31 May 1944.

8. The British confidant of Saud was H. St. John Philby. For origins of the plan, how Churchill and Roosevelt were enveloped in it and the king's alleged anger when he was approached by the president's emissary, Harold B. Hoskins, see Chaim Weizmann to Sumner Welles, 13 December 1943, Silver Papers; Weizmann's autobiography, *Trial and Error* (New York: Harper & Row, 1949), p. 426; *Foreign Relations, 1942*, vol. 3, pp. 550–51, ibid., *Foreign Relations, 1943*, vol. 4, pp. 792–94, 807–14. The whole affair ventilated in a memorandum of a conversation between Sumner Welles and Weizmann, 26 January 1943, File 867N.01/1–2643, State Department Records, RG 59, NA, and in a summary report by Nahum Goldmann, 17 January 1944, in Felix Frankfurter Papers, Box 88, Reel 4, Library of Congress.

9. William A. Eddy, *F.D.R. Meets Ibn Saud,* American Friends of the Middle East, Kohinur Series no. 1 (New York, 1954) is a pro-Arab account and should be compared with Schechtman, *The U.S. and the Jewish State Movement,* p. 107; Halperin and Oder, *Review of Politics;* Robert E. Sherwood, *Roosevelt and Hopkins: An Intimate History* (New York: Harper & Row, 1948), p. 872.

10. New York Times, 2 March and 17 March 1945; Gaddis Smith, *American Diplomacy during the Second World War* (New York: Wiley, 1965), p. 114; Halperin and Oder, *Review of Politics.*

   Further pledges to the Arabs are contained in FDR to Ibn Saud, 5 April 1945, Zionist Archives and Library and FDR to Regent and Heir Apparent of Iraq, 12 April 1945, Official File 700: Palestine, Roosevelt Papers, FDRL. This last letter, dated the day of the president's death, was probably written over Roosevelt's signature and owing to his rapidly deteriorating physical condition, this may also be true of the April letter.

11. *The Memoirs of Cordell Hull,* 2 vols. (New York: Macmillan Co., 1948), 2: 1936; FDR to Hull, 7 July 1942, *Foreign Relations, 1942,* vol. 4, pp. 543–44.

12. Press and Radio Conference no. 945, 28 March 1944, Press Conferences, 23: 120–21, FDRL.

13. FDR to Wagner, 3 December 1944, Wagner Papers. In reply, Wagner told the president on 15 January 1945 that he had once told him that after the present war, we would get "a second bite at the cherry. That bite must put an end once for all to the homelessness of the Jewish people."

   See also, Halperin and Oder, *Review of Politics.*

14. Memorandum of conversations between FDR and Chaim Weizmann, 12 June 1943 and between FDR and Harold B. Hoskins, 27 September 1943, *Foreign Relations, 1943,* vol. 5, 792–94, 811–14. Morris L. Ernst at the Sixth Annual Conference of the American Council for Judaism, *The Council News* (May 1950), p. 2.

   See also, Stevens, *American Zionism,* p. 71.

15. For the president's earlier interest in an extra-territorial solution, see *Foreign Relations, 1940,* vol. 2, pp. 222–24.

   The subject of extra-territorialism is well summarized in David S. Wyman, *Paper Walls: America and the Refugee Crisis, 1938–1941* (Amherst: University of Massachusetts Press, 1968), p. 59.

   The best answer to a Jewish settlement outside of Palestine was given by Sen. Robert A. Taft in a speech delivered before the American Palestine Committee on 9 March 1944, typescript in Wagner Papers. See also Inis L. Claude, Jr., *National Minorities: An International Problem* (Cambridge, Mass.: Harvard University Press, 1955), pp. 106–9.

16. Roosevelt had mentioned the trusteeship plan in rudimentary form to Henry M. Morgenthau on 3 December 1942, John M. Blum, *From the Morgenthau Diaries: Years of War, 1941–1945,* vol. 3 (Boston: Houghton Mifflin Co., 1967), p. 298. FDR first seriously broached the subject to Harold B. Hoskins on 27 September 1943, after the latter's fruitless mission to Ibn Saud on behalf of the Philby Plan, *Foreign Relations, 1943,* vol. 4, pp. 807–10. Thereupon the Division of Near Eastern Affairs that had previously been interested in such a solution had Gordon P. Merriam, its assistant chief, draw up a plan to implement Roosevelt's suggestion, 15 October 1943, ibid., pp. 816–21. From

the content of Murray to Berle, 15 October 1943, File FW 867N.01/2068, State Department Records, RG 59, NA, the president was not prepared for this implementation, for Undersecretary of State Stettinius remarked that FDR had only made to him one hurried remark about a trusteeship for Palestine. When Secretary Hull returned from his Moscow visit of October 1943, he thought the time was not "propitious" and the plan was dropped. Hull, *Memoirs* 2: 1934.

17. For the formation of the *Ihud* movement in Palestine, see *New York Times*, 14 June 1942, and Hurewitz, *The Struggle for Palestine*, p. 160. A memorandum prepared by the Division of Near Eastern Affairs, 6 February 1942, File 867N.01/1797, State Department Records, RG 59, NA, reveals the support of the division for the movement, which is also emphasized in a memorandum, Murray to Welles, 12 December 1942, *Foreign Relations, 1942*, vol. 3, pp. 553–54.

FDR's interest in an Arab federation, which would include an autonomous or semi-autonomous Palestine, is attested by Sumner Welles, *We Need Not Fail* (Boston: Houghton Mifflin Co., 1948), pp. 28–30. See also Kirk, *Middle East*, p. 312 and Halperin and Oder, *Review of Politics*. As in so many other of his plans for a Middle Eastern settlement, the president did not carry through.

18. Edward R. Stettinius, Jr., *Roosevelt and the Russians* (Garden City: Doubleday, 1949), p. 289; Halperin and Oder, *Review of Politics*; Schechtman, *The U.S. and the Jewish State Movement*, p. 113.

19. In his 9 March 1944 speech before the American Palestine Committee, Senator Taft urged that the best time for an imposed Palestinian solution was the present, when the Allied armies were closing in on the Axis (Typescript in Wagner Papers).

Dr. Silver further developed this argument in *Nothing to Lose But Our Illusions* (pamphlet, n.p.,n.d., text of an address delivered at Hotel Commodore, New York City, 21 March 1945).

Historians have also argued that with the fluidity of the international situation in the late war months, such a solution could have been imposed with relative ease. See Hurewitz, *The Struggle for Palestine* and Schechtman, *The U.S. and the Jewish State Movement*, pp. 68–69. Sir Llewellyn Woodward, *History of the Second World War: British Foreign Policy in the Second World War* (London: Methuen & Co., 1962), p. 386, concedes that if Washington had taken a firm stand on the Palestinian issue, London could have hardly resisted an attempt to settle the issue.

For Palestine's contribution to the war effort, an overfavorable account is Pierre Van Paassen, *The Forgotten Ally* (New York: Dial Press, 1943), which should be balanced with Kirk, *Middle East*, p. 320.

Washington's opposition to the formation of a Jewish army is summarized in Murray to Long, 1943, Long Papers, Box 199, Library of Congress.

20. Memorandum prepared by R. H. Buell, 6 July 1944, Laurence Steinhardt Papers, Box 45, Library of Congress.

Assistant Secretary of War John J. McCloy to General Marshall, 22 February 1944, *Foreign Relations, 1944*, vol. 5, pp. 574–77.

Strategic factors are discussed in Eliahu Ben-Horin, *The Middle East: Crossroads of History* (New York: W. W. Norton & Co., 1943), p. 199 and Hull, *Memoirs* 2: 148.

56 SELIG ADLER

At times, Britain had to keep as many troops in Arab countries to prevent uprisings as were deployed by the British against Rommel in North Africa. "The Roosevelt-Ibn Saud Letters," *Jewish Frontier* 12 (November 1945): 3–4.

21. Hull's position on Palestine is stated in his *Memoirs* 2: 1537. His general approach to questions posed by the war is elucidated in an editorial in the Omaha *World-Herald,* 4 December 1942, and in Mark Sullivan's column in the *Washington Post,* 8 August 1943. See also the memorandum by Assistant Secretary of State Brandt, 18 January 1944, File FW867N.01/2183, State Department Records, RG 59, NA.

Possibly Hull was restrained on the Palestine question because his wife was of Jewish origin. The secretary continued to maintain, as he had prior to 1939, that the Middle East was primarily a British concern. He said that while he favored a Jewish national home in Palestine, he opposed an independent Jewish state. As an appointive official, he was much more restrained in voicing public support for the Zionist cause than Roosevelt, who showed constant concern for the urban Jewish voting bloc. For Hull's attempt to restrain the president during the 1944 campaign, see Hull to FDR, 26 July 1944, *Foreign Relations, 1944,* vol. 5, p. 606.

22. Murray (1887–1965) began association with the Division of Near Eastern Affairs in 1927 and two years later became its chief. During World War II, he served as political adviser to the Department of State, but he kept in close touch with Palestinian affairs, writing numberless letters and memorandums, all slanted against Zionism. He was expert in capitalizing upon all Jewish opposition to Zionism, blowing this dissent out of all proportions to its true significance. One of his favorite arguments was that American sympathy for the Zionist cause would lead to an Arab uprising which our troops would have to quell. See memorandum of a conversation between Murray *et al.* with Morris Waldman of the [non-Zionist] American Jewish Committee, 4 November 1943, File 867N.01/686, State Department Records, RG 59, NA.

Murray tried to narrow all American legal and moral responsibilities in the Holy Land to the protection of bona fide American nationals, Murray to Stettinius, 8 March 1944, Breckinridge Long Papers, Box 200.

Murray's intense animosity to Zionism was well known at the time, Representative Emanuel Celler to FDR, 18 August 1943, File FW 867N.01/1985, State Department Records, RG 59, NA; interview between Selig Adler and Dr. Emanuel Neumann, 4 April 1968.

23. This was particularly true of Alexander Kirk and Loy Henderson, stationed at Cairo and Baghdad, respectively. Kirk to Murray, 1 August 1941, File 867N.00/8–141, State Department Records, RG 59, NA; Henderson to Hull, 1 November 1944, *Foreign Relations, 1944,* vol. 5, pp. 628–29; Weizmann, *Trial and Error,* p. 431.

Kirk went so far as to propose that the leaders of the Zionist cause publicly abandon the Balfour Declaration as their share in the defeat of Hitler. Kirk to Hull, 23 May 1941 and 28 June 1941, *Foreign Relations, 1941,* vol. 3, pp. 609–10, 612–14. Kirk evidently impressed Assistant Secretary of State Adolf A. Berle, Jr., who tried to implement the idea, but it was squashed by Undersecretary Sumner Welles with the notation that its implementation would make us more pro-Arab than the British, Welles to Kirk, 15 July 1941, ibid., pp. 615

–16; Herbert Parzen, *A Short History of Zionism* (New York: Herzl Press, 1962), p. 92.

24. For favorable Jewish views of Welles, see Weizmann, *Trial and Error*, pp. 425–35.

    Dr. Emanuel Neumann confirmed Weizmann's view in an interview with the present writer, 4 April 1968. However, the archival material reveals that Welles found large-scale Jewish immigration to Palestine "highly controversial," Welles to FDR, 8 April 1943, Official File 700: Palestine, Roosevelt Papers. The undersecretary also reasoned that many European Jews would want to go elsewhere besides Palestine after the war, memorandum of a conversation between Welles and the Egyptian minister, 30 March 1943, *Foreign Relations, 1943*, vol. 4, p. 767. Welles also joined in the wartime effort to silence Zionist agitation, ibid., *1941*, vol. 3, p. 622. This recognition of Welles's true position has been previously recognized by Parzen, *A Short History of Zionism*, p. 93; Halperin and Oder, *Review of Politics*.

25. In a letter to Silver, 14 April 1943 (Frankfurter Papers, Box 86, Reel 2), the judge stated that he could not speak out on a controversial matter and that he had never indicated to anyone that the right time would come for him to speak out on behalf of Zionism as long as he was on the Supreme Court bench.

26. Fleet Adm. William D. Leahy, *I Was There* (New York: McGraw-Hill Book Co., 1950), pp. 202–95.

    In 1948 Leahy opposed the recognition of Israel. See also, Robert H. Ferrell, *George C. Marshall*, in *The American Secretaries of State and Their Diplomacy* 15, Robert H. Ferrell and Samuel F. Bemis, eds. (New York: Cooper Square Publishers, 1966): 181.

27. Obituary of Forrestal, in *San Francisco Chronicle*, 4 March 1949; Arnold A. Rogow, *James Forrestal: A Study of Personality, Politics and Policy* (New York: Macmillan Co., 1963), pp. 29, 181, 190–94; Forrestal to Hull, 11 December 1944, *Foreign Relations, 1944*, vol. 5, pp. 755–56.

    A memorandum by Forrestal's assistant, 11 March 1944, Forrestal Papers, Box 49, points up the paucity of domestic oil reserves and the consequent need for Arabian oil. But Herbert Feis, *Petroleum and American Foreign Policy*, Commodity Studies Pamphlet no. 5 (Stanford University, 1944), p. 16, reveals that Feis understood in 1944 that our domestic reserves had been badly underestimated and that the United States could depend in the future upon oil imports from non-Arab countries plus the discovery of new domestic reserves as yet unknown.

28. See Brigadier General Hurley's report to the president, 5 May 1943, *Foreign Relations, 1943*, pp. 776–80. The animosity of Hurley to Zionism is further evidenced in Leahy, *I Was There*, p. 187.

    Hoskins was a fluent Arabist, born in Beirut to American missionary parents. Stone to Silver, 18 January 1944, Silver Papers. For background on Hoskins's missions and the reports he rendered, see *Foreign Relations, 1941*, vol. 3, pp. 596–97, ibid. *1943*, vol. 4, pp. 747, 781–85.

    In early 1944 Hoskins circulated to influential senators "The Present Situation in the Middle East," a biased account of his findings, File 867N.01/2229, State Department Records, RG 59, NA.

    For trenchant criticism of the Hurley-Hoskins missions, see I. F. Stone, "Palestine Run-Around," *Nation* 158 (March 1944): 326–328.

29. The basic hostility of the Soviets to Zionism is treated in Hayim Greenberg, "Soviet Russia and the Zionist Movement," *Jewish Frontier* (February 1943) and William A. Williams, *Source Problems in World Civilization* (New York: Octogon, 1958), pp. 30–31.

    With the Yalta Conference in the offing, Murray stressed to his superiors the importance of not allowing an American pro-Zionist policy to vex future relations with the Soviets. Murray to Stettinius, 27 October 1944 and 24 November 1944, *Foreign Relations, 1944,* vol. 5, pp. 624–26, 641.

    Murray wanted Secretary Stettinius to emphasize to the president the danger of Russia winning over to their side some fifty million Arabs by championing their cause against the Jews. Murray to Stettinius, 3 November 1944, File 867N.01/11–344, State Department Records, RG 59, NA. Stettinius, at FDR's suggestion, took up the matter with Ambassador Harriman in Moscow, and the latter's memorandum on the subject was sent to Roosevelt. Stettinius to Murray, 11 November 1944, Harriman to Stettinius, 13 December 1944, *Foreign Relations, 1944,* vol. 5, pp. 636,646–48.

    There was also considerable pressure from American diplomatic officials in the Middle East pointing up the dangers of a Russo-Arab understanding. The most vigorous protests came from Henderson in Baghdad. Henderson to Murray, 4 November 1944, ibid., pp. 631–33.

30. Roosevelt was briefed on the Palestine question should it arise at Yalta, but there is no clear evidence that the president saw this brief nor was the matter discussed there, ibid., pp. 655–57. For Roosevelt's views on the necessity of Russian cooperation in the postwar world, see Robert A. Divine, *Roosevelt and World War II* (Baltimore: Johns Hopkins Press, 1969), pp. 51, 61–63, 87, 90–91.

31. For Churchill's assurances to Jewish leaders, see summary report by Nahum Goldmann, 17 January 1944, Frankfurter Papers, Box 88, Reel 4; Weizmann, *Trial and Error,* pp. 436–37; Hurewitz, *The Struggle for Palestine,* p. 204. The Wagner Papers contain a typed memorandum of a meeting between Churchill and Weizmann, 6 November 1944, in which the prime minister indicated that his task in Palestine would be easier if the United States would cooperate in trying to bring about a settlement. The opposition that Churchill faced in the foreign and colonial offices and in the mandatory government at Jerusalem is covered in Woodward, *Second World War,* pp. 385–87, 393–94, and Welles, *We Need Not Fail,* pp. 26–27. For evidence that Churchill's friendliness toward Zionism was jeopardized by the 1944 assassination of Lord Moyne in Egypt at the hands of the Stern Gang terrorists and that the prime minister resented the fact that the United States was critical of British policy in Palestine while, at the same time, trying to dodge responsibility, see Kirk, *Middle East,* pp. 12, fn.1, 315–16, 331. Zionist leaders believed, and the evidence is on their side, that Britain wanted to use Arab federation for postwar imperialism. In this context, one must recall that Churchill was an unabashed imperialist. Dr. Emanuel Neumann to Prof. Carl J. Friedrich, 27 August 1943, Silver Papers.

American Policy toward Indochina during the Second World War Some Tentative Conclusions

From the Japanese attack on Pearl Harbor in December 1941 to the Japanese acceptance of the terms of surrender in August 1945, American policy toward Indochina reflected the vicissitudes of wartime diplomacy. President Franklin D. Roosevelt personally made the decisions for several years, and his death in April 1945 left a legacy that raised more questions than answers. Actually the major considerations of American diplomacy in the war years focused on Roosevelt's trusteeship idea for Indochina; on U.S. policy toward resistance movements, both French and Viet Minh, in the dependency; and on questions relating to theater command jurisdiction. In these three areas of consideration, decisions were made that affected the contours of the postwar world. On the very same day, September 2, 1945, some of these contours were being drawn: Japan formally surrendered on the American battleship *Missouri* in Tokyo Bay marking the end of one era, while Ho Chi Minh formally proclaimed in Hanoi the independence of Vietnam signaling the beginning of a new one.

President Roosevelt was interested in Southeast Asia, although he did not possess a deep knowledge of it. Some of his comments were casual and superficial; his critics thought him a dilettante or a dreamer. Henry L. Stimson, for instance, once complained that he was "all mixed up" about the Philippines, and the president apparently was not aware of the ethnic breakdown of Indochina with its political implications into Annamites, Cambodians, and Laotians. Yet he had a grasp of the fundamental emerging forces in Southeast Asia such as the rising tide of nationalism and the impending recession of colonialism. He was very sympathetic to Cordell Hull's draft Declaration by the United Nations on National Independence in March 1943 and to a far-reaching memorandum about the termination of colonies in Southeast Asia the secretary of state forwarded to him in September 1944.

Roosevelt viewed American policy on the political evolution of the Philippines toward a fixed date for independence as a beacon that should guide other colonial powers. Over and over again, he stressed this point in discussions in Washington and overseas. He may have offered Gen. Charles de Gaulle some Filipino advisers to assist the French in liberalizing their policy in Indochina. The president also distinguished between what he considered good and bad colonial rulers in Southeast Asia; the French personified the bad, and the Dutch represented the good. Partly as a consequence of his close personal ties with the royal family of the Netherlands and his admiration for the Dutch, he believed he could influence the Netherlands to pursue a liberal colonial policy in the East Indies —one that would lead to increasing self-government and eventual independence. On the other hand, Roosevelt did not personally like de Gaulle and he did not feel sympathetic to the French. The president thought that the French exploitation of Indochina was one of the causes of the Pacific War. Apart from the validity of this viewpoint, it is increasingly evident in perspective that French Indochina was a major consideration in the outbreak of war between Japan and the United States.

Against this background, FDR gave considerable thought to postwar Indochina. Opposed to the outright return of the dependency to France, he considered turning it over to Nationalist China. He even asked Chiang Kai-shek at Cairo in November 1943 if China wanted the territory. The answer was flatly in the negative. Nevertheless, Vice President Henry Wallace was instructed the next year to inform Chiang Kai-shek of the president's interest in China's getting the area. The generalissimo apparently had not changed his mind when Wallace saw him in June. Was Roosevelt actually serious about this solution to postwar Indochina? It certainly stood in contrast to his belief in independence for the dependency. If he ever was serious about this option, it was possibly related to his desire to keep China in the war against Japan.

The president's proposed trusteeship for Indochina was an example of his personal diplomacy. In conversations at home with various people and at summit conferences in Cairo, Tehran, and Yalta he urged the concept. Certainly by early 1943 and then up to the time of his death, he considered trusteeship through various lenses. In late 1943, he mentioned to Gen. Joseph W. Stilwell that a commission of three—an American, a Briton, and a Chinese—should head the trusteeship. About the same time, he suggested to Chiang Kai-shek that the international trusteeship should include Indochinese, French, Chinese, Russian, and possibly Philippine and American representation. The Russians, he noted, were "on the coast." After the Yalta Conference in February 1945, he talked more of France assuming the obligations of a trustee with independence as "the ultimate goal" and of the coming San Francisco Conference where a United Nations trusteeship system would be set up for colonial people. In terms of the duration of a trusteeship, he spoke in Cairo to General Stilwell of "25 years or so" and to Chiang Kai-shek of "perhaps 20 to 30 years."

Roosevelt believed he was firmly supported by Marshal Joseph Stalin and Generalissimo Chiang Kai-shek in his Indochina trusteeship concept, the former at Tehran and Yalta and the latter at Cairo. The president's conversations with Stalin at Tehran in late 1943 and at Yalta in early 1945, in which Indochina was discussed, were apparently not held in the presence of Prime Minister Winston Churchill. But FDR on one occasion summed up the situation by indicating the lineup was three to one— Roosevelt, Stalin, and Chiang Kai-shek against Churchill. In fact, the British prime minister was firmly and consistently opposed to any international trusteeship for French Indochina. Roosevelt believed Churchill's attitude was based on his apprehension about the effects of such a development upon British and Dutch colonies in Southeast Asia. As the president was returning home from Yalta on the American cruiser *Quincy*, he expressed himself in words of considerable bitterness about the colonial attitude of his British colleague.

In retrospect the evolution of the trusteeship concept for Indochina reflected the president's style of operation. As far as can be determined, the concept was never "staffed out" in an expression of Chester L. Cooper or incorporated into a working official document of the White House. Ambassador Patrick Hurley complained a few weeks after Roosevelt's death that he and Gen. Albert C. Wedemeyer received guidance from the president in conversations but not a written directive on United States political policy in Indochina. FDR liked to keep his options open just as long as possible and not to make hasty decisions. Lord Halifax, the British ambassador in Washington, observed that the president employed conversation as other people utilized the first draft of a paper. Ideas could be tried out—accepted, changed, or dropped. W. Averell Harriman, moreover, has indicated that the chief executive was reluctant to take the Department of State into his confidence on the trusteeship proposal, for he considered department officials pro-French. Roosevelt may not have reached a final hard decision on the future of French Indochina. It is certainly difficult to argue that a definite policy existed. Nevertheless, the personal diplomacy of the president and his style of operation cannot be ignored in any analysis of the situation.

What happened to the trusteeship concept, such as it was, after the death of FDR on April 12? One fact emerges: it definitely died. But the circumstances of its decease are not fully clear. It is doubtful if there was a formal decision in the White House to drop Roosevelt's concept. Rather, no person in the highest circles of the government pushed the trusteeship idea. President Truman himself probably did not know about it when he assumed office.

Secretary of State Edward R. Stettinius clearly indicated he did not want any discussions on the future of Indochina, at least during the San Francisco Conference on International Organization (April 25–June 26). The creation of a United Nations Organization was paramount. In fact, the Department of State believed the final determination of United States policy on Indochina depended upon discussions with France, and Stettinius himself on May 8 assured the French at San Francisco that the record was entirely clear of any official United States statement questioning even by implication their sovereignty over Indochina. The French satisfaction about the assurances was indicative of apprehension in Paris about Roosevelt's trusteeship legacy.

Another aspect of the shift in American policy was the greater interest of President Truman as compared with President Roosevelt in the viewpoints of the War and Navy Departments about their desire to get sovereignty over certain Japanese islands in the Pacific for use as American bases. American advocacy of trusteeship for outright European colonial possessions in Southeast Asia would have weakened the arguments of the military in Washington. President Truman was a genuine opponent of colonialism, but he was definitely interested in the acquisition of American bases in the Pacific.

While the San Francisco Conference was still in session, the Department of State on June 10 in response to urgent cables from Ambassador Hurley informed him that President Truman wanted him to know that "no basic change" in American policy toward Indochina had occurred and that a trusteeship for the territory was precluded unless under the auspices of France, which seemed unlikely. The cable from Washington seemed like double talk to Hurley. Twelve days later the department, in a basic policy paper relating to postwar Asia, expressly recognized French sovereignty over Indochina, made no reference to trusteeship, and pointed out the dilemma of the future of how to harmonize backing the French in Europe with supporting more self-government in Indochina. Eventual self-government in the area was the stated American goal.

President Truman in August, shortly after the surrender of Japan, dealt a blow to any lingering trusteeship hopes when he told General de Gaulle in Washington that the United States offered no opposition to a French return to Indochina. Later, on August 29, Truman informed Madame Chiang Kai-shek that, as far as he was concerned, there had been no discussion about a trusteeship for Indochina and that he was satisfied with de Gaulle's statement to him that the French leader favored independence for the area and quick steps toward achieving it.

Roosevelt's policy toward resistance movements in Indochina reflected his desire to prevent the return of the French to the territory. The situation was especially complex there in the closing year of the Pacific War. Involved were the interests of the French, British, Chinese, Japanese, and Americans, as well as those of the Vietnamese resistance. The United States early in the war had given pledges supporting the preservation of · the French Empire to the Vichy government and to the Free French under General de Gaulle. It is true that the pledges mainly came at a time when Washington was concerned lest more components of the empire succumb to the pressure of the Axis and when problems of the postwar world seemed far away. Colonial resistance and American sympathy were obviously related. Roosevelt for his part indicated in March 1943 that he thought the pledges did not extend to Indochina, but Undersecretary of State Sumner Welles reminded him of the contrary. The Vichy French and the Free French, despite their many differences, fully agreed on the objective of preserving the French Empire. General de Gaulle, it is not surprising, was determined to prevent any trusteeship for Indochina.

When Japan took over direct control of the territory from France on March 9, 1945, Roosevelt's attitude toward the French resistance became crucial. The previous October 16 he had firmly told Hull that the United States "should do nothing" about resistance groups in Indochina, although the subject might be brought up later when the situation was "a little clearer." The secretary had cited a letter from Gen. William Donovan, director of the Office of Strategic Services (OSS), on the matter and had stated, subject to the president's approval, that the department would inform the general it was not opposed to providing equipment and supplies to French and native resistance groups that were actually operating in Indochina.

Paris put heavy pressure on Washington after the Japanese coup of March 9 to aid the French forces retreating toward China. Gen. Claire L. Chennault, commander of the Fourteenth Air Force in nearby Yunnan, allowed some supply drops and made some air strikes against the Japanese, but he later indicated that orders from the War Department in Washington to theater headquarters forbade aid to French forces. General Wedemeyer at the theater level subsequently said Roosevelt personally told him in March not to furnish help to the French, and Secretary of War

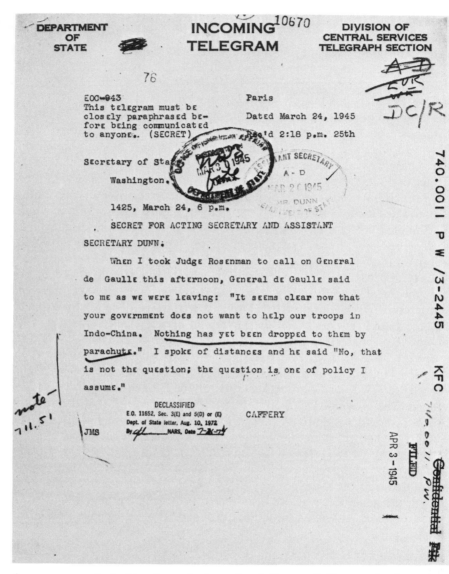

DEPARTMENT
OF
STATE

INCOMING 10670
TELEGRAM

DIVISION OF
CENTRAL SERVICES
TELEGRAPH SECTION

76

EOC-943
This telegram must be
closely paraphrased be-
fore being communicated
to anyone. (SECRET)

Paris

Dated March 24, 1945

Rec'd 2:18 p.m. 25th

Secretary of State

Washington.

1425, March 24, 6 p.m.

SECRET FOR ACTING SECRETARY AND ASSISTANT

SECRETARY DUNN:

When I took Judge Rosenman to call on General

de Gaulle this afternoon, General de Gaulle said

to me as we were leaving: "It seems clear now that

your government does not want to help our troops in

Indo-China. Nothing has yet been dropped to them by

parachute." I spoke of distances and he said "No, that

is not the question; the question is one of policy I

assume."

DECLASSIFIED
E.O. 11652, Sec. 3(E) and 5(D) or (E)
Dept. of State letter, Aug. 10, 1972
By ____ NARS, Date 7-26-74

CAFFERY

JMS

note
711.51

A message on Indochina from Ambassador Jefferson Caffery to the State Department. (RG 59, State Department Decimal File, National Archives.)

Stimson then asked him to mention the matter to Gen. George C. Marshall. On March 13, de Gaulle himself spoke to the American ambassador of the serious consequences should the French public realize that the United States was against France in Indochina.

Adm. William D. Leahy apparently got Roosevelt's approval around March 19 to authorize United States help to the French resistance forces but under the condition that it must not interfere with the Sino-American war effort against Japan. It was officially stated in Washington on April 19 that "an appreciable number" of American missions were flown into Indochina from March 29 to April 13 at direct French request along with other air operations into the territory. General de Gaulle, however, believed that the United States help to the resistance forces of the French was very little and very late. President Truman for his part supported qualified aid to them. In China, it should be observed, cooperation between the Free French and the Americans over resistance efforts in Indochina was certainly not outstanding.

The relations of OSS with Ho Chi Minh in 1944 and 1945 provided another occasion for the United States to help a resistance group in Indochina. The exact circumstances and the exact extent of American aid are still a mystery. Cooper has aptly pointed out from his own OSS experience in the China-Burma-India theater that the Office of Strategic Services was a "freewheeling organization," particularly in "out-of-the-mainstream places" like the southwestern part of China. It is quite possible that one or more OSS agents had established contact with Ho Chi Minh several months before Roosevelt's orders of October 1944 about doing nothing regarding resistance groups in Indochina.

The four secret visits of Ho Chi Minh to OSS Kunming headquarters in late 1944 and early 1945 were quite likely under the auspices of one or more OSS men. Ho wanted weapons and ammunition for which he would provide intelligence through his network of informers in Tonkin, continue to help rescue Allied fliers downed in the jungle, and conduct sabotage operations against the Japanese. Charles Fenn, an OSS agent, later revealed through the press that Ho was enlisted by OSS as Agent 19. Fenn also indicated through the press that he took Ho Chi Minh at his request to see General Chennault, and that the Viet Minh leader agreed to create a rescue team in Vietnam for downed Allied fliers. Paul E. Helliwell, chief of OSS in China during the four mentioned visits of Ho to the Kunming headquarters of the organization, has indicated, however, that Ho's requests for arms and ammunition were each time rejected, as OSS had a policy of not providing aid (in words as quoted by Robert Shaplen) to "known Communists" like Ho and "therefore obvious postwar sources of trouble." A major consideration was the refusal of the Viet Minh leader to promise not to use arms received against the French and only to use them against the Japanese. Nevertheless, Ho did get a few revolvers and some ammunition from Helliwell, and the supply grew in time from various American sources including OSS.

In the spring of 1945, the cooperation of OSS with Ho Chi Minh was much more extensive. By the end of May, a few of its personnel had walked or parachuted into the headquarters of the Vietnamese leader in northern Tonkin. Americans worked closely with Ho in his jungle camp. One of them, an army lieutenant, subsequently revealed that the Viet Minh leader tried to get help from him in preparing a declaration of independence from France. Ho was interested in the words of the American declaration and later actually used some of them. He subsequently said the United States declaration was employed as a model since his people viewed America as the country most likely to sympathize with them. Ho also used the OSS portable radio of the lieutenant to contact the Free French in China about the postwar future of Vietnam. OSS officers through their personal ties were very much impressed with Ho Chi Minh and his guerrillas. The Americans dropped arms to them, and during the final months of the Pacific War, OSS officers were in the words of Cooper "actually leading and training Viet Minh guerrillas."

After Ho Chi Minh took over Hanoi in the "August Revolution" following the collapse of Japan, Americans who arrived on the scene were well received by the Viet Minh. Among the former were OSS personnel under Maj. Archimedes Patti whose task was to make preparations for the Japanese surrender, the Military Advisory and Assistance Group (MAAG) under Gen. Philip Gallagher which was involved in assisting and advising the occupation forces of the Chinese Nationalists, the Military Government Group (G5) under Col. Stephen Nordlinger which was largely concerned with the release and rehabilitation of the Allied prisoners of war, and a number of American journalists. The sympathies of Americans on the scene, OSS officers and journalists for instance, were supporting Ho Chi Minh. (He often met with some of them.) These sympathies, however, were essentially based on Ho's leadership of a nationalist movement and American concern for a colonial people seeking independence.

In retrospect United States material aid to Ho Chi Minh during the closing phase of the Pacific War was probably not extensive. Assistance by the United States to resistance groups in Indochina, as the American Joint Chiefs realized, could obviously not be decisive in the United States objective of defeating Japan at home. But the aid, even though small-scale, could help to maintain active resistance to the Japanese in Indo-china, and this consideration could not be overlooked.

For Ho Chi Minh the American support of his resistance forces against the Japanese had important psychological consequences. He claimed his people were a part of the United Nations war effort against Tokyo. He at least hoped, he may even have expected, that the United States would next back him in winning independence from France. Ho Chi Minh was impressed by Washington's setting a date for Philippine independence and he highly praised the attitude of Roosevelt toward colonialism. The United States did have Ho's good will through much of 1945 and just possibly could have exerted some influence on him in the early postwar years, but there is no available evidence that the highest circles of govern-ment in Washington ever gave serious consideration to working with Ho Chi Minh against the return of France.

Theater command jurisdiction had both wartime and postwar dimen-sions for the Allied nations in Southeast Asia. An outside power that controls military operations in a given territory against the enemy, it should be stressed, is often in a position to influence the course of politi-cal developments there. After the war, military occupation by a victo-rious outside power often facilitates its political goals in a given territory.

The establishment of the Southeast Asia Command (SEAC) and its role before and after the collapse of Japan were significant in the evolution of American policy in Southeast Asia. At the Quebec Conference of Roose-velt and Churchill in August 1943, the British Chiefs of Staff proposed the creation of a Southeast Asia command under a British supreme Allied commander with an American deputy. In the SEAC theater of operations would be Indochina, a suggestion that the American Joint Chiefs accept-ed. On August 21, however, the Combined Chiefs of Staff approved a theater which did not include Indochina, but left it in the China theater under Chiang Kai-shek whose chief of staff was General Stilwell. There was much discussion in Quebec over the command aspects of the China and SEAC theaters in Southeast Asia. On August 23 at a summit meeting, Roosevelt wanted to know if Thailand was in the SEAC theater. Admiral Leahy replied in the affirmative but indicated that Indochina was staying in the China theater at this time.

As far as Southeast Asia itself was concerned, Burma, Thailand, Ma-laya, Singapore, and Sumatra were placed under the new Southeast Asia Command at Quebec and Gen. Douglas MacArthur had the rest of Southeast Asia under his Southwest Pacific Area except for Indochina which remained, as already indicated, with the China theater of opera-tions. Adm. Lord Louis Mountbatten was named the supreme Allied commander of SEAC with General Stilwell in China the deputy commander. The Combined Chiefs of Staff had "general jurisdiction over strategy" in the SEAC theater.

By the time of the Potsdam Conference, July 17 to August 2, 1945, Truman had succeeded Roosevelt, and Churchill himself during the summit with Stalin was replaced by Clement Attlee. The Second World War had ended in Europe, but Japan was still fighting in Asia and the Pacific. Major decisions in theater-command jurisdiction in Southeast Asia were made by the British and Americans at Potsdam. On July 17, it was the United States Joint Chiefs who favored in a memorandum a major alteration in Mountbatten's theater of operations. SEAC would be enlarged to include Indochina south of the fifteenth parallel, with the China theater still embracing Indochina north of the division. SEAC would also be extended to include Borneo, the Celebes and Java, with the area to the east an Australian command under the British Chiefs of Staff. The American Joint Chiefs thought that SEAC with its proposed enlargement would embrace an area of British Empire responsibility with the Dutch, the Portuguese, and perhaps later the French. They pointed out that the initial operational concern of the Americans in the area had substantially declined as they increasingly concentrated on the Japanese homeland. The division of Indochina at the fifteenth parallel, the Joint Chiefs believed, was primarily a subject for the approval of Chiang. What is particularly significant about the American proposal is the division of Indochina between Mountbatten's and Chiang's commands and the much weaker position apparently foreseen for the United States in postwar Southeast Asia, apart from the Philippines.

The final Anglo-American decisions at Potsdam on SEAC followed closely the recommendations of the United States. The division of Indochina was shifted to the sixteenth parallel by the British due to the "run of communications," and Truman and Attlee agreed to undertake efforts to get Chiang to approve the reduction of his theater in the area. Mountbatten's command now included all Southeast Asia except the Philippines, Timor, and, of course, northern French Indochina. He later observed that the decision on the latter area planted the "seed for even greater conflicts in the years to come."

The British and Americans agreed at Potsdam that the French and Dutch would be informed of Anglo-American intentions in any operations directly affecting their territories in the Far East. In fact, the French, Dutch, and Portuguese right up to the surrender of Japan were eager to have a military role in the recapture of their territories in Southeast Asia. General de Gaulle was very persistent about French military participation in the liberation of Indochina. He was critical of American delays, although Truman indicated French forces could be used under certain conditions in the war against Japan. Priorities in American transport and the main objective of defeating Japan at home were considerations in Washington.

Dated August 15, 1945, two significant steps were taken affecting the future of Southeast Asia. First, Truman on behalf of the Allied powers issued General Order No. 1 to General MacArthur which included the listing of areas Japan should surrender and to whom they should be surrendered. Second, Mountbatten, under pressure from Marshall, assumed command of his new SEAC territory. As far as Indochina was concerned, the British occupation of the southern part and the Chinese of the northern opened a new phase in Southeast Asian history.

In conclusion, historians will never know if Roosevelt's trusteeship concept for Indochina could have been implemented had he lived and been in good health. (If his approach to the area had been successful, possibly two bloody and costly wars in Indochina might have been avoided.) Nor will historians ever know if Ho Chi Minh with American support against France in 1945 and 1946 would have predated Tito in outlook and behavior. If so, a Vietnam like the subsequent model of Yugoslavia could have emerged. It is certain, however, that in the late months of the Pacific War the United States did not want its armed forces to play a major role in the recapture of European colonial areas in Southeast Asia and that the decisions at Potsdam signaled an American intention of restricting its postwar role essentially to the Philippines. In the light of the Second Indochinese War, American policy in Indochina back in the Second World War has aroused genuine interest and assumed greater importance. In view of the many variables and the problems of documentation, the final word will probably never be written.

Discussion Summary

In the discussion following these papers, Fifield was asked how much Roosevelt actually knew about the French administration of Vietnam. He replied that the president knew practically nothing about the area. Roosevelt never spoke of the peoples there as "Vietnamese," "Cambodians," and "Laotians," but always used the general term "Indo-Chinese." Why the president selected for his special attention French Indochina from all the dependencies in Southeast Asia remains a mystery.

Responding to a question of the seriousness of Roosevelt's promises to both Zionists and Arabs, Adler indicated his view that the president had not thought that far ahead. Domestic politics had much to do with the promises to the Zionists; those to the Arabs were probably based mostly on economic and strategic reasons. Roosevelt was an eternal optimist, who probably felt he could deal with the conflicting promises when the time came.

Joseph P. Lash felt that Roosevelt's attitude on Zionism was based not only on the Jewish vote but on genuine sympathy as well. Zionist aspirations and Arab nationalism proved to be incompatible, but the statesmen of that period attempted to deal with the problem of doing something for the homeless Jews and at the same time recognizing American interests with regard to the Arabs. Adler disagreed. The dream of Roosevelt and Sumner Welles that the Jewish and Arab aspirations could be reconciled was not then within the realm of political reality, and an abundance of archival evidence demonstrates that this was recognized at the time.

James Watts (City College of New York) asked about Roosevelt's role in excluding Jewish refugees from the United States. Adler replied that Breckenridge Long had received most of the blame for the exclusion and that there was no convincing evidence that the president knew the details of Long's activity. Roosevelt's position was analogous to Lincoln's on slavery: Lincoln said that if he could win the war by freeing all slaves, he would do it; if he could win it by freeing none, he would do that. Roosevelt was personally sympathetic to the Jews. He would have liked to admit them, but for pressing reasons of state he did otherwise.

Robert Milk (Hope College) wondered whether the pro-Nazi position of certain Arab leaders affected Roosevelt's views. Adler did not believe that was the case. Roosevelt's pro-Zionist position was based upon other considerations. His promises to the Arabs were based upon economic considerations, notably oil, and upon the balance of power with regard to the policies of Britain and Russia in the area.

IV

Military Biography

The fourth session of the conference, under the chairmanship of John E. Wickman, director of the Eisenhower Library, was held on the afternoon of June 14. It was designed to explore both the value of military biography and the problems of writing it by concentrating upon two World War II commanders: Gen. Joseph W. Stilwell and Gen. Douglas MacArthur.

Stilwell with Maj. Gen. Claire Chennault in 1943. (United Press International; Office of War Information; National Archives, no. 208-N-14392.)

BARBARA W. TUCHMAN

Sources and Problems
in Writing the Biography of
General Stilwell

I have to begin with a disclaimer. My book on Stilwell is not really a military biography even though the protagonist is a soldier. The book is really two-in-one, like an egg with two yolks: Stilwell *and* the American Experience in China, with the man chosen to represent the experience— to serve, as I stated in the foreword, as vehicle of the theme, which is not military. The larger theme is the Sino-American experience. For purposes of making it comprehensible to the reader, and writing a narrative, it needed a human vehicle. I chose Stilwell for that function, and the more I investigated the more valid the choice appeared. He was, I think, exactly right, but the fact that he happened to be a soldier was, for my purposes, more or less incidental. It was not of the essence; it was merely the form his career took.

With regard to sources for the military aspect, I met only two problems: for the period of World War II there is too much, a problem I will return to later. The second was minor: what happened during the maneuvers of 1940–41? This was when Stilwell earned the great reputation as tactician and field commander that led to his being rated number one corps commander in the United States Army and to his being selected after Pearl Harbor for the first overseas command of the war. Maneuvers do not seem to be a very well documented subject; in fact, for public affairs of the time they have the unique distinction of being *under*-documented. Yet as Stilwell's biographer I obviously had to find out what the maneuvers demonstrated. It is not enough to know the result; one wants to show it happening.

This is a frequent problem in military history: one always knows the result of a battle; the difficulty is in reconstructing the course of events *during* it. It is only when the time comes to write the narrative that you discover that you really do not know what went on. I had that problem with the loss of Alsace in August 1914. In that case I never did find out enough to make it clear in my own mind. I faked it but nobody noticed.

This time I spent endless hours searching. I read all the critiques in the *Infantry Journal*. OCMH (Office of the Chief of Military History) came up with a history of the Third Army in which Stilwell commanded a division during the first maneuvers, but it did not tell me anything. The best source, oddly enough, proved to be the press, which can hardly be said of it later on when the war was for real in China and Burma.

At that stage the American public was reading fairy tales, largely based on Chinese communiqués—which could teach Munchausen a thing or two. For a while, presumably on the theory that you would come nearer to the truth if you got out of Asia altogether, the *New York Times* covered the Burma campaign from *London!* The whole fairy tale of the Chinese war effort became in itself a factor of history because the attitudes and myths it created influenced our policy—but that is another story.

It has led me, however, to the proposition that the press might do well never to publish anything its reporters have not personally witnessed. It would eschew all communiqués, press releases, canned speeches. Just imagine! The news without press releases! We would be reading what happened, not what someone wants us to think happened—it might even be, on some delightful day, nothing at all. I proposed this once to Turner Catledge when the *Times* published a report about an alleged Israeli air raid which Cairo said killed fifty civilians while Tel Aviv said no planes had left the ground. Why not send a reporter to the spot, I asked Mr. Catledge; why bother to print the communiqué and the denial at all? He said something about being a paper of record, but I do not see much point in putting into the record something that may never have taken place, just because some propaganda office has put it into a communiqué. That is simply being a sucker. Communiqués have about as much relation to what actually happens as astrology has to the real science of the stars.

To get back to the maneuvers, the best account of all I found in a press-clipping book kept by the Stilwell family, which was a mine of wonderful things you never would find in a paper of record, but suffered from the disability that neither date nor name of newspaper was supplied for any of the clippings. Needless to say to this audience, the scrapbook was, to put it gently, a nightmare to the researcher.

From the point of view of World War II historians, my research was characterized by two unorthodoxies: no clearance and no tape recorder. As regards the first, I may say that when I first opened relations with the Pentagon I dutifully applied for clearance as I was told to do, had myself fingerprinted, and filled out a questionnaire as long as a Chinese scroll painting—two, in fact: one for the Department of Defense and one for the State Department, though I cannot say I was happy with the thought that I would have to submit notes on classified material, *and* the finished manuscript, for official sanction. The more I thought about it the less the prospect pleased. In the meantime, while the bureaucratic mills were grinding, I was working on the Stilwell Papers in the family home at Carmel and in the Hoover Library, where Stilwell's World War II papers were deposited. At some point *after* Hoover acquired them, the army got to thinking about it, and had gone through the deposit and removed the more "sensitive" (if that is the word) of the classified reports, helpfully leaving a blank sheet of white paper in each place as mute token of its passage. This was not as frustrating as might be supposed since I discovered that duplicates of the removed material remained in the Carmel files. With access to the Stilwell archive and other private collections, and with the amazingly thorough research and documentation by my predecessors, Riley Sunderland and Charles F. Romanus in the military, and Herbert Feis in the diplomatic field, and with the publication of the *Foreign Relations* volumes on China through 1944, what did I need clearance for?

A lawyer who had been consulted on another matter relating to the book, was emphatically opposed to my using any clearance that would require submission of the manuscript. By this time, six months after application, owing either to the murkiness of my past or to bureaucratic torpor (I am not sure which) the clearance had not yet come through. The question was, how does one stop a process even if it is not producing anything? The lawyer advised that I simply write to the Adjutant General and ask that my request be cancelled on the grounds that I no longer needed it, which was accordingly done, taking a load off my mind. Subsequently, whenever I came across reference to a document I wanted to see for myself, I would write to the very obliging people in the Military Division here, or at OCMH, and ask if such-and-such a document could be declassified. In all except one instance, I think, it could. In some cases, for example the episode of Colonel McHugh's intervention through Secretary Knox to have Stilwell recalled that so enraged General Marshall, I was able to establish the facts, through the simple expedient of going to the private source, in this case the McHugh Papers at Cornell, where the top-secret letter to Knox is quietly and innocently—and openly—resting. So much for clearance; it is overrated.

As to not making a tape recording of my interviews with participants, I can only say that a machine makes me quail. This may have something to do with being female. A woman is accustomed to entering upon a conversation as a personal thing, even with a stranger—perhaps more so with a stranger—and I cannot imagine myself plunking a machine down in front of someone and saying, "Now, talk." Besides, I am quite certain I would not know how to make it work. So I took along a notebook instead, one that fitted into my pocketbook and so was always handy for planned or unplanned need. The loose-leaf pages, being the same size as my index cards, could be filed conveniently along with the other research material.

Interviews, of course, proved some of my most useful sources but I have told all about that in a speech to the Oral History Conference two years ago, and as I have a horror of old speeches, I will not repeat it here. There is one aspect however, which I was uneasily aware of all along but more acutely since publication, and that is all the associates of Stilwell whom I did *not* talk to. I have now had innumerable letters from CBI (China-Burma-India) veterans and old China hands, some with anecdotes or phrases or bits and pieces of information which I could have used, but none, I think, or only one, that would have changed my thinking.

An incomparable and, I think, indispensable source for historians of World War II is film. I do not mean merely for illustrations but for physical description, for the realities of place and people that one cannot get any other way, and for flashes of insight and understanding through visual means. I think I learned more about Chinese propaganda from a film of the military parade staged for Wendel Willkie in Chungking, and more about Stilwell from a film showing him lying in the dust next to a Chinese soldier at the Ramgarh training ground and demonstrating how to handle a rifle, than I could have any other way. There is a room upstairs in this institution where one can happily spend days among the reels, learning and learning.

On the same principle, there is nothing like research on the spot, but that of course, in the pre-Ping Pong days, was denied me. As the next best thing I went to Hong Kong and Taiwan to get a feeling of Chineseness and to interview a group of Chinese veterans of the 38th division who fought under Stilwell. Though not on the mainland, these visits were productive of insights: for instance, into the problem created by the Chinese considering it impolite to say No. I knew this caused Stilwell all kinds of agony but I never realized how much until the wife of an American officer in Taiwan told me of her difficulty in giving official dinner parties because the Chinese always accepted whether or not they intended to come. She never knew how much food to order or how many places to set. It is equally difficult to conduct a war if your divisional commanders say yes, they will be ready for action at a time and place, and fail to show up.

So much for research. Actually I would rather talk about the problems of writing, not only because they interest me more but because the average layman underrates writing and is overimpressed by research. People are always saying to me in awed tones, "Think of all the *research* you must have done!" As if this were the hard part. Actually it is not; writing, being a creative process, is much harder and takes twice as long.

The form I use is narrative because that is what comes naturally to me. There is of course another equally important and valid form of history which is written for the purpose of putting the material and the author's conclusions on the record. Such an author is less concerned with communicating than with establishing the facts. He is historian first and writer second, if at all, whereas I am a writer first whose subject is history, and whose purpose is communication. I think of history as a story, myself as story-teller, and the reader as a listener whose attention must be held if he is not to wander away. In my mind is a picture of the itinerant story-teller of India, with his rice bowl, who tells tales of ancient romance and legend to a circle of villagers by firelight. If he sees figures drifting away from the edge of the circle in the darkness, and his audience thinning out, he knows his rice bowl will be meagerly filled. He must hold his listeners in order to eat.

I feel just as urgent a connection with the reader for it does not seem to me that writing has any independent existence until it is read. If it takes two to make love, or war, or play tennis, it likewise takes two to complete the function of the written word. This symbiosis ought to be obvious but it is astonishing how many writers never listen to their own prose nor consider how it will fall on the ear of the reader.

As a form, narrative has an inherent validity because it is the key to the problem of causation. Events do not happen in categories—economic, intellectual, military—they happen in sequence: When they are arranged in sequence as strictly as possible, down to the week and day, sometimes even time of day, cause and effect, which may have been previously obscure, will come clear. However, it is not always possible to narrate everything in straight consecutive sequence because there are always times when events are taking place simultaneously in separate places. In August 1914, the developments leading to the Battle of the Frontiers on the Western front, and to the Battle of Tannenberg on the Eastern front, were unfolding at the same time, putting the narrator in a quandary. The same problem was present with Stilwell when the accelerating deterioration in China and the launching of the last Japanese offensive took place while he was leading the return campaign through Burma. To break off events in one place in order to take up what is happening elsewhere ruins dramatic tension and only accomplishes utter confusion in the mind of the reader—even though that is the way things happen in reality. One has to manipulate reality just a little and carry events through to a natural climax on one scene before moving to the other.

In organization however, if not always in the finished product, chronology remains the spine. When I started writing *The Guns of August* I planned to begin with the guns going off so people should not think this was yet another book about diplomatic origins—Sarajevo and All That. I had worked out an intricate arrangement of four chapters in which war opened in each country and was followed by an internal flashback in each to explain the background. It was as beautifully designed as a Bach fugue, but when I had finished these chapters my editor didn't know what to make of them. On re-reading them, neither did I. He suggested trying it chronologically. This was so simple that I had thought it inartistic, but when the flashbacks were lifted out and put first where they belonged, behold, the result read as simply and naturally as if it had been ordained. I have avoided razzle-dazzle arrangements ever since.

With each book, one encounters new problems of organization and presentation. Obviously the dual theme of *Stilwell*—the biography of a man and the relationship of two countries—was a major difficulty throughout, but it was my choice, and peculiar to this book so I cannot generalize from it—except to say "never again." Every time I started a new chapter I felt like Joseph wrestling with the angel all through the night. Although it was hard work, the dual theme was justified, I think, because the figure of Stilwell as a continuing focus supplies human interest and drama, while the overall Sino-American relationship gives the subject importance.

The Chinese scene of the book was another problem. It meant, as I was aware all the way through, that the reader had no familiar frame of reference. If you write a book laid in Europe or America you can count on the reader having a mental picture of the relative location of France and Germany, or of Texas and Alaska, or where the Rockies are, or the Great Lakes. Equally with people. Once introduced let us say to Francis Drake and Walter Raleigh or Robert Oppenheimer and Edward Teller, he will have no great difficulty in keeping them distinct, but what is he going to make of Sun Li-jen and Li Tsung-jen, two prominent persons in my book, or of Yen Hsi-shan and Wang Ching-wei and Wei Li-huang and Chang Tso-lin and Chang Tsung-chang and all those other triple monosyllables— not to mention the provinces: Kwangtung and Kwangsi, which adjoin each other, Kiangsu and Kiangsi, which do not, Honan and Hunan, Shensi and Shansi, and all the rest. I tried at first to avoid using these names, and to locate places in relation to the more familiar rivers and cities, but this soon proved impossible. China's provinces can no more be avoided than America's states.

Especially in an alien setting like China—but the rule should hold true for all historical writing—I try never to introduce a place name without locating it in relation to some place already mentioned, nor introduce a person without describing some attribute that will fix him in the reader's mind. People and places must be given recognizable identities, otherwise the reader flounders in a sea of unknowns; he will miss the point of this or that and sooner or later, bored by incomprehension, will drift away.

The mere parading of names without taking the trouble to locate or personify them is either simple laziness on the part of the writer or else showing-off, in which case it is no trick; anyone can do it just as anyone can double the length of his bibliography if he has a mind to. I never can understand why historians who go in for this name-dropping make themselves great reputations. In D. W. Brogan's *France Under the Republic*, for example, one can count thirty names to a page, all faceless. Michael Howard recently established himself as a leading military historian with a book on the Franco-Prussian War which one can open at random at any page and find sentences like the following: "The Emperor put Failly's 5th Corps under his command and on 5th August while the divisions of 1st Corps concentrated around Froeschwiller and Felix Douay packed off Conseil Dumesnil's division from 7th Corps by train from Belfort, Macmahon summoned Failly to bring his corps south through the Vosges." In the next sentence we learn that Failly's units were spread between Sarreguemines and Bitche and could not be moved until relieved by troops from Rohrbach. On the same page is a sketch map which shows none of these place names. I am sure Mr. Howard knows all there is to know about the Franco-Prussian War, and his book was highly praised, but it left this reader giddy. I did not gather from it a picture of the battle of Froeschwiller but only how not to describe a battle.

Another difficulty peculiar to the Stilwell book, especially to the second half, was over-documentation. Besides Stilwell's diaries and letters, bringing the scale of events down to a daily basis which I did not want, there was a mountainous mass of military and diplomatic records: messages, reports, memorandums, conference minutes, plus all the material of the China controversy—the White Papers, the *Foreign Relations* series, the interminable testimony before congressional investigating committees in thousand-page volumes. Ever since the advent of mechanical means of duplication there has been a multiplication of material that cannot be dealt with by less than teams of researchers. The twentieth century is likely to be the doom of the individual historian. (Actually I do

not really believe that. Though the doom seems logical, I believe somehow he will illogically survive.) Today we have the opposite problem
from that of the researcher in ancient history who suffers from paucity of
records and must work from coins, tombs, and artifacts. Beginning with
Gutenberg, the sources expand. The nineteenth century is really the great
period with ample information of every kind, yet short of the over-supply
of today.

With the appearance of the tape recorder, a monster with the appetite
of a tapeworm, we now have a new problem of what I call artificial
survival. The effort needed to write a book, even of memoirs, requires
discipline and perseverance which until now imposed a certain natural
selection on what survived in print. But with all sorts of people being
encouraged to ramble effortlessly and endlessly into a tape recorder,
prodded daily by an acolyte of Oral History, some veins of gold and a vast
mass of trivia are being preserved which would otherwise have gone to
dust. I should hastily add here that among the veins of gold two of the
richest sources I found were two verbal interviews with General Marshall
tape-recorded by army historians in 1949. Marshall however was a summit figure worth recording.

As a result of over-documentation I was constantly struggling with the
problems of scale in the Stilwell book. It was as if I had been a cartographer trying to draw a map on a scale of 100 miles to the inch while
working from surveys detailed to a scale of one mile to the inch. Following in the track of the diary and the official documents, I would get caught
up in some issue that was all-absorbing at the time, and spend days
writing the developments from Tuesday to Friday when what I should
have been doing was the overall development from, say, May to November. I had to stop short and remind myself: What does this matter in the
long perspective?

As a result, pages went into the discard—for example, the Henry Wallace mission. Because he was vice president, Wallace's visit and conversations with Chiang Kai-shek assumed enormous importance at the time
and blew up a swirl of passions, intrigues and, of course, prolific reports
by everyone for miles around. The path of research widened out like the
mouth of the Yangtse and the narration likewise in its wake. I had an
uncomfortable feeling, however, that something was wrong. Then one
day someone asked me what actually had been the significance of the
Wallace mission and I heard myself answering, "None." It had really had
no effect on the course of events one way or another.

Because of all the quotable reports it spawned, this affair was a good
example of the bewitching effect of diplomatic documents. An episode

like the Wallace mission exercises the same effect as Everest on Mallory. You write it because it is there. Then it turns out not to mean anything. It would have been false to history to leave out the Wallace mission altogether so I condensed it as much as I could, even at the cost of cutting a wonderful characterization of Wallace by a man who said, "Henry would cut off his right hand for the sake of an idea—and yours too for that matter." I hated to let that go but since Wallace no longer appeared as a personality, it no longer belonged.

The larger scale cannot be achieved by blithely skipping over whole episodes or chunks of time; it requires condensing, which is the hardest work I know, and selection, which is the most delicate. Selection is everything; it is the test of the historian. The end product, after all, consists of what the historian has chosen to put in, as well as chosen to leave out. Simply to put in everything is easy—and safe—and results in one of those 900-page jobs in which the writer has abdicated and left all the work to the reader.

Selection is the task of distinguishing the significant from the insignificant. It must be honest, that is, true to the circumstances, and fair, that is, truly representative of the whole, never loaded. It can be used to reveal large meaning in a small sample. As Robert Frost said, "The artist needs only a sample." At Chiang Kai-shek's residence the glimpse of secret service boots peeking below red curtains, which I took from someone who was present, was a tiny selection that bespoke a whole atmosphere. Likewise the letters of Colonel Carlson to President Roosevelt (which incidentally have not before been printed) crystallized, I think, the American idealized view of China at the time.

One must resist the selection that does too much. By that I mean an item or incident which, by the fact of being made part of the narrative, appears representative and leaves the reader with an impression that may not be entirely justified. The author wields tremendous influence in this way which no one superintends but his own conscience.

I remember facing one such choice at the climax of the debacle in Burma when Stilwell was trying desperately to organize transport and food for the retreat before it collapsed into chaos. The Chinese general who was Chiang Kai-shek's personal liaison officer could not be found because, as it happened, he was elsewhere engaged in organizing the retreat to China of a Rolls Royce which he had delightedly acquired from the British governor-general in trade for two jeeps. I intended to cap this incident with an aphorism I had picked up from the warlord years in the 1920s: "In Chinese warfare commanding officers have never been known to retire poor." While that may have been reasonably true it would have left American readers with the impression that all Chinese generals were venal—which is true only in American terms. I am not an authority on China but I know enough to know that it would be quite false to write about China in the framework of Western values. So I took out the aphorism and the Rolls Royce too. This illustrates the reasoning behind a negative selection.

I seem to be giving you chiefly examples of what I left out, and this reflects what was a constant struggle. I made a vow when I started that I would keep the finished book under 500 pages, and in the course of that effort I discarded or radically pruned everything I thought could be spared or that was not germane to my main theme. I missed my goal by 51 pages but it was not for lack of trying.

Which brings me to another working principle—do not argue the evidence in front of the reader. The author's thought processes have no place in the narrative. One should resolve one's doubts, examine conflicting evidence, determine motives behind the scenes, and carry on any disputes with one's sources in the reference notes, not in the text. For one thing this keeps the author invisible and the less his presence is felt, the greater is the reader's sense of immediacy to the events. For another thing, by eliminating discussion one establishes a tone of this-is-the-way-it-was which the reader quickly accepts. He does not want to be bothered by a lot of maybes and perhapses, on-the-one-hand and on-the-other-hand; he wants to follow along with the action feeling confident this was the way things happened.

In order to identify with the period it is also essential to eliminate hindsight. I try not to refer to anything not known at the time. According to Emerson's rule, every scripture is entitled to be read in the light of the circumstances that brought it forth. To understand the choices open to people of another time, one must limit oneself to what they knew; see the past in its own clothes, as it were, not in ours. To me this is an absolute, although I realize it is one that many historians would fiercely dispute. According to their view, history is properly the interpretation of past events in terms of their consequences, and in the light shed upon them by present knowledge and present values. The history of Kuomintang China, according to this school, is told in the light of the ultimate Communist triumph, although, in fact, no policy maker of the 1930s ever seriously considered that within ten or fifteen years China would be ruled by the Communists. An account told in the light of now must be false to the past, as I see it, whereas the other school maintains that the view from inside the past results in a false judgment for today. The difference is one of philosophic stance and is unlikely to be resolved.

In closing, I may say that though I do not think of myself as a military historian, I agree on the need for military history, if only to bring home to the general public that conflict has been a central theme in the human story from prehistory to the present. Except for specialist studies, military history should be treated, I think, not as a separate category, but along with political, economic, and intellectual history, as part of a whole whose object is to exhibit what a given society was like at a given time. That object, it seems to me, should be the historian's purpose. That is what I tried to achieve in *The Proud Tower*, which is the reason I like it the best of my books.

General MacArthur and aides on Morotai, 1944. (Office of War Information; National Archives, no. 208-N-34197.)

D. CLAYTON JAMES

MacArthur, 1941-1945
Some Problems in
Documentary Research

Not until one is well into research on the career of General of the Army Douglas MacArthur does it become apparent why some scholars begin studies of him that they later abandon. The problems are complex and sometimes insoluble; those in oral history and in the printed materials are as serious as the ones in documentary research. This essay will be confined to a few of the difficulties of research in unpublished sources on MacArthur's role in the war against Japan.

Some of the major problems become identifiable as three questions are asked: Where are the chief unpublished materials and how accessible are they? How helpful are the official histories in delineating and interpreting sources? How revealing of MacArthur are the unpublished sources? Since the research for the second volume of *The Years of MacArthur*, which will cover 1941–45, is not finished at the time of this writing, other problems regarding primary materials will undoubtedly arise.

As to source collections and their locations, only the most important can be mentioned in a paper of limited length. Among federal depositories, the National Archives in Washington, D.C., and the Washington National Records Center in Suitland, Maryland, contain the largest and most useful collections. In the Modern Military Records Division of the former, thousands of messages and documents to, from, or concerning MacArthur are in the Operations Division (OPD) records, especially in the OPD 201 MacArthur file, the OPD Executive Office file,[1] and the OPD 381 Southwest Pacific Area (SWPA) file; the "safe" Secretary of War records' MacArthur file in the Office of the Adjutant General's central correspondence file; and the Chief of Staff's log and the Staff Communications Office file in the records of the Office of the Chief of Staff. The recently opened 273 feet of geographical and general decimal files of the records of the Joint and Combined Chiefs of Staff and Combined Civil Affairs Committee yield disappointingly few new insights on MacArthur's responses to and influence upon strategy making at the top levels. The

State Department records in the National Archives include a Pacific War file which has some documents pertaining to MacArthur,[2] but most major documents have appeared in the *Foreign Relations* volumes.

At Suitland the most valuable collection is the G-3 journal of SWPA General Headquarters; it comprises 239 boxes of assorted documents. Other helpful records at Suitland are those of the headquarters of ALAMO Force, Sixth Army, Eighth Army, and sundry theater task forces. The surviving records of MacArthur's and Wainwright's headquarters during the Philippine campaign of 1941–42 are also at Suitland, but some key files are missing.[3] The Manuscript Division of the Library of Congress in Washington has an inconsequential MacArthur collection, but that division has some MacArthur items of interest in the papers of Generals Henry H. Arnold, Benjamin D. Foulois, George Van Horn Moseley, and Carl Spaatz and Adm. Marc A. Mitscher. No important SWPA commander's papers are deposited in the Library of Congress.

Of the presidential libraries, as expected, the Franklin D. Roosevelt Library in Hyde Park, New York, has the most material relevant to MacArthur during World War II. Interesting items are found in the Harry Hopkins Papers and, of course, in the Franklin D. Roosevelt Papers, including the Map Room file, White House official file, president's personal file, and president's secretary's file. In the Herbert Hoover Presidential Library at West Branch, Iowa, there is a Hoover-MacArthur correspondence file, which, oddly, begins in 1942. Helpful documents relating to MacArthur during the last months of the war appear in President Truman's official file at the Harry S. Truman Library, Independence, Missouri. The Eisenhower principal file, 1916–52, at the Dwight D. Eisenhower Library, Abilene, Kansas, has some wartime items pertaining to MacArthur.

As for collections located at military installations, the Center of Military History (CMH) at Fort McNair, D.C., has retained a wide assortment of documents and other papers compiled largely during the preparation of the U.S. Army's Pacific War volumes. Relevant materials range from notes of researchers' interviews with MacArthur and some of his officers to official and unofficial reports and studies of planning and operations in the SWPA theater, including copies of some Australian documents. This office maintains "miscellaneous 201 files" of a number of SWPA commanders, which, in some cases including MacArthur's, contain copies of documents from the main 201 files of the Saint Louis Federal Records Center. The Philippine army records of 1936–41, also in the CMH holdings when used, are a fruitful source on MacArthur's relations with that organization. In the rapidly growing U.S. Army

Military History Research Collection at Carlisle Barracks, Pennsylvania, valuable, though not extensive, information on MacArthur is in the papers of Generals Charles A. Willoughby, Bradford G. Chynoweth, and Col. William C. Braly. The wartime records of Maj. Gen. Hugh J. Casey, MacArthur's chief engineer officer, are located in the district engineer's office at Baltimore, Maryland. A small collection of documents of MacArthur's headquarters, 1944–45, is in the holdings of the Army Signal Corps Museum at Fort Monmouth, New Jersey.[4]

The Air Force Historical Division at Maxwell Air Force Base has a number of documents on MacArthur's relations with Lt. Gen. George C. Kenney and other air commanders of the theater in its records of SWPA air organizations—Allied Air Forces, Far East Air Force, Fifth Air Force, and Thirteenth Air Force. In the Naval History Division at the Washington Navy Yard, Washington, D.C., items of interest on MacArthur's relations with Pacific naval commanders are found in various operational narratives, private papers, and interview transcripts, the principal contributors being Admirals Thomas C. Hart, Francis W. Rockwell, Thomas C. Kinkaid, Daniel E. Barbey, Chester W. Nimitz, William F. Halsey, and Robert L. Ghormley. Interview transcripts at the Marine Corps Historical Division, Arlington, Virginia, which contain interesting commentaries on MacArthur include those of Generals Oliver P. Smith, Omar T. Pfeiffer, and Thomas E. Bourke.

Of all collections located in university depositories, the most important is the Robert L. Eichelberger Papers at Duke University, Durham, North Carolina, the collection comprising 226 boxes. General Eichelberger was one of the few general officers close to MacArthur who committed to paper extensive and severe criticisms of his theater commander. Sixteen transcripts of the Oral History Collection of Columbia University, New York City, contain observations worthy of notice on MacArthur's generalship and personality, especially among the transcripts of the Naval History Project. Since MacArthur maintained some lively political ties during the war years, the Arthur H. Vandenberg, Frank Murphy, and Joseph R. Hayden Papers of the University of Michigan at Ann Arbor are enlightening. Other noteworthy collections, which contain significant MacArthur materials, are Henry L. Stimson's diary and papers at Yale University, New Haven, Connecticut; the Aaron S. Merrill Collection at the University of North Carolina, Chapel Hill; the Patrick J. Hurley Papers at the University of Oklahoma, Norman; the Robert L. Sherrod Papers at Syracuse University, Syracuse, New York; the Paul V. McNutt Papers at Indiana University, Bloomington, as well as isolated letters in several other universities' holdings.[5]

In the broad category of state, municipal, and private depositories, MacArthur materials of widely varying quality and extent are found in certain collections of the New York Historical Society, Virginia Historical Society, Wisconsin State Historical Society, Mississippi Department of Archives and History, George C. Marshall Research Library, and New York Public Library. The two most useful depositories in this general category are the MacArthur Memorial Bureau of Archives at Norfolk, Virginia, and the Hoover Institution on War, Revolution, and Peace on the Stanford University campus, Palo Alto, California. Although weak on MacArthur's career prior to the Second World War, the MacArthur Memorial has a large body of original documents for the war years and a considerable amount of copies of material found in the National Archives. The collections are in good order, considering the relatively short time the staff has been at work on processing and indexing. The record groups there which are indispensable are those containing files of MacArthur's headquarters as commander of United States Army Forces in the Far East (1941–42), SWPA (1942–45), and United States Army Forces in the Pacific (1945). The record group that comprises MacArthur's private correspondence consists of ninety-three large boxes of letters, many of which date from the war years and some of which concern his wartime political connections, particularly in 1943–44.[6] At the Hoover Institution, the diary and papers of Maj. Gen. Clovis E. Byers are especially valuable. Other collections there which contain letters to, from, or about MacArthur include the papers of Generals Delos C. Emmons, Robert C. Richardson, and Joseph W. Stilwell and Admirals Charles M. Cooke, Raymond A. Spruance, and Charles A. Lockwood.

Among foreign depositories the most important is the Australian War Memorial at Canberra, which has custody of most of the official sources of the Australian army. They are largely war diaries and correspondence files of SWPA headquarters and units, but there are no guides to these collections, photocopying is not permitted, and much material is closed. Documents on MacArthur's relations with Australian political figures and the higher direction of the Australian war effort are in scattered Commonwealth departmental files which have not been opened to researchers. The willingness of surviving Australian commanders of the SWPA theater to share their personal papers and views is partial compensation. Moreover, the frank critiques of MacArthur in the official Australian war volumes suggest that the majority of significant documents were revealed therein. The Australian comments rank with those of Eichelberger as the most refreshingly candid appraisals of MacArthur.

The reports of New Zealand forces serving in MacArthur's theater and papers of some of their commanders are located in the New Zealand National Archives at Wellington, having until recently been in the custody of the Department of Internal Affairs.[7] Liabilities similar to those regarding use of the Australian records exist, but the handicap is not as serious since most New Zealand forces in the war against Japan in the Pacific served in Halsey's theater, not MacArthur's. So far, repeated correspondence has evoked no response from Philippine archives, but MacArthur items are known to exist in the Manuel L. Quezon Papers of the Philippine National Library at Manila. Also, the historical office of the Philippine army headquarters is known to hold some documents of interest. The Pacific War files of the War History Office of the Japanese Defense Agency in Tokyo are of little assistance. Japanese views of MacArthur and his operations are available, however, in the published interrogations of several American occupation agencies, war-crimes trials, and the Strategic Bombing Survey. Visits to the above-mentioned foreign depositories will undoubtedly produce better cooperation than is possible through correspondence.

In addition to the collections in various American and foreign archival holdings, a surprisingly large number of papers are still in the private possession of American officers who served in the Southwest Pacific conflict. Fortunately, a number are willing to share their materials with individual researchers, but too many have adamantly refused to cooperate. It is to be hoped that these personal collections will eventually be channelled into archives, which can properly preserve and organize them for researchers.

The geographical scattering of the various unpublished sources produces nearly insurmountable problems of time and funds for the MacArthur biographer if he teaches as his principal means of livelihood, resides a considerable distance from all of the important depositories, and is seriously limited in funds for travel, photocopy, and secretarial assistance. Ideally, a project of the magnitude of a comprehensive MacArthur biography should be the undertaking of a team of scholars with ample foundation support. If the geographical distribution of sources does not discourage the fainthearted, there are the annoying restrictions on documentary research, including classified-matter regulations of the federal government, legal stipulations of the donor or his heirs, and photocopy limitations of some depositories. Many MacArthur items are still classified "Top Secret" and cannot be examined by nonmilitary researchers, who can get clearance to examine documents only through the "Secret" level. The vast majority of MacArthur documents of the 1941–45 period that are still classified should be downgraded since, by no stretch of imagination, could knowledge of their contents by an "outsider" jeopardize national security or unjustly embarrass surviving participants. Likewise, archival authorities should try with renewed vigor to get donors of primary materials to reduce or to eliminate limitations on their use, especially private collections which could be of unusual historical significance. Drastic revision of policies on classified public documents and restricted personal papers would conserve the time and skills of both researchers and archivists for better use of the documents, but unfortunately such policy changes do not originate at their levels.

The vastness of some of the collections means that the researcher must be very selective. No individual can hope to examine every document on MacArthur's career during World War II. Of course, selectivity is of the essence of any historical research, but for the researcher of a major figure of that war the decision on which materials to examine or to ignore is most unsettling and humbling. Such a researcher cannot help envying his colleague who is writing on a small topic of antebellum American history and who has the confidence of having examined thoroughly the sources. Whether the MacArthur biographer invests four or fifteen years in research, at the end he will still lack a sense of confident mastery of the primary materials.

Reliable estimates of the amount of existing American army records of 1941–45 ran as high as fourteen thousand tons. Although only a small proportion of this is pertinent to MacArthur, the researcher in pursuit of that general must use not only United States Army and Army Air Forces records but also United States Navy and Marine Corps documents and, if possible, Australian, New Zealand, Philippine, and Japanese sources. Moreover, he cannot confine his quest to military records but must also examine diplomatic, political, and public opinion sources. MacArthur was at the same time supreme commander of the SWPA theater and all of its American and Allied ground, air, and naval forces, a close adviser of Prime Minister John Curtin on military and nonmilitary matters in American-Australian relations, a confidant of Presidents Quezon and Sergio Osmena in Philippine affairs, and a potent influencer of public opinion and Republican factionalism in the United States.

Fortunately, the MacArthur researcher can find some solace in the excellent American and Australian histories of the war in the Southwest Pacific. The volumes of the Office of the Chief of Military History on the American army in the SWPA theater offer superb guides to many of the sources which are essential to the writing of a MacArthur biography. It would be vain, indeed, for anyone to attempt alone to cover the documents used in that series as thoroughly as army historians, such as Louis

Morton and Robert Ross Smith, have done. This is true also of the United States Army Air Forces volumes published by the University of Chicago Press, the Marine Corps monographs and historical series, Samuel Eliot Morison's history of naval operations, and the Australian official histories.[8] Not only is it impossible for an individual researcher to retrace the official historians' steps through the legions of documents they used, but also the effort would be pointless because the biographer's task is a different one. He is primarily tracing a man and his career, not an operation, a military unit, or, much less, the whole scope of the war in the Southwest Pacific.

It would be difficult to gain much perspective of MacArthur by relying principally upon the official histories, as valuable as they are. By their nature the volumes on combat operations offer little of his personality, or that of any officer. In both the operational and strategical studies attention is given to headquarters staff planning, but MacArthur's own influence upon the formulation of plans and the process of decision making is not adequately delineated. An in-depth study of MacArthur as theater commander should involve consideration of such factors as the force of personality, motivation, role-taking, prejudices, personality clashes, effect of friendship on judgment, and his self-image as influenced by his public image. Quite properly, the official historians chose not to delve into these matters, but if some of these factors can be identified and explained, new light may be cast on certain decisions and responses of his, ranging possibly from plans for an attack atop a Leyte hill to the development of policy directives at the Joint Chiefs' level.

In the United States Army's official volumes there are some gaps that are only partially filled by the other American and Allied official histories. The Borneo operations of 1945, for example, are omitted from the OCMH Pacific series, and the Australian version is inadequate on the American contribution thereto. Strategy and command in the Pacific in 1944–45, inexplicably, do not rate a separate volume, although the OCMH series does have a volume on strategic and command developments of the years 1941–43. Little attention is devoted to guerrilla activities or civil affairs in territories reconquered by SWPA forces, but these were matters of great concern to MacArthur. As previously mentioned, he was closely involved at times in diplomatic affairs and political relations with Australian, New Zealand, Dutch, and Philippine civil leaders, but, again properly so, his role in such matters is virtually ignored in the official histories.

Other instances in which the biographer cannot be content with the coverage in the official volumes are a number of unsettled controversies, such as the Clark Field disaster, the supplying of Bataan, the results of the Bismarck Sea battle, the relief of certain commanders (especially in the Buna and Biak operations), SWPA censorship policies, the alleged inequities endured by the Australian forces, the possible needlessness of certain amphibious operations, MacArthur's relations with his naval and air commanders and with South Pacific and Pacific Ocean Areas headquarters, and the comparative merits of MacArthur's and Yamashita's defenses of Luzon. Some of these issues are dealt with in the official histories but none in detail as to MacArthur's role. Moreover, in some cases the sources on the controversy are more extensive and varied than indicated in the official volumes. Combat operations and tactics are the chief concern of most of the official studies of the Southwest Pacific War and are rightly presented, for the most part, from the evidence in official documents. On the other hand, the sources for a topic such as censorship should include a variety of other types of primary materials, for instance, private papers, contemporary periodicals and newspapers, and personal statements of key men who yielded little or no information to the official historians. It may be that revision of the official histories' interpretations of certain controversies will not be warranted when further research is completed, but the biographer is obligated to test the evidence for other possible interpretations, particularly in seeking out MacArthur's motivation and responsibility in the matter.

The appearance of a number of sources in books and articles since the publication of the official volumes is another reason that the researcher should not be content with the presentation of sources in the government-sponsored series. Conspicuous examples are Vice Adm. Daniel E. Barbey's account of operations of the Seventh Amphibious Force, MacArthur's memoirs, and the Willoughby edition of the "MacArthur histories."[9] Likewise, some recent and excellent secondary works utilize sources untapped by the official historians, for example, the Belotes' account of the Corregidor operations of 1942 and 1945, Theodore Friend's study of Philippine politics, 1929–46, and David J. Steinberg's work on Philippine collaboration during the Japanese occupation.[10] MacArthur's relations with alleged collaborationists, in the case of Steinberg's study, were significant in determining the influence of the old regime in the reconstituted civil affairs of the Philippines.

In summary, the official histories must serve as a starting point for any study of the facts or search for the documents relating to MacArthur's leadership in the SWPA theater. But those volumes, by their nature, are inadequate for the biographer's purposes and must be revised, supplemented, or updated as to sources for episodes in which he was involved.

Surely the location and accessibility of the unpublished sources and the documentation of the official histories pose difficulties, but the most critical problems of the biographer derive from the third and final question under consideration: How revealing of MacArthur are the unpublished primary materials?

Although there are many thousands of documents covering operations in the Southwest Pacific, some incidents directly involving MacArthur are poorly documented. This is true of his headquarters activities during the first Philippine campaign, with only a portion of his records having been located. Some headquarters records of his SWPA theater and of his later Army Forces in the Pacific command including reputedly large amounts of "Top Secret" documents have never been recovered by the army. An unknown quantity of G-3 planning division files and other headquarters records of the war period were presumably lost in a plane crash in 1947. No records exist covering several of the key conferences between MacArthur and Halsey, MacArthur and Nimitz, and MacArthur and his SWPA ground, air, and naval chiefs. No full documentary record of the famous meeting of Roosevelt, Nimitz, and MacArthur at Pearl Harbor in July 1944 has been located. Thus, whereas a plethora of evidence exists about many activities, especially combat operations, the documentation is sometimes woefully weak or missing altogether in other cases, unfortunately including some critical episodes of MacArthur's decision making.

There is an abundance of MacArthur's messages to the War Department, but some seem to bear the mark of duplicity. On numerous occasions his radiograms to Gen. George C. Marshall, for example, contain affirmations contrary to positions that he actually held, according to the testimony of staff officers in whom he confided. Of course, rare is the officer who is completely candid with his superior on every matter, especially if the former knows his views are the opposite of his superior's. But MacArthur's misrepresentations at times possess an aura of machination. The intensity of his indignation over Wainwright's assumption of command and subsequent surrender cannot be measured from the documents, which convict MacArthur of nothing more serious than misunderstanding the wishes of Roosevelt and Marshall. The unpublished documents tell us only that Prime Minister Curtin repeatedly tried to get Churchill to use his influence on Roosevelt to get a larger logistical commitment to the SWPA theater, though probably few leaders in the War Department had doubts as to the origin of the prompting. A number of men who knew MacArthur well at his wartime headquarters have privately stated that he talked often of politics and was severely critical of the president, but little of this can be found in his messages and papers. If only the documents are examined, MacArthur appears with few exceptions, to be composing paeans of praise to the Australians serving under him; his real opinion may be better judged by the way he used their services. Correspondence in which MacArthur was neither sender nor recipient but instead the subject sometimes reveals his intentions more clearly than his own messages, as in some of the exchanges between General Kenney, his air chief, and General "Hap" Arnold. If the sender was strongly opinionated, as in the case of Adm. Ernest J. King, of course, his remarks about MacArthur must be used with caution. Of some value, too, are reports of journalists and other civilians who visited MacArthur's headquarters; occasionally they reveal nuances of his behavior not seen in any official documents. And where written materials do not tell the story wholly or accurately there is no substitute for interviews with participants, although, again, their statements must be weighed carefully. So far, in this project over one hundred of MacArthur's contemporaries of the wartime period have cooperated in this manner. Even with the bits and pieces supplied by sources other than MacArthur's messages, the charge of duplicity cannot often be substantiated beyond circumstantial evidence. But the researcher must at least be constantly wary handling MacArthur-originated documents. Official Washington surely learned this during the war years when his reports of objectives secured arrived long before the heaviest fighting had occurred and when his reports of Japanese losses and numbers engaged were far from what later checking proved to be accurate.

The question of authorship of messages, particularly radiograms bearing MacArthur's name at the end, is sometimes baffling. His headquarters staff officers vouch that seldom did an important message enter or leave without his cognizance, and rarely was he remiss in authorizing his name on a message which he had not read. Yet at times he seems to have been quite forgetful or perhaps deliberately negligent in regard to messages involving decisions which produced less than desired results. For instance, until his death he disclaimed responsibility for the unpreparedness at Clark Field in December 1941, the researcher being left with the contradictory statements of Generals Richard K. Sutherland and Lewis H. Brereton, as well as sundry views of lesser officers. Likewise, there is the problem of deciding finally how much part MacArthur himself assumed in creating a plan or deciding a tactical move. In a headquarters structure as well organized and efficient as his (and it was both), it is no easy matter to delineate the extent of planning which emanated from MacArthur himself and how much was simply approved by him, the decision being a foregone conclusion from the staff planning and recommendations which reached his desk. Moot subjects, for example, are the credit MacArthur deserves for the ideas which resulted in the Nadzab airborne operation of

September 1943 and the Admiralties invasion of February 1944. Perhaps there are no final answers to such queries any more than to questions of how much credit Roosevelt himself deserves for various New Deal measures, but the biographer has a duty at least to wrestle with these puzzles.

It is difficult to confirm or contradict the public image and professed convictions of MacArthur the man from either public or private papers. Rarely does the biographer feel that the private thoughts and feelings of MacArthur are revealed in the sources, especially official documents. In some collections there have been obvious deletions of papers which could convict him of less than perfection. In other cases, perhaps most, the written record simply substantiates the positions which he publicly professed and omits reference to positions which he expressed to intimates in private conversation or which antagonists felt surely he held. The records of the MacArthur Memorial are especially disappointing in this regard. Papers which suggest contradictions of the outer image that he seemed to cultivate assiduously are rare, exist only outside the Norfolk depository, and are never penned by MacArthur himself. In other words, he covered his tracks well, and some of his devoted colleagues have tried to sweep away what little he left exposed.

The task, then, for which the documentary record does not adequately prepare the biographer is that of penetrating the posthumous reputation of the man and probing the complexity of his personality, particularly as it impressed itself upon his contemporaries and influenced decision making in the war against Japan. Because of his aloof, aristocratic demeanor, few men could lay honest claim to having known him well. Among that intimate group none has yet been found who left papers which afford objective, perceptive analyses of MacArthur the man. They are either blindly adulatory, like Maj. Gen. Courtney Whitney, or bitingly critical, as in the case of Eichelberger, who felt wronged by MacArthur on several counts. So far no contemporary of the 1941–45 period has emerged through papers or interviews who possesses the cool-headed and fair viewpoint expressed by Gen. Dwight D. Eisenhower on the prewar MacArthur.

If the real MacArthur is so elusive and not fully revealed in the documents or elsewhere, if the problems of time, funds, and access to the sources are severe, if the biographer tries his best while aware that his work will be neither objective nor definitive in the final analysis, both writer and reader may well despair of the project. At such moments the advice of historian Henry Steele Commager is helpful:

> If we are to get on with the job, we must agree upon some kind of factual foundation or framework for our histories, if only that Washington was in fact the first President of the United States. . . .

Historians have, after all, surmounted the difficulties that crowd about them, and have given us famous and affluent histories. Gibbon was aware of the difficulties, and Macaulay, Ranke and Mommsen . . . yet all of them managed to write histories which have enlarged the thoughts and lifted the spirits of generations of men. Let the young historian take to heart the lines of the Greek Anthology:

> A shipwrecked sailor, buried on this coast,
>   Bids you set sail;
> Full many a gallant bark, when we were lost,
>   Weathered the gale.[11]

The recent barks of Forrest C. Pogue, Stephen E. Ambrose, and Barbara W. Tuchman overcame intricate problems regarding other great commanders of World War II.[12] This latest bark may get through the gale, though probably not unscathed.

Notes

1. See especially Item 1c, Top Secret SWPA Strategy and Planning Messages; Item 7a, Super Secret Messages to General MacArthur; and Item 7d, Messages from General MacArthur.
2. See File 740.0011PW, Legislative, Judicial, and Diplomatic Division.
3. Part of MacArthur's pre-1917 201 File is in AGO Decimal File 487448, RG 94, National Archives. Even the MacArthur Memorial has been unable to obtain access to his post-1917 201 File.
4. By late 1970, all SWPA records formerly held by the Kansas City Federal Records Center were moved to Suitland. A number of course papers were prepared after 1945 by officers who were studying at army service schools and had formerly served under MacArthur. Some of these papers, especially ones at the Infantry School, Fort Benning, have interesting comments on MacArthur and his key headquarters officers.
5. These include Mississippi State University, Johns Hopkins University, and the University of Texas.
6. The MacArthur Memorial Bureau of Archives' holdings on MacArthur's commands of 1941–45 by record groups and number of boxes therein are as follows: RG 2, USAFFE, 9 boxes; RG 3, SWPA, 160 boxes; and RG 4, USAFPAC, 31 boxes. Of these 200 boxes (about eighty-three feet), 25 are classified matter. RG 9, Radiograms, comprises 74 boxes, but nearly all of these messages postdate World War II.
7. These records were held by the Department of Internal Affairs at Wellington until the New Zealand official war histories were completed.
8. The number of volumes in each official series, which cover Southwest Pacific

operations, is as follows: U.S. Army, 8; U.S. Army Air Forces, 3; U.S. Navy, 8; U.S. Marine Corps, 7; Australian, 4; New Zealand, 1.

9. Daniel E. Barbey, *MacArthur's Amphibious Navy: Seventh Amphibious Force Operations, 1943–1945* (Annapolis: U.S. Naval Institute, 1969); Douglas MacArthur, *Reminiscences* (New York: McGraw-Hill, 1964); Charles A. Willoughby, ed., *Reports of General MacArthur*, 2 vols. in 4 pts. (Washington D.C.: Government Printing Office, 1966).

10. James H. Belote and William M. Belote, *Corregidor: The Sage of a Fortress* (New York: Harper & Row, 1967); Theodore Friend, *Between Two Empires: The Ordeal of the Philippines, 1929–1946* (New Haven: Yale University Press, 1965); David J. Steinberg, *Philippine Collaboration in World War II* (Ann Arbor: University of Michigan Press, 1967).

11. Henry Steele Commager, *The Study of History* (Columbus: Charles E. Merrill, 1965), pp. 52–53.

12. Forrest C. Pogue, *George C. Marshall*, 3 vols. to date (New York: Viking Press, 1963); Stephen E. Ambrose, *The Supreme Commander: The War Years of General Dwight D. Eisenhower* (Garden City: Doubleday, 1970); Barbara W. Tuchman, *Stilwell and the American Experience in China, 1911–45* (New York: Macmillan Co., 1970).

V

Major Resources of the National Archives and Records Service for Research on the Second World War

The fifth session of the conference took place on the morning of June 15, under the chairmanship of Dean C. Allard of the Naval History Division. The papers were intended to provide a description of two types of material in custody of the National Archives and Records Service relating to the Second World War: the records of military agencies in the National Archives and the papers and other historical materials located in the Roosevelt, Truman, and Eisenhower libraries.

ROBERT W. KRAUSKOPF

Military Records in the National Archives on the Second World War

The military heritage of the United States is richly documented in the holdings of the National Archives, and no small part of that documentation relates to that period of violent conflict and upheaval nearly a generation ago that we know as the Second World War.

In the National Archives building and our branch repository a few miles away at Suitland, Maryland, are housed almost 1.1 million cubic feet of permanently valuable records of the federal government, extending back to 1789. Of these, over 50 percent (625,000 cubic feet) were produced by our military establishment, i.e., the War and Navy Departments and their organizational components, and latterly the Department of the Air Force and the Office of the Secretary of Defense, plus several quasi-military agencies created during the periods of national emergency. Of this amount, in turn, about 164 thousand cubic feet, or 26 percent of all the military records in National Archives custody, belong to the period of the Second World War.

It will not be possible to discuss these records in much breadth or depth, or record group by record group. The most that we can expect to accomplish is to examine certain significant aspects of the war and to call attention to some of the official documentation in the National Archives that would be useful for research in those areas.

Most of these records were accessioned by the National Archives over the last two decades in the course of systematic records retirement programs on the part of the agencies that produced them. In one instance, however, the process was something of a windfall: the Department of the Army in 1958, for economy reasons, turned over to the National Archives (complete with its contents and staff) the records depository at Alexandria, Virginia, that held all of its most significant Second World War records. This unit—many of you will remember it as the former Departmental Records Branch of the Adjutant General's Office—was the predecessor of our present Modern Military Records Division, which was established in 1966. The military records at Alexandria were transferred from that depository when it was abandoned a few years ago. Part of these records were sent to the National Archives Building and the remainder to the new branch depository at Suitland.

In discussing the records, I should like to look first at those relating to

Boxes of World War II records in the National Archives. (National Archives photograph, no. NA-5493.)

the antecedents of American involvement; then to those covering the higher direction of the war; those documenting the war on land, sea, in the air, and on the home front; and finally those relating to the aftermath of the war.

Our holdings of official records for the years before the outbreak of hostilities are virtually complete and are therefore of great value in research on the origins and background of the war. Records of the General Staff, particularly of the Military Intelligence Division, report upon, and reflect the reactions of our military leadership to, the effects of Sino-Japanese hostilities in the thirties, the deterioration of American relations with Japan, the Spanish Civil War, Mussolini's aggression against Ethiopia, and Nazi aggression against Austria, Czechoslovakia, and Poland. Together with Air Corps files, they document the implementation of the political decision taken by President Roosevelt in 1938 to give assistance to France and Great Britain in their efforts at rearmament and thereby, fortuitously, to lay the foundations of the great American "arsenal of democracy" that was to sustain our own forces and the forces of our allies for the next seven years. Records of the various planning organs of the War Department document the development of war plans to fit the succession of contingencies faced by the United States, beginning with continental defense and progressing through the hemispheric defense concept of 1940, to our quasi-neutral, quasi-combatant status of 1941. Comparable records of the Navy Department describe the testing in the naval war games of the 1930s of strategic hypotheses and tactical methods applicable to a war in the Pacific, and incidents, such as the sinking of the *Panay* in 1937, that brought the United States prematurely to the brink of war. For the Pearl Harbor catastrophe, the climax of this period, our holdings include the records of the War Department's own investigation of that tragedy, carried out in 1944.

For the serious study of the higher direction of the war, we believe our holdings are of exceptional importance. At the very highest level we are fortunate in possessing the main files of the Joint and Combined Chiefs of Staff, extending from their inception, shortly after Pearl Harbor, to the end of 1945. The 300 cubic feet of this series of records have only recently been reviewed for declassification by the Joint Chiefs and opened to general use by the public. Since all of the major strategic moves and proposed strategic moves of the Allied powers at some stage came under the scrutiny of the JCS or the CCS, there are few aspects of the war, in any theater of operations, and few significant decisions that cannot be traced through these papers.

At the next level, that of interallied operational headquarters, National Archives holdings include the files of Allied Force Headquarters, established in 1942, and Supreme Headquarters Allied Expeditionary Forces, established in 1943. The former of these, headed first by General Eisenhower and later by Field Marshals Wilson and Alexander, directed land, air, and naval operations in North Africa and later in Sicily, Italy proper, and other parts of the Mediterranean. The latter, better known as SHAEF from its acronym, was organized and led by General Eisenhower and executed the cross-Channel invasion of France and the subsequent offensive across France and into Germany that culminated in the collapse of German resistance in May 1945. For the Pacific theater, the National Archives has some records of General Headquarters, Southwest Pacific Area, and Far East Command, dating from 1942, and records of the Southeast Asia Command and United States Forces, China theater.

All of these records are valuable for the study of the diplomatic as well as the military history of the war, for they reflect the close intermingling of political with strategic considerations that always characterizes a war waged by a coalition of allied states.

In a slightly different context, but still at the international level, we have records of the Munitions Assignments Boards, operating in London and Washington from 1941 to 1946, which determined the allocation of available military equipment and supplies to the Allied forces and theaters of war in which they were required, and records of the United States Military Mission to Moscow, which facilitated American-Russian military cooperation and helped to organize such operations as the shuttle bombing raids of 1944, in which American bombers after leaving their targets flew across Germany to Russian bases, which they then utilized for return flights to their home stations in Italy or Great Britain.

Sources for the study of the war on land begin with the files of the War Department General Staff, the Office of the Secretary of War, and the Adjutant General's Office relating to the organization and training of troops and the preparation of plans for their operational employment. The equipment and combat training of these troops in the continental United States, their organization into combat units, and their preparation for overseas movement were the responsibility of Headquarters, Army Ground Forces, the records of which are also in the National Archives. Records of Headquarters, Army Service Forces, document the story of army logistics during the war, covering everything from the acquisition and eventual disposal of army installations, through the supervision of the Army Supply Program and the International Aid Program, to the execution of specific projects of strategic significance, such as the construction of the Ledo Road. The voluminous files of the several technical services of the War Department (Ordnance, Quartermaster General, Engineers,

Transportation, and the like) depict the development and procurement of weapons, munitions, supplies, transport vehicles, and other equipment for the use of the troops. Records of the Surgeon General's Office provide medical statistics for the army during the war and information about significant advances in techniques and methods for the care and treatment of the sick and wounded. The new and larger role of women in the military service is documented in the files of the Office of the Director of the Women's Army Corps.

Finally, at the level of the front-line combat unit, the National Archives holdings contain some eight thousand cubic feet of operations reports, consisting of journals, narrative summaries of events, and supporting documents submitted to the War Department, in accordance with army regulations, by all types of units actively engaged in combat operations.

For the naval side of the war our resources are also abundant, but not to quite the same degree as for the war on land. We hold the unclassified files of the Office of the Secretary of the Navy and Chief of Naval Operations for the war period, plus the logbooks of all commissioned naval vessels that served during the war. Of the records of the several Navy Department bureaus, those transferred to the National Archives include the complete files, classified and unclassified, of the Bureau of Ships, and most of those of the Bureau of Ordnance and the Bureau of Naval Personnel. Taken together, these document the story of the creation of our immense wartime fleet and the provision of its weapons and the trained crews to man it.

For the study of naval aviation, that indispensable arm that added a new dimension to naval warfare in the 1941–45 struggle, the National Archives has most of the wartime files of the Bureau of Aeronautics and some of those of the Office of the Deputy Chief of Naval Operations for Air.

For the student of the development of American military airpower, the files of Headquarters, Army Air Forces, are, of course, a *sine qua non.* Together with the closely related records of the Office of the Assistant Secretary of War for Air, they shed much light on such vital subjects as the position and role of the Army Air Forces within the United States Army; concepts of the employment of airpower; technological advances of the period in aircraft and aero-engine design, including the beginnings of jet propulsion; procurement of combat aircraft and the modification of aircraft designs to meet changing tactical requirements; advances in electronics technology, including the development and application of radar; the introduction of new communications and navigational techniques and equipment; advances in aviation medicine; flying training and technical training; the acquisition and expansion of air base facilities in the United States and overseas; and relations of the army with the aircraft industry.

Also included in the Army Air Forces files are records of Headquarters, Twentieth Air Force, the organization established in 1944 under the immediate command of General Arnold in Washington, to control the operations of American very heavy bombers, the B-29s, in the air offensive against Japan. The mission reports, messages, and orders of this organization relate the successful execution of this final strategic air operation of the war.

The war was waged not only in overseas theaters of combat but on the home front as well—what was known in military parlance as the Zone of the Interior. Some of the records we possess relating to this phase are suggestive of problems of topical interest. Files of the army's Western Defense Command, for example, describe the role of the military in the relocation of the Japanese population of the West Coast states, an unprecedented action in the history of American wars and one about which a lively controversy still persists. Records of the War Department's Bureau of Public Relations depict the army's efforts to keep the public informed of what it was doing through the press and the other news media —a task that was decidedly less difficult and less likely to arouse antagonistic reactions than it is in these days of television programs like "The Selling of the Pentagon." In the files of the Office of the Assistant Secretary of War and the closely related Army and Navy Munitions Board, which were responsible for industrial mobilization planning until the actual outbreak of hostilities, can be discerned the roots of the so-called military-industrial complex that causes uneasiness to some of our fellow citizens today.

Among the records of wartime quasi-military agencies in the National Archives are those of the Selective Service System and of the Office of Civilian Defense, representing two functions of government originally expected to be of a short-term emergency nature that have continued to be carried on in one form or another since the war.

Still other War Department records document the establishment and operation of camps in the United States for German and Italian prisoners of war and the training of army officers and men for postwar military government duties in occupied territory. Others provide the background of the unification of the armed forces, which finally came about shortly after the conclusion of the war, and the controversial Universal Military Training Program, an abortive attempt to provide a substitute for selective service.

The cessation of active hostilities brought with it a transformation of responsibilities and activities for the armed forces. The official records for this period of the aftermath of fighting are equally as abundant as for the years of actual warfare. At the departmental level we possess records of the Civil Affairs Division of the War Department General Staff, which was responsible for the formulation of United States policy for the administration and government of captured or liberated territory. Activities in the field are represented by records of the Allied Commission (Italy) which administered military government in Italy from 1943 to 1947; records of Allied Military Government in the Free Territory of Trieste, a trouble spot that required Allied occupation until 1954; files of the Office of Military Government, United States, better known as OMGUS, which administered military government affairs in the United States zone of Germany until 1949; and dwarfing everything else, the tremendous files (some ten thousand cubic feet) of the Office of the General Headquarters Supreme Commander Allied Powers, in Tokyo, which administered the Allied occupation of Japan and enforced the terms of the Japanese surrender until the Japanese government resumed its functions under the new constitution of 1952.

To determine the part played by airpower in bringing the war to a conclusion, the government in 1945 organized the United States Strategic Bombing Survey. The survey, whose records we now possess, investigated the extent of physical destruction caused by bombing, and the effects of bombing on industry, utilities, transportation, morale, etc., in Japan and Germany and the German occupied areas of Europe. Its files are replete with statistical and documentary material about the condition of enemy plants, industries, and cities and contain reports of interviews with many surviving political, military, and industrial leaders.

Also among the most significant events of the postwar years were the trials by the Allied powers of the major war criminals, held in Nuremberg and Tokyo from 1945 to 1946, and 1946 to 1948, respectively. Their very voluminous files include transcripts of the full court proceedings, several thousand selected official documents admitted as exhibits for the prosecution and the defense, additional thousands of documents assembled but not used by the prosecution, and the final judgments of the tribunals. The collateral value of this great mass of documentation for authentic evidence of the internal policies and activities of the Axis governments during the war and prewar years tends now almost to transcend their value for their original and primary purpose of determining the guilt or innocence of the accused.

To illuminate what took place "on the other side of the hill," so to speak, we have in our custody not only the war crimes trial documents but also an immense quantity of seized German records. Extending well back before the war in most instances, these provide evidence about the development of German foreign policy, naval policy, economic policy, and the racial policies and propaganda efforts of the Nazi party and its various organs, as well as German military policy and military operations throughout the Second World War. Initially exploited for intelligence and official historical purposes, these records were restituted to the West German government between 1954 and 1968, but microfilm copies were made and retained, and these, which total some twenty thousand rolls, have been available at the National Archives for unofficial research for a considerable number of years. A much smaller but significant body of records of the Italian High Command is available, also in microfilm form, to document the major aspects of the Italian role in the war prior to September 1943. The full revelation of the intentions, plans, and operations of the Axis powers and their appreciation of allied efforts, all of which can be found in these files, give the historians of the Second World War a unique and unparalleled opportunity to discern the full dimensions of the events they attempt to describe and to substitute authentic information about our adversaries for mere speculation.

Although our holdings are voluminous and cover almost all conceivable aspects of the war, there are still gaps in them, of which we are keenly aware. Some of these are records of significance still in agency custody that will undoubtedly be offered to the National Archives before the lapse of many more years. Among these are certain wartime files of the United States Navy and Marine Corps that are still in the possession of the historical offices of those services in the Washington area. Records of the Office of Naval Intelligence, that would balance and complement our military intelligence records, are also lacking, and the records of many fleets, task forces, and other seagoing commands are still stored in one of the regional records centers, awaiting the disposal of valueless material before being sent to the National Archives. The Department of the Air Force also still retains some of its wartime records, particularly operational files, for use by the Air University, Maxwell Air Force Base, Alabama. Although we regret the absence of these materials from our holdings, we are confident that they are in capable hands and realize that there are related problems of manpower, funds, and space that would have to be solved before they could be accommodated in the National Archives.

Other gaps are permanent in nature and can never be filled. The files of the Philippine Department, for example, not only for the six-month period of the Bataan-Corregidor campaign but also for a long period of time before the war, were lost or destroyed during the course of hostilities. Professor Morton is perhaps the best authority on this subject, for he had the thankless task some years ago of piecing together the story of the fall of the Philippines from the fragmentary sources that remained. The United States Navy likewise suffered many unhappy reverses in the early months of the war, which account for the absence of the final logbooks of a number of warships that were lost in action.

Still other kinds of wartime military records, although they exist, are absent from the shelves of the National Archives because they are too voluminous to be housed here. For most of our nineteenth century wars, for example, we possess as part of the surviving documentation the equivalent of modern individual personnel records for all officers and men who participated, and even their subsequent pension records. For the first and second world wars, however, the volume of such materials has become far too great even to be considered for storage in the National Archives, and they have instead been assigned to the care of certain of the regional federal records centers.

Reference use of our Second World War military holdings has been heavy for the last decade or more, and, judging from the statistics we maintain, appears to be slowly but steadily increasing. In the years immediately after the war the records were exploited mainly by the military services themselves for the writing of official histories. The best known of these, the *United States Army in World War II* series, planned to fill some eighty volumes, is now almost completed, twenty-three years after the publication of the first volume of the series. The other, less ambitious, efforts were Adm. Samuel E. Morison's *History of United States Naval Operations in World War II*, running to fifteen volumes; the seven volumes of *The Army Air Forces in World War II*, edited by James Lea Cate and Wesley F. Craven; and the five volumes of the Marine Corps' *United States Marine Corps Operations in World War II*. There are also in preparation and near completion certain specialized official histories, such as the Surgeon General's Office's *Medical Department, U.S. Army in World War II*.

As official needs have declined and the records have become more accessible for use by private scholars and students, a prolific flow of monographs, special studies, and articles based wholly or in part upon these records has been coming forth. Literally scores of these works appear each year, and the volume of the flow is unlikely to slacken off so long as interest in the Second World War continues at the present high level. Examples of relatively recent books that have drawn upon our official records include Ambassador Eisenhower's *The Bitter Woods*,

John Toland's *The Rising Sun,* David Irving's *The Mare's Nest,* and John McV. Haight's *American Aid to France, 1938–1940.* In recent years, as many of you are aware, we have made heavy contributions to compilations such as the Eisenhower Papers, and to biographies of Second World War figures, such as Dr. Pogue's life of General Marshall and Professor James's study of MacArthur.

Aside from published works, many hundreds of unpublished dissertations owe much of their substance to these records, and we are confident that several more generations of academic researchers will be able to thrive upon them. There are many nuggets yet to be discovered, and for those already discovered, additional research can reshape and refine them.

Before concluding this survey, I would like to discuss briefly the accessibility of these military records of the Second World War. Military records, like other records in the care of the National Archives, are subject to restrictions on access, imposed for the most part by the agency of origin. These cover a wide variety of subjects and conditions and require respect for the confidentiality of such things as medical information in personnel records, unevaluated derogatory information in investigative records, and any information classified for reasons of national security. This last type of restriction is of most significance and widest applicability in military records. We estimate that more than one-third of all of the recent military records in the National Archives were originally security-classified and only a small part of them have as yet been reviewed for declassification. To be sure, the Department of Defense has issued a number of directives that authorize the declassification of most military records of the war period, but it is necessary for our staff to interpret these directives in any given instance before applying them, and their ambiguity and complexity make this at times a difficult process. In high-level records, futhermore, at the cabinet-office level or the policy and planning level, there is much physical intermingling in the files of material that clearly is declassified by the Department of Defense directives and material that clearly is not, such as documents of foreign origin, or of State Department or White House origin. Under these conditions any rapid and massive declassification work is out of the question.

If a file being reviewed is judged in terms of the highest common denominator of its contents it often has to remain classified. The only alternative, to review and take action on individual documents within a file, is very time-consuming and must result in dismantling the file and leaving a classified residue that will have to be reviewed again at some future date, and making public only part of the story, a solution of sorts, but certainly not the best for either the user of the records or the custodian.

I do not cite these difficulties to imply that access to classified records is impossible but merely to show some of the problems we face in trying to carry out declassification of the records within the limits that now apply. The student or scholar who must do extensive research in records that are still classified can always obtain a security clearance from the agency whose records are involved and thus obtain access. Using this method, over the last twenty years or more several hundred scholars have been permitted to use the records with satisfactory results.

This discussion would not be complete without at least a brief mention of the finding aids that the National Archives has prepared as tools for the control and management of its Second World War military records. Inventories have been produced for all of the National Archives record groups to which the records are allocated; most of these, however, are still provisional inventories, for internal use only, and not of a quality at this stage to permit them to be issued as formal National Archives publications. One reason for this is that the records have been in a rather fluid state for the last ten years or so, many having been reallocated from one record group to another two or three times to respond to changes in policy affecting their control and administration. Another reason is that there have been numerous changes in the physical location of the records over the same period, a condition that has tended to hamper a sustained and consistent effort to complete the inventory process.

Aside from the inventories, however, there are other finding aids available, or soon to be available. I should call your attention, for example, to the imminent appearance of a new edition of the *National Archives Guide*. This publication, which contains summary descriptions of all National Archives holdings, has been revised for the first time since 1948 and will now include, in this new edition, the first published descriptions of many of our Second World War records. Another finding aid, one that has been with us for a good many years but is still useful, is our two-volume publication, *Federal Records of World War II*, the second volume of which, totalling over one thousand pages, is devoted to military records. Its descriptions of the records, the organizational entities that produced them, and the functions they reflect are still accurate, although the physical locations and custodial agencies have in some instances changed since the publication came out. It can still be recommended as the starting point for any student undertaking a major research project in the official records of this period.

As for the German records we have microfilmed, we are in a relatively good position with respect to finding aids. The series of guides to these materials that we have been preparing over the last thirteen years has now reached sixty-five in number and we will probably produce another twenty before we come to the end of the task. We hope eventually to produce similar guides to the very extensive series of evidentiary documents for the Nuremberg trials, which we are now also beginning to microfilm.

I think we can claim without exaggeration, finally, that we possess in this building and in our Suitland branch one of the richest concentrations of official source material in the United States for the scholarly study of the Second World War. We encourage you to make use of it. Work in the records is sometimes arduous, but the reward is usually well worth the effort expended. We will undertake to assist you to the full extent of our resources with your research problems. We encourage you also to give us the benefit of your thought, your advice, and your suggestions as to how we may better serve you and your needs, and through them and beyond them the broader interests of Second World War scholarship.

BENEDICT K. ZOBRIST

Resources of the Presidential Libraries
for the History of the
Second World War

The presidential libraries of the National Archives and Records Service offer unique opportunities for researchers interested in the Second World War. Indeed, the very first in the series of presidential libraries established by the federal government—the Franklin D. Roosevelt Library at Hyde Park, New York—concerns itself considerably with the coming and prosecution of this second great war of the twentieth century, although all of the presidential libraries presently open for research have some materials relating to the war.

The Presidential Libraries Act of 1955 gave statutory recognition to the importance attached by the federal government to the preservation of papers and other historical materials of the presidents of the United States. However, the six presidential libraries now in operation—representing Presidents Hoover, Roosevelt, Truman, Eisenhower, Kennedy, and Johnson—contain not only the papers and files of these presidents but also scores of collections of personal correspondence, diaries, and other historical materials of the men and women, both military and civilian, who served with them or who played important public roles during their administrations. The libraries also have large collections of books and other printed materials, as well as still pictures, motion pictures, television tapes, oral history interviews, and innumerable memorabilia that bear on the historical periods with which these presidents are associated. As part of the National Archives record-keeping system, these vast collections are administered by the same agency that has responsibility for preservation of the official records described by Dr. Krauskopf.

Recently, we have been impressed with the continued and wide-ranging interest of researchers in the Second World War, many of whom have used the sources of the presidential libraries. A cogent review article,

The author wishes to thank the Harry S. Truman Presidential Library staff members who have assisted him in compiling the information presented in this paper.

written by one of our conference participants, sums up the situation this way, "The demand for books on World War II seems insatiable, the supply inexhaustible. World War II . . . offers an almost unlimited supply of subjects for the enterprising writer. . . . Nor is there, apparently, any lack of readers."[1]

True as these words may be in describing the present situation, it was with some degree of interest that I discovered an article in the current issue of *Daedalus,* which gives a corrective to the boundless energies of the military historian and suggests approaches which would lend themselves to the types of source materials—some still unworked—to be found in the presidential libraries.

Prof. Peter Paret of Stanford University asserts rather harshly that: "Far too much military history is being written in America" and notes that "with few exceptions, the character of the work produced is extremely conventional—descriptive history, centering on leading figures, campaigns, and climactic battles, often with a strong antiquarian bent." Attributing these shortcomings to an "indifference to problems of methodology" and to a willingness "to jog along in the old narrative ways," Paret proposes that military historians make greater use of other disciplines, particularly the social and behavioral sciences, and expand their efforts in the "conventional" genres of history. He gives as examples the application of economic theory to the history of war, the economic aspects of the management and expenditure of force, the interaction of war with science and technology, and he places special emphasis on what he terms to be the central element of military history: violence.[2]

These and other subjects can be studied with profit in the sources of the presidential libraries. For the sake of both clarity and brevity, I am commenting basically on major sources pertaining to the Second World War, with particular reference to those collections that have been seldom used by researchers.

One approach to the coming of the Second World War can be gained from the sources of the Herbert Hoover Presidential Library.[3] Hoover opposed American involvement in the early phases of the war and led several attempts to bring American relief to war-torn Europe—organizations such as "Finnish Relief," "Food for Small Democracies," "Polish Relief," and others. Although the war began, Hoover's services were not requested, but he kept himself abreast of the world food situation and he found much to criticize in our failure to provide wartime relief and in the conduct of our wartime rationing. In the immediate postwar years, he influenced the reversal of our "German Policy" and served President Truman through his Emergency Famine Relief Studies and by his fact-finding trips to Germany, Austria, Latin America, and the Orient. Many of these aspects of Hoover's later career have not been fully investigated.

Also in the Hoover Library are two not widely used collections that shed light on the isolationism of the 1930s and the America First Movement—the papers of Hanford MacNider and Sen. Gerald P. Nye. And recently the library has acquired the papers of Verne Marshall, Pulitzer Prize-winning editor of the *Cedar Rapids Gazette* and head of the "No Foreign Wars Committee" at the outbreak of World War II.

The Japanese attack on Pearl Harbor can be studied in the papers of Rear Adm. John Franklin Shafroth in the Hoover Library. They deal mainly with his investigation of the attack and his correspondence with certain of the "revisionists." Rear Adm. William Outerbridge's papers, which are deposited in the Eisenhower Library,[4] describe his command of the destroyer U.S.S. *Ward,* which sank a Japanese submarine just prior to the attack on Pearl Harbor, as well as his later command of the U.S.S. *O'Brien* during the Normandy invasion, and his postwar career. This indicates how many of the collections overlap and extend beyond the wartime period.

Moreover, papers in older collections are being continually reviewed and opened for research as the specific situation may permit. Recently, an early war episode documented in the Roosevelt Papers was opened—the type of material that gives color and substance to men and events. In late December 1941, Charles A. Lindbergh, the outspoken critic of American foreign policy, offered his services to the Army Air Corps. The Roosevelt file contains a strong letter from Secretary of the Interior Harold E. Ickes, old curmudgeon himself, to President Roosevelt in which Ickes labeled Lindbergh "a ruthless and conscious fascist," and went on to write, "I ardently hope that this convinced fascist will not be given the opportunity to wear the uniform of the United States. He should be buried in merciful oblivion." The president responded: "I agree . . . wholeheartedly."[5] Secretary of the Navy Frank Knox, writing to the president on January 1, 1942, and stating that "I give you my sober reflection," concluded: "If it were a Navy question and were put up to me, I would offer Lindbergh an opportunity to enlist as an air cadet, like anybody else would have to do. He has had no training as an officer and ought to earn his commission."[6]

A few days later, Secretary of War Henry L. Stimson spoke with Colonel Lindbergh personally and reported this meeting to the president. He told Lindbergh that he would welcome any information or suggestions that would help in the work of the War Department,

> but I also told him that I would not be frank if I did not make it clear to him now that from my reading of his speeches it was clear to me that he took a very different view of our friends and our enemies in the present war from

not only that of myself but a great majority of our countrymen, and that he evidently lacked faith in the righteousness of our cause. I told him that we were going to have a very difficult and a very hard war on our hands and that I should personally be unwilling to place in command of our troops as a commissioned officer any man who had such a lack of faith in our cause as he had shown in his speeches. . . .

Although evidently rather set back by my frankness, he thanked me cordially for seeing him and for giving him this opportunity for even limited service.[7]

Turning to grand strategy, the most important presidential library collection as to content concerning the Second World War is the president's secretary's file of the Franklin D. Roosevelt Papers. Spanning the years from 1933 to 1945, this file consists of papers of particular importance to President Roosevelt and were kept close at hand for ready reference. The "safe file" portion was kept in a safe in his office, the rest just outside his office. The president's secretary's file includes documents about many of the wartime conferences, reports from foreign capitals before and during the war, and much of the early Churchill-Roosevelt correspondence. Recently declassified British-American exchanges concerning atomic energy, for example, are located in the Harry Hopkins subject file, while an Einstein letter and other early correspondence on atomic energy are located in the safe file material under Alexander Sachs, an occasional advisor to the president. Material concerning American relations with China early in the war are filed under Lauchlin Currie, the presidential assistant, who was especially concerned with Far Eastern affairs.

The president's secretary's file should be used in conjunction with the Map Room files, also at the Roosevelt Library. The White House Map Room was established in January 1942, under the supervision of the naval aide, as a military information center and communication office for the president. The files include the messages exchanged by President Roosevelt and Prime Minister Churchill, Marshal Stalin, and Generalissimo Chiang Kai-shek, and much of the president's correspondence with the secretary of war, the secretary of the navy, and the Joint Chiefs of Staff. There is also considerable material on the wartime meetings of the Allied leaders in the Map Room "trip files." The original file has been used very little by researchers because of the need for security clearance. About 80 percent of the files still remain classified.

The Harry L. Hopkins Papers at the Roosevelt Library recount Hopkins's many duties as special assistant to the president, including his trips to London and Moscow, his lend-lease work, and his aid to Roosevelt during the wartime conferences. Despite Robert Sherwood's supposedly definitive work on *Roosevelt and Hopkins*, largely based on the Hopkins Papers, remember that this study was done twenty-three years ago.[8] Hopkins's wartime missions can now be told more fully with the availability of the Map Room files, as well as other related collections.

To give you a taste of the heady wine provided at this level of exchange, may I quote briefly from the William D. Hassett diary entry on the so-called shotgun wedding at Casablanca:

> But the really funny incident of the Casablanca pilgrimage came when the President was trying to bring about a reconciliation between General Giraud, High Commissioner for French Africa and General De Gaulle, leader of the fighting French who had come over from London.
>
> "My job," said the President, "was to produce the bride in the person of General Giraud while Churchill was to bring in General De Gaulle to play the role of bridegroom in the shotgun wedding. . . ."
>
> At one conference (with De Gaulle) the President said De Gaulle said again and again that he represented the spirit of France—the spirit of Jeanne d'Arc which drove the English out of France five hundred years ago. . . .
>
> At another conference F.D.R. said De Gaulle told him that in the present emergency he felt that he must play the role of Clemenceau with Giraud acting as Marshal Foch.
>
> "I almost laughed in his face," remarked the Boss. "On Friday you are the reincarnation of Jeanne d'Arc and today you are Clemenceau. That was going from one extreme to the other.
>
> "But after long-drawn out negotiations De Gaulle consented reluctantly to sign with Giraud a simple declaration that the liberation of France was the one thing closest to the hearts of all loyal Frenchmen regardless of political affiliation."
>
> So finally Winnie produced the bridegroom; the boss gave the bride away and the marriage took place—a typical shot gun union. We shall see how it turns out.[9]

Still on the high political level, may I point out other sources before we examine the military side of the war. This material falls into two categories: the personal papers of individuals holding official positions of prominence relating to the war effort, and special committees, boards, commissions, and missions appointed by the president.

The Henry A. Wallace Papers in the Roosevelt Library relate chiefly to his term as vice president and to his duties as chairman of the Board of Economic Warfare, which was established by executive order on July 31, 1941, to fulfill United States needs of raw materials and to control the export of finished products. The Board of Economic Warfare material has not been used extensively by researchers. The Wallace Papers, by the way, are being made available on microfilm by a project jointly sponsored by the Roosevelt Library, the Library of Congress, and the State University of Iowa, all of which have substantial holdings of Wallace material.

Little use has been made of the papers of Leon Henderson, who headed the Office of Price Administration during the early years of the war. The Harold D. Smith Papers constitute a small but valuable collection describing Smith's significant role as director of the Bureau of the Budget. The Smith diaries are of particular interest because of Smith's perceptive insights into meetings with President Roosevelt and many other leading figures. The Smith Collection is complemented by the papers of Wayne Coy, who was assistant director of the Bureau of the Budget during 1942 and 1943.

Other significant collections that deal with the prosecution of the war include the papers of Oscar Cox, who held responsible positions with the Lend-Lease Administration, the Office of Emergency Management, and later, the Foreign Economic Administration. The papers of John M. Carmody reflect his wartime role as a member of the United States Maritime Commission. The Herbert Marks Papers recount his service as assistant general counsel to the Office of Production Management and, later, the War Production Board. His activities were concerned largely with electric power and petroleum.

And not to be overlooked at the Roosevelt Library are the Eleanor Roosevelt Papers, which constitute a major source for the entire Roosevelt period. Her so-called White House papers, measuring 490 linear feet, are concerned with Mrs. Roosevelt's public and private life in Washington and elsewhere as the wife of the president of the United States. Many of the letters are from the general public, in which tens of thousands of demoralized citizens sought her assistance, intercession, solace, and advice. Other correspondence is personal and reflects and documents her interest and service in such fields as labor, youth, civil liberties, education, and public welfare. Mrs. Roosevelt's papers through 1945 will be opened to scholars in October 1971, while the remaining material will be made available in the year following.

The records and files of several presidential committees, commissions, and boards have also been deposited at the Roosevelt Library. Among them are the records of the Advisory Commission to the Council of National Defense, an early and somewhat unsuccessful try at mobilizing the productive forces of the nation. The papers of the president's Rubber Survey Committee, headed by Bernard Baruch and empowered "To proceed to speedily produce a report on the feasibility of artificially producing a rubber or rubber-like substance," provide an untapped source describing an early effort to answer the need for this critical raw material. The records of the president's Soviet Protocol Committee, covering the period from June 1941 to September 1945, document the implementation of the American government's policy to support the Union of Soviet Socialist Republics in its defense against German aggression. Included in the records are copies of the protocols and supporting documents, the report of the Harriman mission to Moscow, correspondence, memorandums, schedules, incoming and outgoing cables, G-2 military reports,

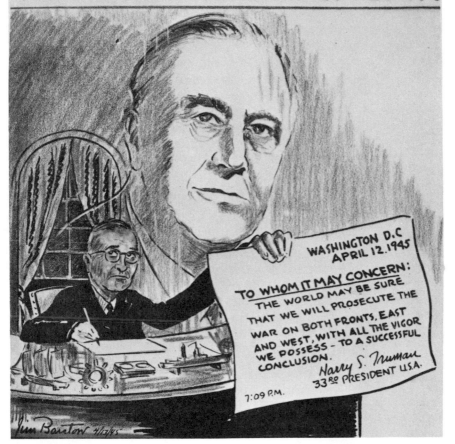

A cartoon on Truman's succession to the presidency, April 1945. (Harry S. Truman Library.)

newspaper clippings, and files of the Joint War Aid Committee, United States Section. On the home front, the records of the president's Committee on Portal-to-Portal Travel Time deals with the 1943–1944 dispute relating to portal-to-portal pay for the miners and is reflective of labor troubles during the war.

Concerned with China's ability to continue in the war with Japan and with China's postwar future, President Roosevelt asked Donald M. Nelson, chairman of the War Production Board, to go to China as the president's personal representative in 1944. The records of the mission, which became known as the American War Production Mission in China, are also in the Roosevelt Library. A last example of such holdings would be the records of the War Refugee Board, established by presidential executive order to combat the Nazi campaign of persecution and extermination of helpless people because of their race, religion, or political belief. This material will undoubtedly be used far more extensively by researchers in future years.

In the Truman Library[10] may be found other supporting collections, such as Harry S. Truman's senatorial and vice presidential papers, which deal largely with domestic problems. These sources have not been used extensively with reference to World War II, except for the activities of the Truman Committee, a story that has been fairly well told. The papers and files of Edwin A. Locke, Jr., who succeeded Donald M. Nelson as head of the American War Production Mission in China in May 1945, might be used profitably with the official records of the mission already noted as being in the Roosevelt Library. The Philleo Nash Papers, also at the Truman Library, contain material dealing with race relations and minority group problems. During the war, Nash, who later became an administrative assistant to President Truman, served as assistant to the director of the Domestic Branch in the Office of War Information.

The John F. Kennedy Library at Waltham, Massachusetts, is anticipating the arrival of the James P. Warburg Papers, which also contain material relating to Warburg's service with the Office of War Information. Undoubtedly, all of the presidential libraries will be acquiring additional personal papers of major individuals involved in the Second World War, but it would be somewhat premature to speculate further on this point.

Turning to the military side of the war, I must begin with a delightful letter written to Gen. Dwight D. Eisenhower in the midst of the war by the eminent American historian, Douglas Southall Freeman:

Dear General Eisenhower:
    Much as I dislike to trouble so busy a man, my long studies of American Command have made me very anxious to see that you, General MacArthur

and General Marshall were keeping full memoranda of your principal decisions. In writing my long life of General Lee, and my more recent "Lee's Lieutenants," I had very little difficulty in ascertaining what happened but I had hell's own time, on occasion, in finding out why it happened. . . .

Whether I or some other military historian has the privilege of writing of your great achievements, I beseech you, if you can do so without too much hardship, keep enough memoranda, please, to explain the major decisions and the reasons for them. Unexplained decisions rob military history of almost all its instruction to the future soldier.

Admiringly yours,

/s/ Douglas Southall Freeman[11]

A copy of this letter should be issued to all military commanders prior to their engaging in battle!

At the Eisenhower Library, the pre-presidential personal papers of Dwight D. Eisenhower comprise a major source for studying the European War. Over a third of this material pertains to the period of December 1941 through May 1945. During the war years, Eisenhower's pre-presidential papers are supported substantially by the Gen. Walter Bedell Smith Collection. As General Eisenhower's chief of staff from August 1942 through 1945, General Smith compiled two very significant files: the Cable Log, which consists of extracts or complete texts of incoming and outgoing messages, and the Eyes Only Cables file, consisting of especially important messages, intended for the exclusive view of the person addressed. These major collections are buttressed by the microfilm records of the secretary of the General Staff of Supreme Headquarters Allied Expeditionary Force, the records of the United States Army Historical Division in the European theater, and over one thousand linear feet of United States Army after action reports, dating from 1941 through 1945. The Eisenhower Library also has complete microfilm records of after action reports for the Eighty-second Airborne Division, the First Armored Division, the First Infantry Division, and the Fourth Infantry Division. Much of the official record, of course, remains in the National Archives, but the Eisenhower Library has made a studied effort to establish itself as a major research center for the military history of the Second World War by collecting inventories and finding aids to pertinent material scattered throughout the world.

The Eisenhower Library also has significant personal collections that have barely been touched by researchers. The career of Lt. Gen. Henry S. Aurand, while not in the dashing, romantic tradition of military history deplored by Professor Paret, delineates the major responsibilites of a continental United States Army area service commander, the commander of the Normandy Base Section in 1944, the chief of the Services of Supply in the China theater in 1945 and, subsequently, in the Africa-Middle East theater. The Aurand Papers measure 30 linear feet. The Gen. Courtney H. Hodges Papers present material for a study at the army command level. General Hodges led the First Army, which was first to land in Normandy, to break through at Saint Lô, to liberate Paris, and eventually to make first contact with units of the Soviet army in Germany. The logistical support of the army through the Services of Supply in the British Isles, the Mediterranean, North Africa, and southern France is documented in the papers of Lt. Gen. Thomas B. Larkin. Airborne operations during the Second World War are a significant part of the papers of Lt. Gen. Floyd L. Parks. At the end of the war, General Parks was named United States sector commander in Berlin. The papers of Lt. Gen. Harold R. Bull, assistant chief of staff, G-3, Supreme Headquarters, Allied Expeditionary Forces in the European theater, along with other closely related assignments, contain detailed information pertaining to the invasion of Europe. In addition, the Parks material contains almost fifty-six hundred photographs, while the Hodges Papers hold more than twenty-two hundred photographs.

Papers and records of many types and from varied sources are contained in the presidential libraries. Some are still closed to researchers—a matter that will be discussed in the next chapter—and more are yet to be acquired by these libraries. Many small but significant collections have, of necessity, been omitted from my limited text. It is therefore appropriate to point out that highly trained archivists, as well as published listings and finding aids, are available to assist the researcher in all of the presidential libraries.

In view of the world turmoil that continues to proceed from this greatest of all wars of the twentieth century, our comprehension of war and violence appears, indeed, to be inadequate. Would that the mightiest efforts expended during this destructive, as well as formative period of history, could have been directed into more constructive effort. Nonetheless, this significant period of world history does tell, for better or worse, what man's determined effort can do. I would submit to you then that military history in its broader and more imaginative context—as we have addressed it from sources in the presidential libraries—does have something to teach us after all.

Notes

1. Louis Morton, "World War II: A Survey of Recent Writings," *American Historical Review* 80 (December 1970): 1987.
2. Peter Paret, "The History of War," *Daedalus* (Spring 1971): 376–96.
3. Located at West Branch, Iowa.
4. Located at Abilene, Kansas.
5. Ickes to Roosevelt, 30 December 1941; Roosevelt to Ickes, 30 December 1941, PSF (Ickes), Roosevelt Papers, Franklin D. Roosevelt Library, Hyde Park, New York, hereafter cited as FDRL.
6. PSF (Navy-Knox), Roosevelt Papers, FDRL.
7. Stimson to Roosevelt, 13 January 1942, PSF (War-Stimson), Roosevelt Papers, FDRL.
8. *Roosevelt and Hopkins: An Intimate History* (New York: Harper & Brothers, 1948, rev. 1950).
9. Hassett Diary, 7 February 1943, FDRL.
10. Located at Independence, Missouri.
11. Freeman to Eisenhower, 5 November 1943, Eisenhower Papers, Dwight D. Eisenhower Library, Abilene, Kansas.

Discussion Summary

James Hewes, Jr., (Office of the Chief of Military History) commented upon the Douglas Southall Freeman letter to General Eisenhower, which Zobrist had quoted, suggesting that the only sure way to document decisions and the decision-making process by military commanders was to assign historians to their staffs to make certain that all signficant documentation was preserved. Donald Detwiler, speaking from his knowledge of the war diary of the *Oberkommando der Wehrmacht,* compiled by Percy Ernst Schramm, agreed with this solution, provided the man had the talent to do the job well, for it was bound to be a difficult and tricky task.

General James L. Collins, Jr., (Chief of Military History) observed that the present policy of the Department of the Army was to assign qualified historians to the principal headquarters of army units. Normally these were civilian historians, assisted by junior officers also possessing some historical training. At lower echelons and in combat areas, they were mainly military personnel, insofar as possible with a degree of some sort in history. His problem, however, was to get commanders to have confidence in their historians. Sometimes relationships were good and results were excellent. In other instances commanders might not see the value of their historians, who would end up by being made responsible for other tasks. At least there was a policy, it was being implemented, and OCMH was doing the best it could within the limits of the resources available for the purpose.

Seymour Pomrenze (Department of the Army) pointed out that some of the records described in the two-volume *Federal Records of World War II,* mentioned by Krauskopf, had been disposed of since that work was compiled, and to that extent the guide was out-of-date and could not be completely relied upon by researchers. Krauskopf expressed his thanks for this useful reminder. Any such records had, of course, gone through the records appraisal process and been judged to have no further historical or other value and their disposal had been duly authorized by Congress. Although the absence of such materials would have to be kept in mind, it seemed to him that it did not substantially detract from the value of the publication as a starting point for research in the history of the Second World War.

VI

Accessibility of Sources for the History of the Second World War

Paul Ward, the executive secretary of the American Historical Association, served as chairman of the conference's sixth session. The topic was conceived of as a dialogue among an agency official, a nongovernment historian, and an archivist on the problems of making sensitive records or papers available for historical research. The initial publication of the "Pentagon Papers" by the New York Times *two days earlier gave the session an unanticipated timeliness.*

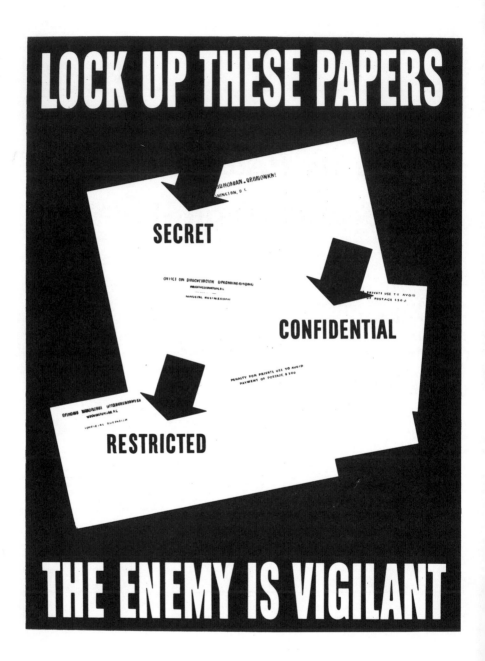

A 1943 Office of War Information poster on the need for security of documents. (Office of Government Reports; National Archives, no. 44-PA-206.)

RUDOLPH A. WINNACKER

Declassification of
World War II Military Records
The Agency's Viewpoint

It seems appropriate to discuss with World War II historians the size of the review task required for the government's holdings of World War II records. The National Archives has approximately two hundred sixty thousand feet of records for the years 1940–45. At a conversion rate of 2,500 pages per foot, this collection would contain 670 million pages, to which must be added at least 100 million more to include holdings of the United States Army, Navy, Marine Corps, and Air Force not yet turned over to the National Archives. Let us round off the total of 770 million pages to 750 million or three-fourths of a billion. What are 20 million pages, more or less?

Public release involves screening these 750 million pages not only for information that might still deserve classification in accordance with Executive Order 10501 but also for privileged information, including personnel and medical data, investigatory reports, proprietary rights, and financial and other information given to the government in confidence by individuals, foreign nations, corporations, or other organizations. These exemptions are listed in Section 552 of Title 5, United States Code.

Much of the originally classified material has already been cleared either by paper-by-paper review or by automatic declassification. We estimate that there remain about 100 million classified pages in our World War II records—80 million in the National Archives and 20 million in departmental holdings. A rather formidable review task, one must admit.

What makes the review task so formidable is the nature of the files. If the records had been retired on the basis of the "forbidden fruits," i.e., the type of information that must be protected by statute and executive order, we would have no problem. Unfortunately, this is not the case. We have, for example, specific personnel and medical files, inspector general records, and files of intelligence officers—our most troublesome areas—but information from these files has seeped into numerous other collections. In fact, still classified and privileged information might be found anywhere.

Moreover, there are no master files in the military departments, the review of which would flag a still sensitive paper by number for the reviewers of other files. (Only the Joint Chiefs of Staff and the Combined Chiefs of Staff have such master files.) Thus, all files must be reviewed for their total content.

In addition, there are not even State, War and Navy Departments files in the strict sense of the word. The files of each department are full of classified documents from other departments and, worst of all, from foreign governments. (One rough estimate of classified British papers in War Department files comes to one million two hundred thousand pages.) Obviously, a single agency review would be of little value. A joint effort is indicated.

This brings me to my final topic, the review process.

First, I would like to point out that, in spite of what some of you may believe, we have not been completely idle. The numerous declassification actions taken since 1945 were summarized in a 1958 Department of Defense directive which directed the automatic declassification of a vast amount of World War II records—related necessarily, however, to the lower command echelons in which most of you are not interested. Throughout these years, the *Foreign Relations* volumes of the Department of State kept rolling off the presses, including special volumes on the international conferences of World War II. On December 21, 1970, the United States and British governments announced the completion of their review of CCS as well as of JCS papers.

The *Foreign Relations* volumes and the CCS-JCS review were particularly important because the classification of the highest echelon papers determines that of most supporting documents. We have now reached the stage where the review of lower-echelon files could become a worthwhile operation, instead of being a futile gesture. One may assert that we should have reached this stage long ago. We might even agree to a certain extent and still feel, in view of the difficulties that we encountered, a certain sense of accomplishment in being where we are today.

In recent months, we have been reviewing the major remaining problems in the release of our World War II records, particularly with a view toward reducing the cost of the operation.

This cost rises every time a document cannot be cleared at the National Archives and, in order to determine its proper current status (classified or privileged), must be pulled from its file, forwarded through numerous departmental offices for a decision, and then returned the same way to its original resting place. The paper work in this process is rather astounding. What we need above all are more specific release criteria that will permit the reviewers at the National Archives to make determinations without referral to the originating agency. Since these documents are now more than twenty-six years old, we are expecting substantial improvements in the applicable criteria.

A substantial review problem will remain, requiring a good number of intelligent people endowed with common sense—a quality not in overabundance in either the public or private sector of the country. All employees cost money and good ones cost even more. We doubt that the reviewing task can be completed within a reasonable time with the currently available staff. Only experience will determine how many files will require a paper-by-paper review and how many can be released with a relatively hasty review or no review at all.

I regret that this fact prevents me from predicting exactly when our World War II records will become available for research. The best that I can venture at this time is that fine bureaucratic expression "in the not too distant future." And, if this comes true, the United States will be ahead of most of its Allies in World War II and not far behind some of them.

JAMES E. O'NEILL

The Accessibility of Sources for the
History of the Second World War
The Archivist's Viewpoint

About sixty years ago, before there was even a First World War, John Franklin Jameson described the advance of historical learning as something like the advance of an army. In the front were what Jameson called "the workers in organized institutions of research," who moved out ahead "like pickets or scouting parties making a reconnaissance." Behind them came "the light cavalry of makers of doctoral dissertations, then the heavy artillery of writers of maturer monographs, both of them heavily encumbered with ammunition trains of bibliography and footnotes." There followed next "the multitudinous infantry of readers and college students and school children, and finally, like sutlers and contractors hovering in the rear, the horde of those that make textbooks."[1] Both warfare and history have changed somewhat in these sixty years. The battalions are bigger, the weapons are more powerful, and the sutlers have been augmented by reprinters, microfilmers, and those that make audiovisual kits.

Somewhere in Jameson's army, presumably among the "pickets or scouting parties," were the handful of archivists of 1912, indistinguishable from their fellow scouts—the Jamesons and Waldo Lelands—and not numerous enough to make a decent-sized platoon. Probably no part of the army has undergone such profound change in the intervening years as have the archivists. They are not only more numerous, but they now have their own part of the field, and a very large and very difficult part of the field at that. In 1912 there were only a dozen state archives, the Library of Congress had barely begun the remarkable expansion of its manuscript holdings, and, of course, there were no National Archives, no regional archives, no federal records centers, and no presidential libraries. The total volume of federal records scattered among the government's offices in 1912 amounted to something in the vicinity of a million feet, a mass of

This article was also published in *Prologue: The Journal of the National Archives* 4, no. 1 (Spring 1972): 21–25.

material that even the ordinarily unperturbable Leland found "well-nigh appalling."[2] Since then we have become the beneficiaries (or victims) of a paper explosion. The federal government today creates over five million feet of such records in a single year, a fact that is not simply appalling, but positively frightening.

This sheer mass of material with which the archivist must now cope—a phenomenon which even the prescient Jameson did not foresee—has created a problem of staggering proportions. This is not only a problem for the archivist, who must struggle to gain control of the documents; it is a problem for the historian as well. The National Archives system contains more than two hundred million documents related just to the Second World War. To these, of course, would have to be added the Second World War material (perhaps forty to fifty million documents) still with the departments and agencies. Even if the "Top Secret" stamp had never been invented, historians would have difficulty finding what they need, or want, amidst such a large volume of material. Accessibility in any meaningful sense is not only the legal right to see, but the ability to find, and sifting the mountain to find the scattered nuggets is a bleak prospect indeed.

In the long run the most serious problems that both the historian and the archivist must face are those of dealing with the mass of material which modern society generates. Immediately, however, this is the source of less anxiety and less frustration than the problems posed by legal restrictions on access to documents. Archivists and historians have come to accept bulk as an unavoidable fact of their professional lives. They share a common concern and they can find common comfort in damning paperwork bureaucrats or the copy-machine industry. But when it comes to closed or restricted documents, they part company. The archivist is guarding secrets that the historian wants. The historian is demanding documents that he cannot have. As a result, the archivist is no longer seen as a bold scout moving before the historical army to reconnoiter the way. No longer is he like Hawkeye or a Stephen Crane hero. He is more like the antihero of a John le Carre or a Len Deighton novel: the double agent whose loyalty is questioned by both sides.

From the archivist's point of view he is the man caught in the middle, trying to serve two masters whose interests conflict. On one side he must deal with the officials of government departments—officials who are sometimes nameless, usually distant, and always powerful. He must follow their rules and guard their papers from the prying eyes of the uncleared. On the other side he must deal with the historians—who are neither nameless nor distant and whose lack of legal power is more than compensated by the persistency of their demands.

As the archivist sees it, there are three different types of restricted materials. For convenience they can be called agency-restricted material, classified material, and donor-restricted material. They share several common features. They are either closed entirely or they are accessible only under certain conditions and with the permission of someone other than the archivist who has custody over them. But each has its own peculiarities and problems.

Agency-restricted material comprises the unclassified back files of the departments and agencies of government. These are official records; they make up the bulk of the restricted official records of the agencies and departments for the years prior to the Second World War, when formal classification of documents was the exception rather than the rule. But they are still numerous for the wartime period. Basically such material is closed on the grounds that confidentiality is still essential to the efficient operation of that particular department or agency or on the grounds that their availability could constitute an invasion of citizens' privacy. The Freedom of Information Act has curtailed such restrictions. Nonetheless, when files are transferred to the custody of the National Archives and Records Service and are placed either in a federal records center or in the National Archives itself, there are frequently such agency-restrictions upon access to them.

The second category of restricted material is that of classified documents. Although security classification began in 1917, for most agencies it became a customary practice only during the Second World War. Technically, classified material has a relevance to national security. It is marked "Top Secret," "Secret," or "Confidential," and it is closed or restricted under the terms of either a statute of Congress, which is the case with Atomic Energy Commission material, or executive orders issued by the president. (The basic executive order governing classified material is Executive Order 10501 and its subsequent amendments.) Such material can be found scattered in many different parts of the National Archives system, including the collections of otherwise privately owned papers which have been given to the presidential libraries.

The third category, donor-restricted material, is the kind of material that is, in fact, most commonly found in the collections of personal papers in presidential libraries. Legally the papers of a president are his own; they are not official papers. Legally a president or any other person owning papers can, in giving them to a repository (whether a presidential library, the Library of Congress, or a university manuscript collection), place upon those papers restrictions on who will see them, or restrictions which in effect state that no one will see them either for a given period of years or until the original grounds for the restriction have disappeared. At least initially most collections given to a presidential library are protected by such donor-restrictions.

To the archivist these three classes are different. To the historian—as a man seeking the material—the distinction is not particularly relevant. To him, whether a document is an agency-restricted document, whether it is a classified document, or whether it is under some kind of donor restriction is not nearly so important as that it is closed, that he cannot get at it. To the archivist, however, the distinctions are important. They tell him

"Poor Chap — He Was Just Declassifying A Paper When A New Batch Dropped On Him"

The declassification problem as seen by cartoonist Herblock in 1971. (From *Herblock's State of the Union* [Simon and Schuster, 1972].)

where he must go to try to remove the restrictions. They tell him as well what kind of penalties he is likely to face if he makes the documents available illegally. Most important, though, these different types of restricted material present different practical problems for the archivist.

Agency-restricted material, which is often very bulky, is probably the easiest for the archivist to manage because, by and large, an agency will either restrict the whole of its back files before a certain date or set restrictions upon easily distinguishable series of files, such as personnel files or the files of a particular project or operation. The archivist can easily segregate whole blocks of material, entire series, or conceivably the whole files of a department or agency for particular years.

Donor-restricted materials present greater difficulties. Sometimes donors in their deeds-of-gift or in their wills incorporate what both archivists and historians regard as at least whimsical if not downright unreasonable restrictions. Occasionally a donor, frightened by the publicity that some friend has received from the premature publication of his letters, sets a date for the opening of material so far in the future as to make the papers unusable for historians for several generations. The real difficulty in handling the donor-restricted material, however, comes from the fact that it is not in neat blocks. Rather, it tends to be scattered throughout a man's papers. Thus for the archivist there are frequently two parallel sets of files: one consists of open material; the other consists of material drawn from the same original files which is still closed under the restrictions of the donor. Rarely can the archivist open all of this material at once. It requires a page-by-page, and in some cases a line-by-line, review—a slow and time-consuming task.

The problems of dealing with agency-and donor-restricted materials are as nothing compared to the problems of dealing with classified documents. By the latest count no fewer than forty-six different departments or agencies of the federal government have the legal authority to classify their own documents. These range from such obvious bodies as the Central Intelligence Agency and the National Security Council to such unobvious ones as the Peace Corps and the Civil Aeronautics Board. Not all of these agencies approach classification in the same way or with the same zeal. More important, not all approach the problem of declassifying their documents in the same way. It would be exaggeration to say that there are forty-six different systems, different sets of ground rules, but there are probably at least half that many.

The largest and most important agencies, the Department of Defense and the Department of State, approach declassifiation differently. The Department of Defense has issued very elaborate orders indicating the types of material that can be declassified and indicating other types (such as intelligence data) which can be downgraded but which still remain indefinitely closed. For the archivist this is a very difficult system. He must, in effect, make at least a document-by-document if not a page-by-page review, for the categories in which indefinite classification applies are broadly defined and it is not at all obvious from the particular file in which a document is located or from the particular area within the Department of Defense in which the document originated whether it falls into one of those categories of indefinite classification.

From the archivist's point of view the approach taken by the Department of State has many advantages. It uses a chronological rather than a subject classification approach. At the present time Department of State records are open through the end of 1941, restricted (which means a historian can see them with the department's permission) for the period 1942 to 1945, and closed for the period after 1945. There are, to be sure, exceptions. Certain material within the wartime period is not merely restricted but totally closed, while certain types of files cutting across these date lines remain restricted if not totally closed.[3]

Still a third pattern in this at times Byzantine world of classifying and declassifying documents is represented by the Treasury Department. For a very long time, one could justly say, the Treasury Department had no workable system for declassifying its documents. When it finally developed a system some three years ago it did so by simply declaring declassified all classified documents dated prior to November 5, 1953, the date of Executive Order 10501. Classifying officers in the department who felt a particular early document still needed classification could then go back and reclassify it. For the archivist this represents the most satisfactory approach of all to the tangle of classified documents.

These three examples represent three different ways of handling classified documents, and there are others. The archivist's main difficulty is that he must juggle so many sets of declassifying rules. The same folder or box may contain a State Department memorandum on the Casablanca Conference which is open, a naval intelligence report which is still closed, a SHAEF planning document for the Normandy invasion which can be seen with departmental permission, a "cover and deception" document on the same topic which cannot be seen, a declassified Treasury Department document, and perhaps a half-dozen other classified documents originating elsewhere. In effect, the archivist must tear this file apart to make those portions of it available that *can* be made available to a given researcher. And in trying to open its contents he must apply a different criterion to each different item.

For the archivist the problem of classified documents is not a problem of keeping the historian away—that contributes annoyance and irritation and sometimes leads to angry letters to the *New York Times*. But if all of the material is closed, the archivist has no problem handling it; if all of it is open, his problems are those of reference service and bulk—professional archival problems. His real difficulties come when classified documents (or for that matter agency- and donor-restricted documents) fall in the no-man's-land between the totally closed and the completely open: when some of the material for a given period or on a given topic is open and other such material is not, when some researchers can gain access and others cannot. To his other duties have been added those of policeman and censor.

The apparatus sounds complicated because it is complicated. It sounds inconsistent because it is, at least at times, inconsistent. And certainly it is troublesome and time-consuming. There are within the National Archives and Records Service system approximately sixty-four million documents dating from the Second World War that remain classified. To declassify these documents under the present regulations would mean almost a case-by-case or document-by-document review, requiring the full-time services of one hundred additional archivists working for more than eleven years. Since the Second World War marks only the beginning of the age of passionate classification, we face the prospect of falling further and further behind, unless some better way of declassifying documents is devised.[4]

I would like to offer some personal observations on this subject. It seems to me that the system of classified documents is not working well. I am not in a position to judge whether it does, in fact, preserve the secrets of national defense that must be preserved; but from my own experience (or endurance) of this problem in the last several years I think I can say that it is not meeting the other objective it was established to meet. Executive Order 10501 which is the basic document for this classification system begins "it is essential that the citizens of the United States be informed concerning the activities of their government." Unless we are to regard these words as window dressing (and I am not willing to do so), we must assume that President Eisenhower issued the order not only with the idea of preserving material essential to the national security but with the objective of preventing the indiscriminate closing or restriction of material. Over the years, however, I believe that the emphasis of the entire system has been in the other direction: toward the need to keep material closed in the interest of national security. The need to make it available to citizens has received insufficient attention.

I am oversimplifying a bit, but I think one could characterize the present arrangement in this way: a document, once classified, requires the positive action of some official in authority to be declassified. It may be that consideration should be given to reversing this approach, to declassifying automatically all documents after a reasonable number of years. This implies, of course, the elimination of the categories of indefinitely classified material. It seems to me unimportant, at least at the moment, whether we are talking of ten years, as James MacGregor Burns has suggested, or of twenty or thirty years, or of something in between. What does seem to be important is reconstituting the system so that there is, in all cases, automatic declassification. It may well be that there are certain documents which even after the passage of ten, twenty, or thirty years are still so vital to the national security that they must be kept closed. I would suggest that here positive action be undertaken and that *individual* documents of such high sensitivity could be reclassified for a limited period, hopefully for a very short limited period.[5]

In his most recent book, Lewis Mumford has recalled to our attention the historic connection between the preservation of the secrets of power and the preservation of power itself and has pointed once again to the inherent danger which this represents for a democratic society in the twentieth century. Some means must be found to achieve a better balance between the government's need for secrecy and the public's right to know. Solving the problem of classified documents would contribute to that balance. Then we could all rejoin our ranks and the historical army could continue its inexorable march.

Notes

1. J. Franklin Jameson, "The Further Uses of History," *American Historical Review* 65 (October 1959): 61–62, reprinted from *History Teacher's Magazine* (February 1913).
2. Claude H. Van Tyne and Waldo G. Leland, *Guide to the Archives of the Government of the United States in Washington,* 2d ed. (Washington, 1907), p. vi.
3. Since this paper was presented in 1971, the Department of State has opened its records through the end of 1947.
4. In 1972 the president issued Executive Order 11652 substantially revising the security classification system and placing the emphasis on declassification. The National Archives and Records Service was provided with funds by the

Congress in 1972 to inaugurate a large-scale, systematic declassification program beginning with World War II documents. A description of the revised security classification system can be found in the author's article "The Security Classification of Records in the United States," *Indian Archives* 22 (January-December 1973): 35–45.
5. "Automatic declassification" (or, perhaps, more accurately "semi-automatic declassification") along the lines suggested here is included among the provisions of Executive Order 11652.

12 November 1944

From: U.S. Military Attache, London, England

To: The President of The United States

Nr: 821, 12 November 1944   Filed 121616Z

        Prime Minister to President Roosevelt personal and ▇▇▇▇▇

No 821.

        I have seen your directive of 1st November to the U. S. Secretary
of War about the Italian grain ration, and I hope you will not mind my
saying that you have jumped a good many fences. It will be difficult
to give our ex enemies in Italy more than our Allies in Greece and
Yougoslavia, and I hope your people will bear this in mind.

        You will understand why I am rather anxious about commitments
of this sort, which are bound to tie up so much shipping. I trust
that the U.S. War Department will take steps to provide the additional
tonnage, which we cannot ourselves provide, to carry the increased
supplies.

        As regards economic assistance to Italy generally, dealt with
in NAF 810, MacMillan is coming here soon and has asked that this
question should be kept open until he has taken over as Acting President
of the Allied Commission.   REGRADED UNCLASSIFIED by British
                                         Govt., State Dept. tel., 3-29-72
                                         By R. H. Parks   Date MAY 6 1972

File Copy

LLOYD C. GARDNER

Past Secrets and Present Security

The Historian's Viewpoint

No historian, so far as I can tell, views the present situation regarding access to American archival materials from the World War II period to the present as satisfactory. The chief villain usually cited is the State Department; but I hasten to add that not all scholars agree on the source of their troubles. Because most diplomatic historians working in this area sooner or later (generally sooner) seek out State Department records, the brunt of criticism has fallen on that agency. In my opinion, deservedly so.

However favorably it might compare with that of other countries, the record of the State Department in its dealings with scholars does not constitute a happy chapter in the history of American diplomacy. I am perfectly aware of all the explanations (past and present) given by the department for not granting access to records in the so-called closed period, i.e., twenty-five years back from the present. I find those explanations self-serving on several levels and at odds with any serious definition of an open society. Moreover, I suggest they are of dubious legality under American law.

Fortunately (or perhaps unfortunately as I shall explain later), one of the worst features of restricted access seems to have disappeared in recent years. I refer to the practice of granting certain historians special privileges to restricted materials in order to get an "objective" account to the American people, before the field is invaded by "partisan controversialists." In the case of the famous Langer and Gleason volumes on American entry into World War II (*The Challenge to Isolation* and *The Undeclared War*), one historian raised such a fuss that he, too, was allowed into the still-classified files. I do not know the details of how that was managed, but the important point is that the remainder of the profession—and the public—was left to debate the issue on the merits of the views put forward by Langer and Gleason, or those asserted in Charles C. Tansill's *Back Door to War*. Another diplomatic historian, a former policy maker himself, has recently joined in denouncing governmental secrecy. It is helpful to have his voice added to the cause; it would have been even more helpful if Herbert Feis could have expressed himself just as vigorously when he was writing books based in part upon privileged access to State Department records.

Perhaps it is unfortunate that this practice has been abandoned. For one thing, if it were still being carried on today, the uproar would be so great that the walls might come tumbling down. A second reason is that it could be argued that even a few snippets of the record, gathered from a re-reading of official volumes, are better than none at all. That there was not a greater protest against this practice by the profession at the time is unfortunate, because it set a bad precedent.

The opposite practice, of denying certain historians access to all records in the restricted period, also seems to have disappeared. I stand to be corrected on this point, in part because of statements made to me which I have no way of verifying, and in part because of solid evidence that the practice did exist at one time. When it was done, it was done with discretion, and written records may not exist of all instances of this abuse. The requirement of a security clearance to look at classified records in this period has been used to limit what papers can be seen, even where access is granted.

Of recent date, I have heard some diplomatic historians make the argument that general access to postwar archival materials will provide ammunition to refute the most recent wave of cold war revisionism. I do not share that view, nor the curious notion that by making new sources available one reduces the number of possible interpretations, but if it persuades the guardians of the archives, fine. I am all for it!

In 1951, and again in 1952, committees of the American Historical Association, chaired by Prof. Jeannette P. Nichols, proposed resolutions to the general membership concerning the increasing gap between the actual events and the State Department's publication of the record of American diplomacy in its official *Foreign Relations* volumes. Professor Nichols warned that the gap had already reached eighteen years and that scholars were being denied a chance to review the path America took to war. Her committees' resolutions were strongly worded, eloquent appeals to the best in the American democratic tradition. The gap today has reached twenty-five years plus. And I fear we would be grateful even to return to the situation condemned by Professor Nichols and her committees. The best way to remove such temptations would be to heed the Nichols committees and their successors.

From its origins until after the turn of the century, volumes in the *Foreign Relations* series were published within a year or so of the actual events; they were attached to the President's annual message as House Document no. 1. As America rose to world power, the volume of documents naturally grew. So, too, did the secrecy surrounding diplomatic doings. President Franklin D. Roosevelt once expressed doubts about the publication of Wilson's Big Four conferences at Versailles, on the grounds that statesmen could not speak freely if their doings were to be open to all at some future date. Because Roosevelt was involved in the process of wartime diplomacy, his position was perfectly understandable but not acceptable to historians in a free society. It is a *sine qua non* of such a society that policy makers must be held accountable to the people and to their representatives in Congress.

The very fact that the publication of diplomatic documents pertaining to World War I had been so long delayed should have been a warning signal to the profession and the public. I am not making the argument that by giving historians access to nearly contemporary documents we add another quasi-constitutional check or balance on the excesses of governmental power. I will make the argument that long-term secrecy promotes excesses. Today's papers offer new proof, if any is still needed, of that proposition. A twenty-five-year plus moratorium on documented criticism (as opposed to the easily refuted assertions of contemporary figures— even of chairmen of the Senate Foreign Relations Committee—who can easily be dismissed with an all-knowing, "Well, if you saw the documents, you would not take that position, etc.") is simply too long a time for the welfare and continued vigor of political democracy. We may regret that policy makers have to run the risk of public criticism and that their views may be thrown up against them by old enemies. I do not minimize the problem; however, criticism is a lesser price we all must pay than the present and future expense of mistaken policies, continued and propelled by the force of inertia through a secrecy-sealed tunnel to some safe landing place twenty-five years hence.

I am speaking now as a citizen (as well as a historian) concerned about the welfare of the nation and not simply with the publication of historical interpretation. Historical interpretation will take care of itself, with or without access to recent documents in the archives. I am convinced that a full memory is important to nations as well as to individuals. An amnesia gap of twenty-five years is more than disadvantageous to both; indeed, it is impossible. However distorted, the blank spots will be filled in, most often with the memories or memoirs of those who participated in the events. In the early cold war period, for example, the original interpretations of events leading to the breakdown of the "Grand Alliance" were often little more than compilations of such memoirs edited by the historian into a passable narrative. Until access to the records of those events is open to all, we will have a one-sided memory based upon the evidence as selected and published by the disputants themselves.

I do not know when the objectionable practice of requiring security clearances for scholars working in even twenty-five-year-old records began, but it should be ended as a first step toward freeing the historian from the chains of governmental censorship. Can it really be argued that access to such records—even by severe critics—imperils the nation's security? If so, we ought to consider what kinds of policies we are pursuing that require that their origins be kept a state secret for nearly three decades. Presumably, the record of American diplomacy (as opposed to the nefarious activities of the Soviet Union and other powers) has been a search for a world order based on the creation and maintenance of honorable agreements. We cannot assess that record so long as the documents remain closed to legitimate scholars.

The Department of State already retains the research notes of scholars granted access to its records in the restricted period in order to clear whatever material has been taken from foreign documents. One would think, therefore, that the government has an adequate check on the flow of information potentially embarrassing to other nations, without insisting that all documents on the day-to-day development and implementation of foreign policy must remain secret for so many years.

In years past, diplomatic historians often found some of the materials they were seeking in other manuscript collections in the Library of Congress or in private libraries. The private papers of ambassadors and secretaries of state are prime examples. Recently, something of a footrace takes place every time a new collection is deposited in a research library. If the historian gets there first, he is rewarded by access to records closed elsewhere. If the department gets there first, it seeks to persuade the library to close its holdings in conformity with its own time-frame regulations, regardless of whether the papers include nonclassified, or personally classified items. Moreover, the Historical Office of the Department of State will then undertake to determine what the individual himself intended when he classified a document, e.g., how long it was to remain "secret" or "confidential." The Historical Office also seeks to extend its control over records physically located in other government agencies or in presidential libraries. It presumes to assert that, by right of origin, its regulations cover the intentions of a former president in ordering the document and then depositing it in his papers when he leaves office. What monsters grow when regulations are left to feed upon themselves!

To scholars who question these practices, the department recommends that historians would all be better off if everyone supported the Historical Office, because in that way, at least, they will be guaranteed access after the set time period has elapsed, that is, if the *Foreign Relations* volumes for the years they wish to research have been published. But it cannot guarantee that the publication of those volumes will continue to be at a twenty-five-year interval after the events. It is not today. Some hope that it would not fall too much more behind thirty years. We are assured that every effort is being made to push the publication of these volumes, but for a variety of complex reasons, including sheer quantity, difficulty of obtaining clearances from other departments, etc., the lag is inevitable.

The Historical Office is to be congratulated on recent volumes in the series; they set a standard to be envied by all historians and foreign countries. That is not really the answer to the questions raised by historians and by other scholars. If the magnitude of the documents is so great as to preclude earlier publication, then it behooves the department all the more to work out a system for allowing researchers to investigate the record of American diplomacy—and come to their own conclusions.

The present system is not just "not working well" (a bureaucratic euphemism for nothing can be done); it is working too well, but against the public interest. Some historians have proposed that automatic declassification procedures should be introduced so as to permit research within eight to ten years after the events. As a general proposition, I would argue that a ten-year gap makes sense, although there are obvious exceptions, such as papers connected with weapons systems and the need to protect sensitive information about foreign policy makers. There are other exceptions, but my own experience in working with formerly classified materials makes it clear that the bulk of the record on any subject does not involve such exceptions.

There are many interpretations of the law concerning the classification of government documents. Those who question the government's current interpretations (and they vary considerably from department to department) are not unaware of the complexities of the issues. I hope that this discussion will help us to confront the central problem with an eye toward serving the public interest. It cannot be properly served so long as the only people permitted to determine these questions are working for the policy makers alone.

Discussion Summary

The discussion was initiated by Julius Epstein (Hoover Institution), who narrated his unsuccessful attempts to obtain access to classified records relating to "Operation Keelhaul," attempts which included appeals through the Federal court system to the Supreme Court. Winnacker noted that "Keelhaul" was a joint operation; its records were protected by an agreement with the British government, which was unwilling to permit their declassification.

Arthur L. Funk (University of Florida) suggested that the basic conflict lay between the needs of historians and those of the government. Public officials must feel free to express themselves frankly without fear that what they say will be released to the public prematurely and in such a way as to hamper the government's activities. He felt that such a conflict between good administration and the historians' interests was inevitable.

Barbara Tuchman wondered whether completely automatic declassification of documents after twenty years would not be feasible. Winnacker replied that even if all the classified material were automatically declassified, it would still be necessary to review the files for material protected on other grounds, such as potential invasion of privacy. He added that the closer the material was to the present, the more material would have to be kept closed, requiring still further review later.

William M. Franklin (Director of the Historical Office, Department of State), saying that he appeared "not as an advocate of the devil, but as the devil himself," described at length the access policies and procedures of the State Department. He noted that with the Second World War the United States became a major world power and the records of the State Department inevitably became more sensitive. The Department, he felt, made its records available within a reasonable period of time—twenty-five years at present, tied to the publication of the *Foreign Relations of the United States* volumes. Low level material might be made available sooner, but it would be of little value until the really important documents were released.

Lloyd Gardner commented upon both Winnacker's remarks and Franklin's. In view of the varied ground-rules on access noted by O'Neill, he questioned whether the issue were really the government's priorities versus historians, and he wondered whether government officials were the best judges of the public interest in such a matter. Moreover, the State Department seemed to tell different historians different things when they asked for access. Gardner also questioned the authority of the State Department to place restrictions on access to papers in university repositories.

Louis Morton (Dartmouth) closed the discussion by describing the work and prospects in the area of access of the Committee on the Historian and the Federal Government, a joint committee of the American Historical Association and the Organization of American Historians.

VII

Science and Technology in the Second World War

The seventh session was one of two concurrent sessions held on the afternoon of June 15. The chairman was Nathan Reingold of the Smithsonian Institution, and the papers were devoted to an exploration of the use of archival materials in writing the history of science and technology.

CARROLL PURSELL

Alternative American Science Policies during World War II

During the decade of the 1930s, American science, like the economy of which it was a part, was heavily concentrated in the private sector. Also like the American economy in general, the private sector of science was heavily concentrated in a small number of large institutions. Despite the hopes of some and the fears of others, Franklin D. Roosevelt's New Deal did little to alter the basic distribution of economic power in the country during the Great Depression, and analogous proposals to make fundamental changes in the support and pursuit of science were likewise rejected.[1] As a result, both the economy and the community of science entered upon a war mobilization program in 1940 which was characterized by a virtual abandonment of even the pretense of New Deal reform and the further concentration of economic power.

Perpetuated into the postwar period, these patterns have recently led to an increasing criticism of the basic structure of American scientific support. Like many other social reforms of the Depression years, the democratization of science represented a problem deferred rather than solved. The wartime science effort is usually celebrated for the technology it provided to a surprised military and for the subsidy it arranged for a sometimes suspicious academic community. An equally significant result, however, was the perpetuation of inequalities and priorities not always in the larger national interest.

In 1939, on the eve of mobilization, only half the manufacturing firms in the United States employed more than five hundred workers, and since World War I a consistent quarter of the nation's total manufacturing work force had been concentrated in firms employing more than one thousand.[2] The American ambivalence toward monopoly had dictated the New Deal's approach to this problem: the desire for economies of scale and planning had been at constant war with a commitment to the tradition of trust-busting.[3] The emergency of the Depression, like the nearing emergency of war, appeared to argue for both policies.

Scientific activity in the United States was similarly concentrated and carried on primarily through three agencies: one-sixth of research support came from the government, an equal amount from colleges and universi-

151

ties, and two-thirds from private industry. Only a very small amount was supported by private philanthropic foundations. Within the government's sixth, the largest share of research money (one-third) was spent by the Department of Agriculture, far from the concerns of industry. Within the colleges and universities, 10 percent of the institutions accounted for the great bulk of the perhaps $50,000,000 spent annually. Within industry in 1938, thirteen corporations employed a third of the research workers and a comparable share of the total of $250,000,000 put into industrial research.[4] Despite a number of schemes put forward to involve the federal government more heavily in the support of American science, most were rejected, and this basic pattern prevailed.[5]

One dramatic result of the war mobilization that the United States undertook in the spring of 1940 was a massive infusion of government funds into both the economy generally and the practice of science specifically. From June 1940 through September 1944, the government awarded prime contracts for material, valued at $175 billion, to 18,539 corporations. Two-thirds of this amount ($117 billion) went to 100 corporations—and half of this $117 billion went to 10 corporations.[6] Contracts for research and development were also greatly expanded and similarly concentrated. By 1944 the government was spending $700 million a year—ten times what it had in 1938. Between 1940 and 1944, government science agencies had dispensed $1,879,183,000 in research and development contracts. Nearly half of this was spent in private industrial laboratories: 68 corporations got two-thirds of the money, and the top 10 contractors received nearly 40 percent of the total.[7] The change can be seen clearly in the case of one firm, the Bell Telephone Laboratories. The research arm of American Telephone & Telegraph Company (which was the eighth largest recipient of prime contracts for material during the war), Bell Laboratories in 1939 spent $20,000,000 on research, only 1 percent of which came from the government. By 1944 Bell Laboratories had more than tripled its research effort, with the federal government now providing 80 percent of the funds.[8]

Through fiscal year 1944, the War Department dispensed more research and development funds than any other agency, over $754 million. The second largest granting agency was the Navy Department, with $348 million. Close behind was the newly established wartime agency, the Office of Scientific Research and Development (OSRD) with total expenditures of nearly $337 million.[9] These three agencies accounted for the bulk of R & D funds. Although the OSRD was not the largest spender among science agencies, its wartime total of $450,000,000 (of which $50 million was for medical research) and the way in which it was spent make it the most important of the group.

The Office of Scientific Research and Development grew out of the National Defense Research Committee (NDRC), which had been established in June of 1940.[10] The prime mover of the new OSRD was its chairman Vannevar Bush, president of the Carnegie Institution of Washington, chairman of the National Advisory Committee on Aeronautics, and vice president of the Massachusetts Institute of Technology.[11] Working through Frederick A. Delano, a trustee of the Carnegie Institution and uncle to the president, and through Harry Hopkins, Bush was able to commit the president to support a new and independent agency charged with developing and improving instruments of war. With him on the NDRC Bush associated James B. Conant, president of Harvard University; Karl T. Compton, president of the Massachusetts Institute of Technology; Richard Tolman, of the California Institute of Technology; and Frank B. Jewett, head of Bell Laboratories and the recently elected president of the National Academy of Sciences.

It was hardly a representative group, but it would be difficult to find one more closely connected with the centers of corporate, scientific, philanthropic, and collegiate power in the nation. They were, as a group, strong supporters of the Allies and advocates of all-out aid to Great Britain in her coming showdown with the Axis. Furthermore, although they had been involved during the 1930s in various schemes to tap relief programs for the benefit of education in general and science in particular, they were not strong admirers of Franklin Roosevelt and had a hearty distrust, bordering on dislike, for New Dealers.[12] It was a group intimate and at ease with the most powerful and progressive business interests of the nation.

In beginning their operations, the members of the NDRC had adopted the same two guidelines which were to lead most other aspects of the nation's economic mobilization program.[13] The overriding purpose was to be the speedy defeat of the Axis powers. Second, this was to be done with as little disruption of peacetime power alignments as possible. When President Roosevelt dismissed "Dr. New Deal" and called in "Dr. Win-the-War," he was announcing a policy very much in line with the thinking of the leaders of the scientific community. Both desires, to avoid delay and to avoid disruption, dictated a break with the precedent of World War I. In 1940 it was decided that, as much as possible, scientists were to be used *in situ* rather than mobilized in government laboratories. In securing research, as in securing guns and tanks, the contract was to be the primary instrument of procurement.

An analysis of research and development spending through September 1944 shows that the pattern set by the OSRD was unique in that two-thirds of its funds went to educational institutions and foundations, with most of the remainder being spent in industrial laboratories. In contrast, the Department of Agriculture spent the bulk of its funds in its own laboratories and the War Department spent two-thirds of its funds with industry.[14] When looked at institution by institution, however, the pattern shows the same concentration of funds: through June of 1945, MIT had received far and away the most money from OSRD, nearly $117 million. Along with the California Institute of Technology, Harvard University, Columbia University, and the University of California, it accounted for well over half the funds spent by the OSRD during the entire war.[15] The top two industrial contractors were Western Electric (like Bell Laboratories a subsidiary of AT&T) and the Research Construction Corporation, an organization created to build the Radiation Laboratory at MIT.[16]

Massive government spending channeled into a small number of industrial and educational giants was a salient feature of this wartime mobilization, and came almost immediately under attack from those who feared that once again, as so often in American history, the martial trumpet was drowning out the call for reform. Although there was, at least after December 7, 1941, no disagreement with the need to speedily defeat the Axis, there was a persistent realization that the way in which the war was fought at home would help determine the shape of the peace to come.

Needing the cooperation of big business and believing in its ability to organize and produce, Roosevelt acted to dispel or, at least to neutralize, the antiadministration posture of the business community. Mobilization was placed largely in the hands of dollar-a-year men operating through such agencies as the War Production Board. Leaders of the largest industries were selected to direct the home-front war effort. General Motors did not receive the largest amount of prime contract during the war simply because William S. Knudsen left the presidency of the world's largest corporation to become production chief of the National Defense Advisory Committee—rather, both facts were the result of Roosevelt's basic decision to take the economy of the nation where he found it and begin mobilization from that point.[17] It was the same decision which Vannevar Bush made for the nation's science.

The policy was quickly challenged. "Monopoly," charged the *Nation*, "is the worst enemy of the technological progress so essential to national defense."[18] Critics were quick to point out that, however reluctant the president might be to conceptualize the postwar world, business kept one eye firmly on the likely postwar results of wartime economic policies. Monopolies based on the control of scarce resources—be they patents, research brains, physical plant, high-grade ores, or production know-how —were not anxious to lose that advantage if the war could be won with their privilege intact. Since research and development were great solvents of the industrial status quo, their mobilization was as much a threat as an opportunity for the nation's largest interests.

There were three basic criticisms leveled at the way in which science was mobilized, especially by the Office of Scientific Research and Development. First, it was said to have fallen far short of utilizing the entire research capability of the country; second, it concentrated on the development of weapons to the neglect of needed improvements in industrial production; and third, funds were distributed in such a way as to perpetuate and even to strengthen the uneven prewar pattern of research capability and, therefore, of economic and educational power.

The charge of underutilization was a difficult one to either document or to refute. Periodicals as diverse as the liberal *Nation* and the business-oriented *Fortune* worried that the country was allowing the waste of precious research talent.[19] Leonard Carmichael, head of the newly established National Roster of Scientific and Specialized Personnel, estimated in 1943 that there were perhaps "between 400,000 and 500,000 trained or qualified scientific men and women in the country," and he guessed that over three-quarters of them were to some extent involved in war work.[20] If James B. Conant was anywhere near correct in his estimate that 10,000 to 15,000 scientists and engineers had worked for OSRD contractors during the war, the dimensions of the problem are clear.[21] While thousands found work through other channels (the chemical industry claimed that every one of its people was doing war work[22]), it remains true that Bush's OSRD was the closest thing to a central scientific agency in wartime Washington.

The reasons for underutilization were many. A central fact was that the OSRD hierarchy was heavily skewed in favor of physics, chemistry, and electrical engineering, and saw its major effort in terms of creating what Hunter Dupree has called "an electronic environment for war." James Conant later wrote that "we all rode to a position of influence on the backs of those physicists and electrical engineers who were concerned with this new instrument of war," radar, which had played such a dramatic role in winning the Battle of Britain in the first weeks of the NDRC's life.[23] To a large extent, geologists, biologists, astronomers and many other specialists were irrelevant to this effort.

The problem of full utilization was also complicated by a frankly elitist attitude on the part of OSRD's leaders. It was axiomatic to them that, being at the top of their profession, they knew personally the others at the top and that they together represented the talent in the field. Capable journeymen scientists at small, southern or western teaching colleges were not known to them personally and had no good way of coming to their attention. The prewar precedent of distributing research funds geographically was abandoned in favor of a policy of supporting excellence and existing capability. A professor of physics at the University of North Carolina complained in 1943 that "as much as 50 percent of my colleagues in the southeastern part of our country" had been given no war work to do.[24]

Vannevar Bush and James B. Conant receiving decorations for their wartime achievements from President Truman, 1948. (National Park Service; National Archives, no. 79-AR-946A.)

Vannevar Bush came at the problem of mobilization from a concern over new weapons and counter-measures against them. From its establishment, the NDRC was exclusively concerned with what were always referred to as "instrumentalities of war," excluding only the airplane which was left to the National Advisory Committee for Aeronautics. In 1941, when the OSRD was established and Bush moved up to its chairmanship, medical research was made a coordinate responsibility with weapons, but this was not a concern which directly engaged any of the original NDRC group and represented only a small part of OSRD's effort. The largest area left out, or at least the one which caused the most concern, was the more traditional (and controversial) area of industrial research. If aluminum, for example, was in short supply, might not research discover new sources or production methods to make it more plentiful? It was the sort of question which Bush scrupulously avoided.

Early in the mobilization such a question might have been asked of the National Academy of Sciences, a body referred to by the liberal journalist I. F. Stone as "a 'stuffed shirt' organization, full of technical men who are mouthpieces for powerful industrial interests."[25] Late in 1942, at the instigation of New Deal politicians operating within and without the War Production Board, an Office of Production Research and Development was set up to act as the scientific arm of that agency. In 1944 it spent an insignificant $4.5 million—evidence enough that federal intrusion into industrial research failed to win the vigorous support of either business or government. This failure, of course, contributed to the related problem of underutilization.[26]

Both the underutilization of research potential and the failure to vigorously pursue production problems were closely related to the general problem of monopoly. Like their dollar-a-year counterparts in the economic mobilization agencies, the leaders of the OSRD, on loan from Bell Laboratories, Harvard, Cal Tech, MIT, and the Carnegie Institution, were in the happy position of being able to serve at the same time the nation, their own idea of what was good for American science, and their familiar institutions, with little apparent conflict of interest. As Conant later remarked, the NDRC was not only a means of mobilizing science but also "a mechanism by which all the universities and many of the colleges contributed their scientific staffs to the war effort."[27] In other words, the agency had a conservative as well as an innovative mission. A school like MIT had long been accustomed not only to leadership in American science and engineering but also in service to the federal government. This moment of the nation's crisis seemed a particularly inappropriate time to contemplate a pulling down of the mighty and a lifting up of the weak.

In the midst of such a crisis, the agency with a plan and an ongoing purpose had an enormous advantage over critics who were discontented with the status quo. Furthermore, the already considerable record of NDRC's success stood up well against the less than spectacular results of such democratically conceived agencies as the National Roster of Scientific and Specialized Personnel or the National Inventors Council. Both were dedicated to the proposition that everyone with potential for invention or research should be integrated into the mobilization machinery. The Roster eventually registered over half a million specialists but served more often to identify the exotic than the typical scientist. Certainly the OSRD made precious little use of it, preferring to rely on a decentralized version of the old-school-tie system. The Inventors Council was eventually able to put into production only 106 of the 208,975 ideas received from the general public.[28]

Besides a greater reliance on such new agencies, a second alternative to the OSRD might have been an increased dependence upon the old-line scientific agencies of the government, some of which had been serving the nation since the early nineteenth century.[29] Conant's fear was that such a procedure would have led to a "competition among at least a dozen government bureaus or their equivalent for the best scientific brains and the technical skill of the country. We should have had an enormous expansion within a governmental framework already in existence. Furthermore, all policy decisions even on matters of applied research would have been in the hands of regular officers of the Army and the Navy."[30] He was doubtless correct on all three counts. The scientific effort was already being criticized for being too decentralized, an expansion of the federal bureaucracy would have set ill with many, and the military had already proved itself institutionally and psychologically unsuited to appreciate the possibility and benefits of weapons innovation.

A third alternative, and one which caused considerable concern within the OSRD as well as within the industrial community, was the possible creation of a centralized, politically responsible agency which, both during the war and possibly after as well, would direct all science and technology for both weapons and production innovation. Such an agency had been suggested during the Depression as a mechanism for breaking the power of industrial monopoly and harnessing technical innovation to the needs of both recovery and reform. Now it was proposed to do the same for wartime needs and opportunities.

The suggestion came from many quarters. Some of the most innovative reforms proposed during the New Deal had come from lower echelon functionaries in the various government agencies, and this proved to be true during the war as well. Those within the War Production Board who sought the establishment of the Office of Production Research and Development, for example, saw that it might be expanded to become such an agency. Waldemar Kaempffert, science editor of the *New York Times,* urged the need for such centralized planning and control, but he thought that the excellent record of the OSRD with weapons suggested that it might be expanded to fill the need.[31] Bush had no such ambitions and stoutly resisted any such move.

Just as the Truman Committee served as a constant watchdog and critic of the general economic mobilization program, so did the Subcommittee on War Mobilization of the Senate Committee on Military Affairs (chaired by a Truman Committee member) serve to provide a platform for alternative science policies between 1942 and 1945.[32] Chaired by the freshman senator from West Virginia, Harley M. Kilgore, the subcommittee brought forth an elaborate and broad-scale plan to federalize and centralize the science and technology of the nation. A steady stream of witnesses complained of underutilization and overconcentration in the science effort. In response, the committee suggested creation of an Office of Technological Mobilization with power to "mobilize for maximum war effort the full powers of our technically trained manhood and similarly to mobilize all technical facilities, equipment, processes, inventions, and knowledge."[33]

Almost all aspects of the proposed operations of the new agency were threats to existing interests. Instead of a war effort led by the largest concerns, under conditions very much to their advantage, the Office of Technological Mobilization was to draft knowledge just as the military drafted men. A special effort was to be made to enlist the contributions of small manufacturers, small schools, and independent inventors. Research was to be encouraged which would break monopolies, and the resulting patents were to be freely available to all. It was in the finest tradition of New Deal reform thought, but it would have been completely alien in the wartime Washington of the 1940s. Long since dismissed, "Dr. New Deal" was not to be called back for consultation.

The major result of the Kilgore hearings, and the other agitation for a more democratic mobilization of science, was to force the hands of the OSRD leadership in preparing plans for the postwar support of science. Neither the architects around Bush of the wartime scientific efforts nor its critics around Kilgore had been unaware of the fact that the shape of that mobilization owed as much to postwar hopes as to prewar failures. The spectre of New Deal reform hung low over the debates of 1941 to 1943, and the battle over postwar science policy fit easily into the ill-fated revival of the reform impulse during 1944 and 1945.

The emerging picture of a scientific community, internally controlled by a well-placed elite and externally put at the service of the most powerful economic and political interests of the nation, sat ill after a decade and a half of fighting monopoly at home and fascism abroad. Questions of patent policy, the extent and mechanism for political control of science policy, geographical distribution of funds as opposed to support of individual excellence, and similar matters survived the war to torment postwar planners. Their resolution in favor of established interests was the last victory of the OSRD group before it ended its service to science and the nation; but the alternatives were merely rejected, not defeated. They have survived a quarter of a century and have emerged again in the growing revolt against the power and direction of American scientific and technological supremacy. The seeds of that revolt were planted by the NDRC and its organizers in 1940.

Looking back on the effort soon after the war, James B. Conant, prominent chemist, industrial consultant, president of Harvard University, and active interventionist, declared, "I believe that the mobilization of science in 1940–1945 was an effective means of shortening the period of hostilities and assuring victory to our side."[34] He was undoubtedly correct, and it is no small victory to celebrate. The price of this accomplishment, however, was only half acknowledged at the time and is still being paid today.

Notes

1. On the economic results of the New Deal, see Douglass C. North, *Growth and Welfare in the American Past* (Englewood Cliffs, N.J.: Prentice-Hall, 1966), p. 179. On science, see Carroll W. Pursell, Jr., "The Anatomy of A Failure: The Science Advisory Board, 1933–1935," *Proceedings of the American Philosophical Society* 109 (December 1965): 342–51.
2. U. S., Congress, Senate, Special Committee to . . . Business, *Economic Concentration and World War II: Report of the Smaller War Plants Corporation*, 79th Cong., 2d sess., 1946, p. 21.
3. See Ellis W. Hawley, *The New Deal and the Problem of Monopoly* (Princeton, N.J.: Princeton University Press, 1966).
4. U. S., Congress, Senate, Subcommittee on War Mobilization to the Commit-

tee on Military Affairs, *The Government's Wartime Research and Development, 1940–44, Part 2: Findings and Recommendations,* 79th Cong., 1st sess., p. 20.

5. See, for example, Carroll W. Pursell, Jr., "A Preface to Government Support of Research and Development: Research Legislation and the National Bureau of Standards, 1935–41," *Technology and Culture* 9 (April 1968): 145–64.

6. Senate, *Economic Concentration,* p. 29.

7. Senate, *Government's Wartime Research and Development,* p. 22.

8. Ibid., pp. 21–22.

9. Ibid., pp. 66–67.

10. The best history of the NDRC-OSRD is Irvin Stewart, *Organizing Scientific Research for War: The Administrative History of the Office of Scientific Research and Development* (Boston: Little, Brown & Co., 1948).

11. For some of his recollections, see Vannevar Bush, *Pieces of the Action* (New York: William Morrow & Co., 1970).

12. See, for example, remarks in James B. Conant, *My Several Lives: Memoirs of a Social Inventor* (New York: Harper & Row, 1970).

13. An excellent short piece on economic mobilization is Barton J. Bernstein, "America in War and Peace: The Test of Liberalism," in Bernstein, ed., *Towards a New Past: Dissenting Essays in American History* (New York: Pantheon Books, 1968), pp. 289–321.

14. Senate, *Government's Wartime Research and Development,* p. 5.

15. James Phinney Baxter 3rd, *Scientists against Time* (Boston: Little, Brown & Co., 1946) p. 456.

16. Ibid., pp. 456–57.

17. An angry interpretation of this policy is I. F. Stone, *Business as Usual: The First Year of Defense* (New York: Modern Age Books, 1941).

18. *Nation* 152 (February 1941): 143.

19. See, for example, I. F. Stone, "Brains for Defense," *Nation* 152 (January 4, 1941): 7–8; "A Technological High Command," *Fortune* 25 (April 1942) and "The Bottleneck in Ideas," *Fortune* 27 (May 1943). For comparison, read Joseph Needham, "The Utilizaton of Scientists in England," *Science and Society* 7 (Winter 1943): 32–35.

20. Leonard Carmichael, "The Number of Scientific Men Engaged in War Work," *Science* 98 (August 13, 1943): 144–45.

21. James B. Conant, "The Mobilization of Science for the War Effort," *American Scientist* 35 (April 1947): 197.

22. Charles Albert Browne and Mary Elvira Weeks, *A History of the American Chemical Society: Seventy-five Eventful Years* (Washington, D.C.: American Chemical Society, 1952), 156–78.

23. Conant, "Mobilization," pp. 203–4.

24. U.S., Congress, Senate, Subcommittee of the Committee on Military Affairs, *Scientific and Technological Mobilization: Hearing before the Subcommittee of the Committee on Military Affairs,* 78th Cong., 1st sess., 1943, 3: 237.

25. Stone, *Business as Usual,* p. 105.

26. The OPRD is touched upon in Bruce Catton, *War Lords of Washington* (New York: Harcourt, Brace & Co., 1948).

27. Conant, "Mobilization," p. 197.

28. See U.S., Department of Commerce, National Inventors Council, "Admin-

istrative History of the National Inventors Council'' (processed, NIC, Dept. of Commerce, n.d.).

29. The standard work on this subject is A. Hunter Dupree, *Science in the Federal Government: A History of Policies and Activities to 1940* (Cambridge: Harvard University Press, 1957).
30. Conant, "Mobilization," p. 201.
31. U.S., Congress, Senate, Committee on Military Affairs, *Technological Mobilization: Hearings before the Subcommittee of the Committee on Military Affairs*, 77th Cong., 2d sess., 1942, 1:67–69.
32. See Donald H. Riddle, *The Truman Committee: A Study in Congressional Responsibility* (New Brunswick, N.J.: Rutgers University Press, 1964). No scholarly study has been made of the Kilgore subcommittee.
33. The text of the bill may be found in *Technological Mobilization* 1: 1–3.
34. Conant, "Mobilization," p. 210.

MEYER H. FISHBEIN

Archival Remains of Research
and Development during the Second
World War

Topical analyses of voluminous records, in contrast to descriptions of discrete files for specific agencies, are impressionistic, personal interpretations of records rather than simple enumerations of types of materials, volume, dates, and topics. The composer surveys masses of paper to find elements that suggest the whole or that may excite the interest of certain specialists. Few, if any, significant subjects on United States history are unrepresented in the National Archives. The topic, research and development during the war, is so well represented that a relatively brief guide should give me free range of the materials to select illustrative and important items. Yet, my subject led me a tortuous route through the maze of scientific research and development.

Students of science learn to make careful notes of project objectives, observations, and conclusions. Few of them, however, adhere to these standards when they reach their professional seniority. Notes for several projects are intermixed in lab books, jargon is intermixed with esoteric scientific terms, and abbreviations are made particularly obscure by obvious lacunae in note-taking. Furthermore, many governmental scientists take their notes with them when they leave federal employment. Such alienation is illegal, but the incomprehensible notes may be of use only to the producer. This determination should be made by agency officials rather than the producer himself.

The centralization of scientific research into one agency, the Office of Scientific Research and Development, should presumably simplify the descriptive process until we remember that the office farmed out projects to other federal agencies, numerous universities, General Electric, Western Electric, Radio Corporation of America, Remington Rand, DuPont and Company, and other private organizations. Each may have retained the original research notes as well as copies of the contracts and final reports.

Finally, everyone concerned with the disposition of the records must

163

determine what parts are truly unique; that is to say, that they document the process of innovations inadequately described in monographs or professional journals. Such determinations are rarely based on thorough examination of the literature and comparisons with source records.

These disclaimers must be explicitly stated. It seemed best to begin with certain inadequacies of the records before discussing their positive values for research. I can well appreciate the frustrations they impose on researchers in the history of science and technology or research and development.

I have organized this tour of research and development records roughly in the order that they came to my attention. In this way, you will gain some knowledge about an archivist's approach to records. My use of the term "research" refers to applied science designed to solve specific problems, including medical and other research of general public value. "Development" carries these scientific projects beyond the theoretical solution of problems to constructing and testing models and producing the required quantities. This distinction is not always clear and precise.

The vast body of literature that is known as technical manuals is not explored in this paper. Most manuals for the war period are being retained until we find a method of selecting those of permanent interest.

My earliest experience with research and development records for the Second World War occurred about April 1947. At that time, about one thousand cubic feet of records of the Office of Scientific Research and Development (OSRD) had been retired to the National Archives and another two thousand were awaiting transfer.

As the records were well organized and retrievable with reasonable ease, and access to the records could only be granted by the Department of Defense, my detailed study of the records would be of limited value to researchers. I was, however, dubious of one expert's opinion that the records were largely valueless because the published and unpublished reports contained all the information of use for the history of its achievements.

Whatever work an archivist performs on records, he tries to locate files or even items of unusual interest. An item relating to an OSRD project filed among the records of the Office of War Mobilization and Reconversion caught my passing attention. The Office Director, James F. Byrnes, sent a memorandum to President Roosevelt on March 2, 1945, noting the expenditure of close to two billion dollars on the Manhattan Project with "no definite assurance yet of production." "I know little of the project," Byrnes continued, "except that it is supported by eminent scientists." He proposed a reexamination of the project because it could fail. How much did Byrnes know at that time? Was he unhappy at his lack of knowledge or was he predicting failure? We know only that the president gave the letter to Secretary of War Stimson who, in turn, referred it to the Manhattan Engineering District.

Requests for records relating to science during the war were rare in the immediate postwar period. Researchers were however increasingly interested in technological innovations. This interest was unrelated to scholarly concerns; instead, the researchers hoped for monetary gain from their examination of certain records in the National Archives. The war generated considerable litigation over patent rights. Several members of the staff, therefore, devoted their attention to sources for inventions.

Probably the most active records on inventions related to research and development concerning synthetic rubber. The main source for this documentation appears among the records of the Reconstruction Finance Corporation (RFC) and, within this record group, the records of its subsidiary, the Rubber Reserve Corporation. The subsidiary's records include the articles of incorporation; records about the organization and functions; minutes of meetings of the Board of Directors; and operating records of the Copolymer Development Committee, the Butadiene Producers Technical Committee, and the Research Compounding Branch.

The Rubber Reserve Corporation was chartered on June 29, 1940, to "buy, sell, acquire, store, carry, produce, process, manufacture, and market raw and cured rubber." At first it devoted its resources to stockpiling natural rubber. At its meeting on November 26, 1941, the Board of Directors decided to expand the production of synthetic rubber as essential to the national defense. It therefore financed plants under rubber and chemical company management in several cities. A few days after the Pearl Harbor disaster, Jesse H. Jones, administrator of the Federal Loan Agency, notified the board to substantially increase the projected annual production of 40,000 tons. It was therefore decided to permit a free exchange of research and development information among all producers. Research was accelerated to improve the quality of synthetic rubber and to find methods of producing a necessary ingredient, carbon black. Some of this research involved basic findings on polymers, with considerable spinoffs after the war.

The corporation's records are importantly supplemented by the records of another RFC subsidiary, the Defense Plants Corporation, which include detailed case files on the construction and operation of synthetic rubber plants. Related materials also appear among the carbon black records of the Office of War Mobilization and Reconversion and the synthetic rubber records of the War Production Board. The WPB records document American rights to German technology, the role of the Standard Oil Developing Company in initiating the industry in this country, the apparent lead by the Soviet Union in the industry before our entrance into the war, a 1942 state of the art report for the Soviet Union, the production and distribution of the product, and problems of dislocated rubber workers.

Another source for data on synthetic rubber technology is the Strategic Bombing Survey records. The report relating to the Huels Synthetic Rubber Plant, for example, shows that the firm, located about twenty miles north of Essen, produced 4,079 tons of synthetic rubber in 1944, making it the second largest Buna rubber plant in Germany. Its technology and labor supply (chiefly slaves) are described in some detail.

The Patent Office played a minor role during the war. Sources for major inventions at the time of conception appear among the records of the National Inventors Council led by the commissioner of patents and Charles F. Kettering, president of the General Motors Corporation. Anyone could send his ideas for inventions to the council, which referred those of seeming merit to the War and Navy Departments. The council's records have not as yet been transferred to the National Archives, although most of them are in our Washington National Records Center. We do have custody of some related documents among the records of the Office of the Secretary of Commerce. These documents show the organization and operating methods of the council.

The earliest document is a letter from Secretary of Commerce Harry Hopkins to Kettering, dated July 11, 1940, that stated in part: "I am about to create, with the full concurrence of the President, a National Inventors Council. Confidently counting on both your competence and your consent to serve as head of the Council, I appoint you its chairman. . . . I feel that in the present exigency, as never before in the life of this country, we should master American inventive genius in the cause of national welfare, defense and security."

Since 1962, my activities within the National Archives have been devoted mainly to the appraisal of records; hence, I am rarely concerned with reference service and the preparation of finding aids. For this paper, I had to renew my acquaintance with the records mentioned above and a considerable body of materials about which my knowledge had been quite limited. It seemed obvious that most of my investigation would be largely concentrated among the OSRD records. Limitations on access to the records of the type that I encountered in 1947 would have severely restricted any descriptive data. Fortunately, more than 90 percent of the records were open to researchers by a Department of Defense memorandum of August 2, 1960. The exceptions are Atomic Energy contracts, the

records of the Miscellaneous Weapons Division, and all documents originally classified "Top Secret" and not subsequently declassified.

My first task was to digest the most important of the available literature
about the OSRD. These studies refreshed my memory about key people,
the organizational pattern, and the significant achievements of the agency. Analyses of certain files about these people and their contributions
would, I believe, be more suggestive of research values than a general,
superficial description of the approximately three thousand cubic feet of
records. These comments about the OSRD records will illustrate also
interrelations with the records of other agencies that were concerned with
research and development.

My reference to the OSRD records includes not only the archival remains for that office, with its subordinate offices, committees, and panels,
but also the files of the National Defense Research Committee (NDRC)
and its subordinate offices, committees, subject area divisions, and panels. Each of these elements is represented by specific files that show its
management and activities. Unlike many other terminated agencies, we
did not have to reconstruct the files. The managerial staff planned the
retirement and preservation of the records in accordance with the archival principle of provenance, that is, retaining the records with due regard
to their origin.

Plans for the efficient management of the records were completed early
in 1944 when the administrative staff developed methods for arranging
and controlling all documentation. Folders were clearly labeled, and all
files were inventoried. Regulations for the maintenance of security were
carefully drawn. To assure that projects were adequately documented,
the OSRD borrowed a member of our staff, David C. Duniway, to evaluate the system and suggest improvements. Booz, Allen and Hamilton, a
consulting firm, also provided assistance. The chief sources for information about research projects (contract case files, contractors' reports, and
the summary technical reports) account for more than four hundred fifty
of the three thousand feet.

Records relating to the leadership, delegations of authority, and the
structure of the federal scientific community are largely centralized
among the files of the Offices of the Director of OSRD and the Chairman
of the NDRC. Biographical data about leading scientists appear in files of
the OSRD, the War Production Board, the military agencies and the
National Advisory Committee on Aeronautics (NACA). The personnel
files of officials supply useful information to the degree that they can be
made available to researchers. Dead or alive, several of the leaders still
exert an important influence on the scientific establishment.

Files for several of these leaders show their essential roles. Frank B.

Jewett as president of the National Academy of Sciences and of the Bell Telephone Laboratories developed the roster of leading scientists for staffing research institutions in 1940. His official records as a member of the NDRC from its establishment on June 27, 1940, until its termination at the end of 1947, are completely indexed. They document his role in recruiting scientists for war duties. Leonard Carmichael of the Smithsonian Institution and the National Research Council provided assistance in his capacity as chairman of the War Manpower Commission's Committee on Scientific Manpower.

The leading figure in planning and directing and manning the scientific program was, the records seem to testify, Vannevar Bush. His first federal employment, I learned, was his position of subinspector in the Navy Department in 1915. Bush's appointment was certified by Franklin D. Roosevelt as assistant secretary, who also noted that his name was incorrectly spelled "Vannevan" and his legal residence was Massachusetts instead of New York. He resigned his summer job on September 15, 1915, to return to Tufts College. When the war started in 1939, Bush was chairman of the NACA and president of Carnegie Institution.

Bush became chairman of the first National Defense Research Committee established by the Council of National Defense on June 27, 1940, to plan and administer scientific and technical research. His organizational plan, which was outlined at the committee's first meeting on July 2, 1940, set the wartime pattern for research and development programs. Each member was delegated direction of a subject area division. Each division would let out contracts to organizations and individuals that appeared capable to examine problems posed by the War and Navy Departments in its subject area, such as ballistics, subsurface warfare, or radar, and contract them to expert organizations or individuals for solution.

Bush established special committees for unusually complex and urgent problems. At its first meeting, for example, Bush organized the Committee on Uranium under Lyman Briggs, director of the National Bureau of Standards (NBS). This committee received $102,300 from the United States Army and Navy to separate an uranium isotope. In his letter to Bush announcing the appointment, President Roosevelt delimited the NDRC and later the OSRD concerns to accelerating "the creation or improvement of the instrumentalities of warfare." This limitation was clearly in Bush's mind throughout the war.

When Bush was made director of the OSRD, he resigned from direction of the NACA and the NDRC, although he remained influential in both. In a letter to Senator Kilgore in 1943, Bush expressed his belief in centralized control over science and its application during war. But in peacetime, he asserted, scientists should be given a maximum of freedom and a minimum of control from any source.

One key to Bush's leadership in the field of research was undoubtedly his dominance in this field over the military. He demanded that scientists be treated with full honors in dealing with military officers, whether in Washington or on the field of battle. Bush could not determine what officers would provide liaison with OSRD; nevertheless, he was instrumental in the establishment of the New Developments Division in the War Department (October 1943) and other units concerned with research that supplemented the OSRD programs. The first director of the New Development Division, Maj. Gen. S. G. Henry, wrote to Bush that the division could properly be called the "Vannevar Bush Division." Bush was also helpful in establishing the Naval Underwater Sound Laboratory (October 1942) under the command of Rear Adm. Julius A. Furer, a specialist in naval construction.

Bush's scientists insisted on and obtained the right to inspect the military's use of inventions. When they received a poor reception at Wright Field, Bush told the commanding general that civilian agencies were best suited for certain duties rather than by bringing everything under military command. "The scientists as well as the military have a problem in the adaptation under war conditions to unusual circumstances," he noted. Bush also won a battle against Gen. Lucius Clay over control of projects concerning radar research.

James B. Conant succeeded Bush as chairman of the NDRC under OSRD. He had been a committee member and chairman of its committee on explosives. His conception of his role seems typified by a letter to President Roosevelt, "It is my understanding that the position will not involve full time, but that I can carry it on a two day a week basis in addition to my normal load as President of Harvard University."

Karl T. Compton, president of the Massachusetts Institute of Technology, played a role in wartime research that came closest to matching that of Bush. Compton's assignments were of such importance to the war effort that even his personnel file is security classified. A considerable portion of his time was devoted to the OSRD Field Service, with secret trips to England, Australia, New Guinea, Bikini, and elsewhere. Within the NDRC he was head of the division for investigating new missiles and was a consultant to the War Department's Chief of Ordnance. For this service his compensation ranged from $25 to $50 per day. His last federal employment at the time of his death on June 22, 1954, was commissioner for the National Security Training Commission. Compton's office files are excellent sources for relations with the military, plans for research and development in radio propagation, plane-to-plane fire control, protection against bombing, and computers.

Though the records show occasional differences of opinion and a rare display of acerbity, the American scientists come through as a strongly cohesive group. To some extent the community of professional interest extended to foreign scientists as well. The first foreign contacts were actually initiated by the War Department. The British mission under Sir Henry Tizard, rector of the Imperial College of Science and Technology and scientific adviser to the Ministry of Aircraft Production, arrived late in August 1940, with a box of secret scientific data.

In September, Assistant Secretary of War Robert P. Patterson wrote Bush: "It is the hope of the War Department that you and your associates will take the opportunity of getting in touch with Sir Henry Tizard and the members of his staff and will discuss freely with them all problems that have to do with national defense."

Bush's reply about two weeks later reported that the meeting had taken place and that in the future the NDRC would deal directly with British scientists. Secretary Stimson concurred with the proposal for free exchange, with the exception of data on the atomic bomb, the bomb sight, and ballistic tables. Copies of this and related correspondence are located among OSRD and Manhattan Engineering District records.

The question of limitations on British access to certain information occupied considerable attention. The records show that President Roosevelt discussed some of them with Prime Minister Churchill. Atomic research seemed to go under the code name "tube alloys" instead of "Manhattan Project." The reasons given by the Americans for lack of free exchange was the additional possibilities of information leaks. Problems of proprietary interest in patents were resolved by the British-American Joint Patent Interchange Committee, whose records (1941–46) also include reference to the Tizard mission.

This British visit was reciprocated by Conant's mission to London in 1941. Thereafter, exchanges were frequent and, with the exception largely of data on the atom bomb design and the installation at Oak Ridge, quite open. There was complete exchange of information about medical findings and synthetic rubber. Some of these exchanges were shared also with the Soviet Union. Research findings about penicillin, blood plasma, malaria, dysentery, shock, and insecticides were exchanged with the Russians from 1943 to 1945. One mission to Moscow made a study of the curriculum in a medical school where the 216 hours of Principles of Marxism exceeded the hours on pathological anatomy.

More has been published about the atomic bomb than probably any other invention of the war; yet, most records relating to it are still highly classified. One key document, the famous letter from Albert Einstein to President Roosevelt, dated August 2, 1939, is accessible at the Franklin D. Roosevelt Library. Minutes of the NDRC meetings contain references to uranium and other related research. Bush created the S-1 Committee on December 6, 1941, to recommend action on fission research. In just one year, scientists achieved the first nuclear chain reaction.

The largest file in the National Archives relating to the bomb was received from the Manhattan Engineering District, 1942–48. Researchers may find here some records relating to the transfer of the project to the Corps of Engineers, the role of the Military Policy Committee composed of Bush, General Styer, and Admiral Purnell, the "Diplomatic History of the Manhattan Project," and information about General Groves. This file may be supplemented by thirty cubic feet of General Groves's personal papers. The OSRD records include scientists' comments about the bomb after Hiroshima.

Apparently, it was decided long before Hiroshima that the bomb would be carried by plane. In any case, developmental difficulties resulted from the seemingly insurmountable problem of making the bomb small enough to be carried by an airplane. Most research problems posed by the military, in fact, concerned either methods of increasing the attack capabilities of aircraft or defenses against air attack.

Aerodynamics and technical problems relating to the aircraft itself were outside the OSRD jurisdiction. From 1915 to the establishment of the National Aeronautics and Space Agency in 1958, research on flight was promoted by the National Advisory Committee for Aeronautics (NACA). Only a small fraction of the committee's records have been transferred to archival custody by NASA. The remainder has been made the subject of a special study by our staff with the objective of selecting the permanently valuable segment. [These records have recently been transferred to the National Archives.]

Although the volume of NACA records in our custody is still relatively small, the files provide useful sources for an examination of its organization, program, and activities. They include minutes of committee meetings, technical reports, abstracts of periodical literature, the aforementioned biographical file, progress reports, a chronology of the Langley Research Center from 1917 to 1966, and a 110-page survey of NACA research. Significant projects included studies of supersonic and pilotless aircraft, compressors, rocketry, turbines, thermodynamics, and nuclear energy as a power source.

At its meeting of April 24, 1941, the committee recalled an early member, William F. Durand, to head a special committee on jet propulsion because General Arnold had requested urgent attention to the project. Durand was born somewhat before the air age, March 5, 1859.

The records that are being surveyed for potential permanent preservation include the committee's general correspondence, records of the NACA's research centers (Langley, Lewis Flight Propulsion, and Ames Aeronautical Laboratories), the main body of technical publications, and airplane construction files.

A few OSRD projects were of such importance that they occupied the attention of leading scientists throughout the war. Radar and radio propagation research had one of the highest priorities. Tizard's famous black box included a summation of all that the British had learned about radar. The military kept up a sustained demand for methods of improving radar for blind flying and countermeasures against enemy radar by jamming. Special research centers, the Radio Research Laboratory and the Radiation Laboratory, were created by the office and placed administratively within MIT where Compton could assure their high priority. The OSRD records include considerable details about organizing, financing, and operating the installations.

Significant research was also generated in 1942 by the expert consultant to the Secretary of War Edward L. Bowles and the Joint Committee on New Weapons and Equipment under the direction of the Combined Chiefs of Staff, as shown by the CCS files. Admiral Furer's significant role in coordinating radar and related research is documented among naval records. Additional sources may be found among the records of the Radio Propagation Section, National Bureau of Standards. The records of the British Radio Board should be rich in similar documentation. Other British sources are probably included among the records of the Committee on Research on Air Defense and centers like the Cavendish Laboratory. All these sources seem essential for any definitive history of the development of radar and of ultra-high radio frequencies that unfortunately promoted television.

A special unit, Section-T, was established to develop the proximity fuse for use largely in bombing missions. Most of the work on the fuse was carried on by the Applied Physics Laboratory attached to Johns Hopkins University, which presumably still maintains developmental records. Other records were transferred to the Navy Department, which supplied most of the leadership for the section. Some correspondence and reports remain within the OSRD record group. The remaining records were retained or destroyed by Western Electric and the Erwood Company of Chicago.

Requests from the military for advice about the selection, training and protection of airmen led to psychological studies and aviation medicine. The former are documented among the records (about fifty cubic feet), of the NDRC Applied Psychology Panel. The records of the Committee on Medical Research deal, in part, with such problems as the conservation of oxygen, the bends, and night vision.

Rocketry and jet propulsion cover a wide range of technologies and are described among the records of a number of civilian and military units. The NACA has already been mentioned. The Joint Committee on New Weapons and Equipment, the Research and Development Division of the Naval Bureau of Ordnance, the Rocket Development Division of the Naval Bureau of Ordnance, as well as the Rocket Development Division of the Army Ordnance Department all contributed developmental resources. To some extent research on jet propulsion was coordinated by the NDRC under the supervision of George B. Kistiakowsky and the Director of the Chemical Division, Richard C. Tolman.

The research projects that have been mentioned were proposed jointly by the army and the navy. Numerous projects were generated by one of the two services and most of the research and all developmental programs were carried on by that service. Many of the elements of these relationships are contained in the OSRD file entitled "Cooperation." The Office of Production Research and Development, War Production Board, worked closely with the services to assure priorities in obtaining the critical material for the projects. This office was a successor to the Office of Technical Development and was established "to plan, direct, and coordinate the scientific and engineering evaluation, research and development work" within the WPB. It usually provided liaison between the military and industry in developmental and production programs.

The records of the WPB office indicate that it was more closely allied to the War Department and, of course, the OSRD, than the navy. The projects are described in a September 1948 history of the office and its successors.

The task of planning and coordinating research for the navy was assigned to the Office of the Coordinator of Research and Development within the Office of the Secretary. Its director, Rear Admiral Furer, was one of several principal advisers to the secretary of the navy, in which capacity he could exert considerable authority to establish priorities. He served as chairman of the Naval Research and Development Board, comprising representatives of the naval bureaus, and appointed naval representatives to numerous research and development organizations. The valuable records of his office were transferred to us by the successor Office of Naval Research.

Furer corresponded with Lee DuBridge, director of the Radiation Laboratory, about radar, radio circuit components, blind flying tests, and the need for computers. The admiral's assistant director, Comdr. Robert P. Briscoe, provided liaison with the Naval Research Laboratory, which operated within the Bureau of Ships. The laboratory was concerned chiefly with improving the performance of ships and their war potentials. It is of some interest to note that the OSRD was occasionally bypassed on antisubmarine research.

The records of his office include Furer's correspondence, photographs, and blueprints of various devices, scientific and technical reports, and notes and memorandums documenting research programs and projects. Project files about SONAR, acoustically actuated mines, transducers, rockets, torpedo stations and lighting devices may also be included among the archival remains of the Underwater Sound Laboratory at New London, Columbia University (a major contractor), and the U.S. Radio and Sound Laboratory at San Diego. Frederick V. Hunt's personal papers in the Harvard University Archives probably provide supplemental documentation, as Hunt was a leading physicist at the Underwater Sound Laboratory.

The War Department's research and development programs were considerably more complex than the navy's. The army had no one man equivalent to Rear Admiral Furer. Its liaison officer for the OSRD and representatives in the National Defense Research Committee had some coordinating responsibilities with regard to research projects. In addition, the Joint Chiefs of Staff organized the Committee on New Weapons and Equipment that also coordinated activities with the OSRD.

The United States Army Chief of Staff organized the New Developments Division, in October 1943, to be a part of the War Department Special Staff for coordination of R & D matters. The division maintained direct or indirect liaison with the navy, the National Inventors Council, the Joint Army-Navy Testing Board, and the OSRD Field Service, and the British army. This liaison concerned technical problems, such as those posed by jungle warfare, chemical warfare, mine detection and removal, locating invisible targets, and the reduction of ambient noises for artillery crews. Although the records refer to medical problems, particularly with regard to jungle diseases, it is clear that the division deferred to the OSRD and, secondarily, to the surgeon general for basic research in medical science and development of drugs. It was the Surgeon's General's Office and the naval Bureau of Medicine and Surgery that posed the problems, engaged in some of the research, and organized the field tests.

Control over applied medical research was delegated by the president to the Committee on Medical Research (CMR) within the OSRD. The chairman and three members were appointed by the president and, three additional members, by the secretaries of war and the navy and the federal security administrator, respectively. Like records of other subject area units, the CMR files consist largely of contract case files, technical reports, and general correspondence. One of its most dramatic accomplishments was the discovery of a method of producing penicillin in the quality and quantity needed to meet war needs.

Fleming's discovery preceded the war by a decade. Although the British assigned high priorities to its production in quantity, its Medical Research Council had failed to solve the problem. Howard Florey, as a member of the mission to the United States in 1941, asked for assistance. The British Council, the Imperial Chemical Company, and the Therapeutic Research Corporation continued their research while the CMR contracted for research in this country after a conference in October. The chief contractors were several pharmaceutical companies and the Department of Agriculture. A subcommittee was established under Hans T. Clarke, a leading biochemist, to assure continued and efficient effort in this project. Later Clarke, as special assistant to Bush, took over the project personally.

The OSRD records indicate that the pharmaceutical firms first sought methods for producing penicillin without federal assistance, but the major breakthrough was achieved by the Department of Agriculture. On February 4, 1944, Bush wrote that "early leadership in developing superior strains of molds and improving fermentation production methods was provided by the Peoria Laboratory" of the Department of Agriculture.

The results of all experimentation had been tested clinically on Guadalcanal patients about a year earlier at the Brigham Young Hospital in Utah. Later tests were conducted at the nearby Bushnell General Hospital. Records relating to the tests are among the records of the naval and army medical units. Research on the chemistry of penicillin produced about four-hundred OSRD studies during 1944.

My inquiry to our Federal Records Center in Chicago quickly located the basic records of the Peoria Laboratory relating to the development of improved penicillin in quantity. We discovered, in addition, that the Laboratory also retired records about the production of alcohol and chemicals for synthetic rubber. I regret that other laboratories were less concerned about the future needs of historians of science.

In its study of wartime medical research, the committee referred proudly to the "unrivalled value of DDT" [E. C. Andrus et al., eds., *Advances in Military Medicine* (Boston: Little, Brown & Co., 1948), 2:540]. Until the last few years, most experts would have agreed. The records about DDT research and development appear among the files of a number of federal agencies.

About the time we entered the war, the army had determined that existing insect repellants and insecticides were inadequate since some of the most effective chemicals had been produced in Japan. While referring the problem to the CMR, the army continued its own investigations, using Sanitation Corps entomologists who had been first assigned to the elimination of malaria in southern army posts. By 1942 more than 80 percent of these specialists were assigned to overseas posts to combat insects.

The Medical Department considered proposals for the development of insecticides through CMR and provided technical assistance in their use; the Quartermaster Corps procured and supplied insecticides, rodenticides and related equipment; and the Corps of Engineers supervised the installation of insect control systems.

Although the basic formula and some characteristics of DDT were known when the war started, it was just one of a number of chemicals under study. By early 1943 it was apparently decided to find the best all-purpose insecticide for major study. Gen. Henry H. Arnold, among others, asked Bush to speed research. At that time, the best insecticide was a chemical that was effective for five hours and thirty-seven minutes. Within a few months the Agriculture Department's Bureau of Entomology and Plant Quarantine and the Gorgas Memorial Laboratory had improved DDT to the point that it was considered superior to all other competitors. About the same time, the Office of Production Research and Development granted priorities to the Shell Chemical Company to obtain supplies required for experiments on DDT.

In August the Agricultural Research Service developed plans for testing several insecticides, including DDT. About six months later, the Service determined that DDT posed no hazard to human or animal food "although it would be desirable to put treated plants through the series of toxicological tests customarily used in the case of new insecticides." The tests are described in numerous reports. Apparently most of the source records were destroyed.

In June 1944 the findings were made known to the public and in September Bush established the Insect Control Committee under the CMR to coordinate developmental programs with the Agricultural Department, the Fish and Wildlife Service, and the Public Health Service. Thus, continued progress was assured until *Silent Spring.*

The production of amphibious vehicles was also generated by an urgent army request to OSRD that originated in the Motor Transportation Ser-

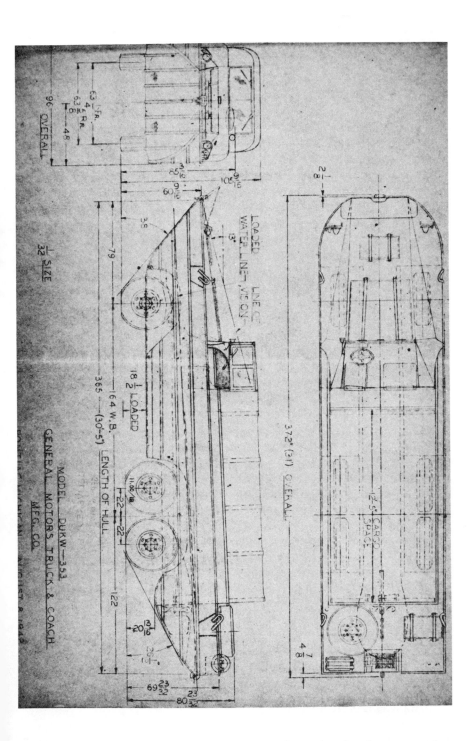

A drawing of the amphibious DUKW, which was developed under contract for the Office of Scientific Research and Development. (RG 227, Office of Scientific Research and Development, National Archives.)

vice, Quartermaster Corps. The Yellow Truck and Coach Division, General Motors Corporation, was the chief contractor. It designated its pilot project as DUKW, better known as "Duck." The rapidity of its development seems astonishing. The Research and Development Division placed their first order for the vehicles in June 1942 while the New Developments Division sought a battle-ready company to test them. General Eisenhower and Admiral Mountbatten later wrote so enthusiastically about the Ducks' performance under battle conditions at the Sicily landing that General Eisenhower requested many more. By January 1944, the army had forty-eight DUKW units ready for future amphibious landings.

Two other military-generated projects assigned to the OSRD deserve at least a brief mention because of their postwar impact: the development of computers, and experiments with operations research. Bush corresponded with the Bureau of Ships about an electric computer to develop firing tables for its 90 mm gun in July 1941. Later, Army Ordnance also asked for faster computers for similar use. This time OSRD found no rapid breakthroughs. A contract with the Bell Telephone Laboratory resulted, about September 1942, in the construction of an experimental computer with a memory capacity for missile computations.

The theoretical formulations for computers were contracted to MIT. Compton noted that by January 1942, Norbert Wiener had "a general mathematical theory of prediction and determining the characteristics of electrical networks for carrying it (sic) out." These and other related problems were assigned to the NDRC Applied Mathematics Panel. At the panel's request, the University of Pennsylvania and the National Bureau of Standards put their best minds to the development of electronic computers. Most of the records relating to ENIAC and its successors are still in the custody of federal agencies.

As the panel consisted of leading mathematicians and logisticians, the military requested assistance in simulation techniques. One problem posed to the panel was the determination of the optimum B-29 formations and flight procedures that would provide a balanced protection from fighter planes and flak and effective strike capability. Such problems led the OSRD into operations research. By the end of 1943, the Office of Field Service was being asked to check the efficiency of numerous battle operations, including recommendations about the best use of scientific and technological innovations, procedures and techniques for repairing the inoperative telephone system in Paris, and checking the efficiency of units working with jet-propelled missiles, radar equipment and antisubmarine and antimine devices.

The OSRD thoroughly documented the plans and administration of its own termination. Its plans for the history of research and development during the war and the correspondence relating to the disposition of the records should be of interest to historians of science.

The earliest reference in the OSRD files to the history program was a March 1943 decision to prepare a history of the Radiation Laboratory. When Henry E. Guerlac was designated for the task, it was decided that he would operate at the headquarters level and broaden his study to record all aspects of radar research. This history was not published but the typescript copy, 1,300 pages, is included in the OSRD files. Rear Admiral Furer had reviewed the text and had it reduced by about one-third. Furer himself, promoted the preparation of government-wide histories of World War II research in a memorandum of March 9, 1944. Anyone interested in the research and development programs should become familiar with these histories before searching the records.

The OSRD resisted attempts to scatter its records to the many agencies that engaged in research and development during the postwar years. A considerable portion of the records was nevertheless transferred to the National Academy of Sciences, the Central Intelligence Group (now CIA), the Office of Naval Research, and the Atomic Energy Commission.

The records staff kept inventories of records and demanded the return of files on loan to OSRD officials and historians. Researchers are thus assured of fairly complete documentation on the disposition of records, including their transfer to the National Archives.

This analysis of certain personally selected records relating to research and development will prove suggestive for many studies. One author phrases our motto thus: "The past is prologue in research and development as in other institutions." [Richard Tybout, ed., *Economics of Research and Development* (Columbus: Ohio University Press, 1965), p. 8.]

A more thorough guide would have described records of many additional governmental units. Congressional records, to cite one example, contain rich data about the scientists and their role during and since the war. Eventually, scholars will explore the related archival resources of the National Academy of Sciences, universities, and private contractors. Much of the wartime scientific research documentation outside the federal government has already been destroyed; nevertheless, a considerable portion should remain. In any case, requests for access will convince these institutions that destruction of such records wastes an important resource.

Discussion Summary

The question was asked of Pursell whether there really were policy choices or whether the necessities of the situation made certain policies inevitable. He replied that some individual scientists or classes of scientists, because of the nature of their specialty, really had little choice because they were not much in demand and thus inevitably could not be utilized, but in the wider policy context many possibilities existed other than those that were followed, and no course of action could be said to have been inevitable.

Philip Lundeberg (Smithsonian Institution) asked whether there was a conscious effort, when the immediate and urgent demands after Pearl Harbor developed, to seek out and pursue scientific excellence to meet the emergency. Responding again, Pursell held that basic choices had been made and courses determined by Conant and Bush and other leading figures as early as the spring of 1940, long before Pearl Harbor and our entry into the war. As for seeking out scientists of the best quality, this tended eventually to favor the faculties of certain leading universities, and although this was usually justified, it occasionally resulted in the neglect of equally valuable scientific talent available elsewhere.

VIII

Wartime Emergency Agencies

The eighth session, like the seventh, was a concurrent session held on the afternoon of June 15. The chairman was Stanley Falk of the Industrial College of the Armed Forces, and the session examined nonmilitary records of the Second World War and their research use.

ALBERT A. BLUM

Mobilization of Men and Machines during the Second World War

As I cast my eyes back to explore the kinds of research needed to understand better how men and machines were mobilized during the Second
World War and the implications of that mobilization, I find myself looking
at the problems differently from when, in 1951, I first became lost among
the mountain of papers dealing with that issue filed in Alexandria and at
the National Archives in Washington. Although the Korean War was then
upon us, an interest in manpower and economic mobilization was mainly
that of an antiquarian—of one in love with the past and seeking an understanding of it but with no necessary relationship between the studies past
and the active present. In fact, the felt irrelevance of the Second World
War experiences in manpower and economic mobilization is perhaps reflected in that only eighty-five out of the 23,493 doctoral dissertations in
history, political science, and economics completed from 1946 through
1968 dealt with any aspect of economic or manpower problems of the
Second World War.

But now twenty years after I first started to do research in this field, a
present-minded historian ought to be more concerned with the period
(even though the evidence of doctoral dissertation research indicates he is
not). Otherwise, Santayana may prove right in his over-quoted statement,
"Those who cannot remember the past are condemned to repeat it."
Although it is, of course, true that historians should not let the present
affect how they describe the past, it is also nonetheless true that the
present affects the topics they choose (for example, it explains why I, a
labor historian, will focus in this paper on manpower mobilization more
than on economic mobilization). Moreover, new techniques should influence the methods by which historians analyze the past. Such current
problems as a military-industrial complex, selective service, the need for
economic and manpower planning, and inflation as a byproduct of war,
plague us again. Many of these current problems were dealt with during
the Second World War; and they, therefore, should attract scholars who
might wish to explore their meaning during the Second World War in
order, perhaps, to secure added perspectives concerning these issues
today.

Of course, there is a risk in present-minded research that one will start out with a conclusion and later find the facts to prove the case. Recently, I spoke on manpower mobilization at the Thirteenth Congress of Historical Sciences. It was clear that many of the participants were using propaganda to parade as facts. They tried to show that all of their citizens either rushed to serve in the military or worked as hard as they possibly could in factories or on farms. I felt rather unpatriotic because I kept my paper short (since one measure of patriotism seemed to have been the length of the papers) and even criticized some aspects of the United States' manpower mobilization during the Second World War.

Another instance of the force-fitting of facts evolves around the concept of a military-industrial complex. One somehow wonders why any American scholar should feel impelled to show that there are close ties between the military and industry in the United States. In a country where corporations are so powerful, and where the military has become increasingly powerful, one need not have to waste one's time to keep proving the obvious. It seems to me that if one wants to do research on the military-industrial complex, one might instead be fascinated by those situations when these powerful groups failed to get what they wanted and try to explain and understand why the obvious did not occur.

One example might suffice. Recently, Paul A. C. Koistinen, in his article, "The Industrial-Military Complex in Historical Perspective: The Interwar Years," published in the March 1970 issue of the *Journal of American History,* argues at great length that during the 1920s and 1930s, the military worked closer and closer with industrial executives in pushing forward various industrial mobilization plans. He is, of course, correct. But the interesting fact which I tried to examine in a paper dealing with "The Birth and Death of the M-Day Plan," published in Harold Stein's *American Civil Military Decisions* [University of Alabama Press, 1963], is that, although it was true that the military and industry had had sufficient intimate relationships to claim joint parenthood of many of the economic mobilization plans, this very relationship helped kill the plan. There were other countervailing forces at work: a growing labor movement; a conflict within the military and among industrialists concerning appropriate policies, as well as a lack of concern with the M-Day Plan by some of these powerful people; a changing ideology reflected in the New Deal; and a president who was sensitive to these new groups who were gaining in power as well as to his own sense of who should be ultimately responsible for running the war effort, namely himself, not the War Resources Board thought up by the military and some industrialists.

The failure to understand these countervailing forces not only weakens our understanding of what has been called the military-industrial complex, but it also helps us miss the drama of other manpower and economic mobilization disputes during the Second World War: why the passage of the Selective Training and Service Act had to await the sponsorship of a civilian group; why the Selective Service System was placed under the War Manpower Commission for only a period of time; why there was a constant fight over the size of the army; why the drive for a national service law failed; why claimed manpower shortages on the West Coast required special manpower projects; why pressures to release soldiers to work in industry and agriculture developed in certain industries; and why special treatment accorded farmers by the Selective Service System made the farm the safest place for a young man to be during the Second World War. Researchers seeking answers to those questions would indicate, I am sure, that the answers are not always the ones favored by the supposed military-industrial complex. The military-industrial complex may have provided the greatest input, but there were other inputs which affected the ultimate decisions.

The activities of the War Manpower Commission might be a place to start if one wanted to examine further the issue of countervailing forces, although the WMC merits further study in any case. This agency, criticized by the military, disliked by the industrialists and their representatives on the War Production Board, has been relatively ignored by students of the Second World War. And yet this agency was supposedly the key agency dealing with civilian manpower problems during that war. Moreover, it was in this agency that organized labor's voice was supposed to be heard at its loudest. And it was this agency, of all of the public agencies other than the War Labor Board and the Department of Labor that was concerned with those at work at home.

Present-minded historians, looking for perspectives from the past, moreover, should be fascinated by the War Manpower Commission. In recent years, we have tried to develop, however badly, a manpower policy for the nation. The War Manpower Commission also had tried to develop a manpower policy during the Second World War. The WMC, therefore, had to deal with such issues as training the disadvantaged and others, integrating black workers into the labor force, developing programs for the female worker, organizing procedures to facilitate manpower planning within the firm as well as within society, providing adequate housing, and launching massive manpower programs within communities. These same issues are now being debated throughout the country and are being studied by scholars at the universities, but usually as if these techniques and issues were new and as if at no other time in its history had the United States ever tried to deal with them.

Another agency that should attract the present-minded historian is the Selective Service System. The draft has, of course, provoked bitter hostility. Nearly everyone has an opinion concerning the debate over a conscripted versus a volunteer army. But nearly all of these opinions are based on ignorance of how the post-World War II selective service system evolved out of the system created during the Second World War. As a result, some of the policies that developed during the Second World War and perhaps were justified then prevented a selective service system from working appropriately. Thus, the ideas that the military needs only young men; that only those young men physically and mentally fit for combat duty should be allowed in the armed forces; and that local boards, based in the communities, would know best which young men should be drafted continued on as accepted truths. These myths continued even though the little research that had been done indicated that they were either false then or irrelevant today. Thus, there are many jobs in the armed forces which could be satisfactorily filled, as they were during World War II, by older men and by those with physical and mental qualifications lower than those determined by the Department of Defense. After all, the number of white-collar jobs in the military has been increasing at a higher rate than in the civilian sector of the economy (jobs that a man with a trick knee surely could perform) and there are a host of jobs for men with low IQs. But these myths continued, preventing the armed forces from becoming the microcosm of American society that it should be. And, of course, there was the myth of the local board—a body, created by the military which had learned its lesson from history—namely, that draftees and their families should blame civilians in the local boards for the fact that they had been inducted, rather than the military-dominated Selective Service System. Again, whatever research that has been done indicates that these local boards neither necessarily represented nor were a part of the local community, nor knew best who should be drafted or who should be deferred. They were consistently attacked for their mistakes during the Second World War by all those involved in manpower planning. Again my point is that more detailed studies of the origins of some of these ideas and how they have worked out in practice, might have laid to rest some of the myths concerning conscription which confuse the present-day student of this controversial subject. Such studies might have also provided enough information so that the recent decision to make a volunteer army might have been based upon facts rather than on *a priori* values and "hunches," or whether a volunteer army or a conscripted one would but secure these values.

I have touched on the agencies involved, but there were also leaders of these agencies, and research concerning their ideas and policies is neces-

sary for an understanding of the workings of the wartime agencies. Sometimes their role is overemphasized. Such has been the case with Bernard
Baruch and his supposed important role in pre-World War II and World
War II economic mobilization. Baruch is a myth in terms of influence—a
myth created partially by himself. But then there are such persons as Paul
V. McNutt, the head of the War Manpower Commission whose dreams of
becoming president were perhaps destroyed by his experiences at the

Lord Halifax, General Marshall, and Admiral King with Bernard M. Baruch,
1944. (U.S. Navy; National Archives, no. 80-G-286654.)

WMC. There is Lewis B. Hershey who, for a while, appeared as if he were going to be the permanent head of the Selective Service System. There were the host of bright young men who handled labor relations matters for the army: James P Mitchell, later secretary of labor under President Eisenhower, and William J. Brennan, Jr., now a member of the Supreme Court, just to name a few. All of these individuals merit more scholarly studies than have appeared concerning them.

But one should not only look at the leadership. One of the problems with the history of wars is that historians too often focus on the dramatic, the hero, the politician, the diplomat, and the general. But wars affect soldiers and society too. Surely the war made the "khaki-collared worker" or soldier an important segment of the labor force. His role in manpower planning and labor relations could no longer be ignored. Surely, the war moved Americans around the country. Surely, the war developed some industries and destroyed others, and by so doing, destroyed some jobs, skills, and cities while creating other jobs, skills, and cities. Surely, the war helped to make a labor movement reach its peak of membership from which it has not grown markedly since. Surely, the war brought a host of fringe benefits to blue-collar workers and arbitration to dispute settlement. Surely, the war helped to end the excessive unemployment rate that had lingered on through the 1930s. Surely, the war helped to make relatively permanent what the Great Depression and the New Deal which followed in its wake, really started, namely, a United States committed to a mixed economy and ready-to-use government to bring about maximum employment and production—now required by the Employment Act of 1946 passed one year after the end of the Second World War. Surely, the war helped to convince American workers of all colors that they would no longer be willing to be the foolish laborer in Yeats's poem, "who wastes his blood to be another's dream."

These dramatic developments, brought about at least in part by manpower and economic mobilization during the Second World War, merit the attention of the scholars of the Second World War at least as much as the bullets, the battleships, and the bombardiers. In fact, they all developed a somewhat strange and symbiotic relationship—a relationship still relatively ignored by scholars of the Second World War.

JOSEPH HOWERTON

The Record of Federal Emergency Civilian Control

Most World War II writings have been devoted to the historian's approach to that "lethal chess game" that was the shooting part of World War II; the military personalities who captured the imagination of the public; and the relations between governments interacting at that level of abstraction called diplomacy, which is largely confirmation of decisions already taken at the level of operations at which humanity operates. In this paper, I am attempting to discuss records documenting activities, reaching closer to the level of operations on which World War II was really decided.

By way of leading into my observations on wartime civil controls, I must regress a bit to consider some relevant prior developments.

It has been remarked that nations, in the periods between wars, make plans to fight the previous one. In 1939 and 1940, in the preliminary phases of World War II, the tactics of the major participants were based on their preliminary planning. Thus, the French had constructed a stupendous series of comfortable trenches convenient to their border with Germany, which the German army bypassed with a motorized version of the Schlieffen Plan, this time succeeding in overrunning France. The British "—again late with little—" had poised their forces to take advantage of any weakness in the German right wing but were swept into the sea. Thereupon, having won the First World War, Hitler, forced into improvisation, made a virtuoso attempt to reverse historic military campaigns that had decided the fate of the world in ages past. First sending his bombers, like lumbering fourteenth-century armored knights, to devastate the British Isles, he was countered with an aerial equivalent of the longbow. He then launched a campaign aimed at a Napoleonic hegemony of Europe, taking the road to Moscow and sending forces to the Mediterranean and to North Africa to confront England in Egypt. The British, presciently, chose for their wartime leader a historian.

Meanwhile, back at what was soon to be very aptly called the "arsenal of democracy," the United States began gingerly to prepare for defense and summoned a body named the War Resources Board to consider plans to mobilize her economy. Specifically, the board was to study the "Protective," "Procurement," and "Industrial Mobilization" plans prepared by the Joint Army and Navy Munitions Board. As is the case with so many other elements of World War II, the origins of the machinery envisioned in the service plan for industrial mobilization can be traced back to the First World War. Many of the agencies that emerged in World War II had their counterparts in agencies created during World War I. In many cases, the names, even, were similar.[1]

The Joint Board's Industrial Mobilization Plan reputedly had been originally outlined for the army by Bernard Baruch, fresh from his experiences with the War Industries Board. It had been honed by the Army Industrial College up to the 1930s when the navy began cooperating under the aegis of the Joint Board. The basic parts of the plan, published in several revisions,[2] were analyzed by the political scientist, Harold J. Tobin. "The basic principle of the plan," said Professor Tobin, "was that victory demands the disciplining of most civilian activities so that they will make the fullest contribution to the national strength. All the nation's resources must be at the disposal of the government as long as the emergency lasts."[3] From this sample, it will be seen that Professor Tobin explains the plan much more candidly than the Joint Board would have dared in its published versions, and I will, therefore, continue with his analysis.

As expounded by Tobin, control of civilian activities fell into three categories: first, manpower for armed forces and for war production, necessitating a nationwide employment service, restrictions on competitive hiring practices, a national system for settling labor disputes, stabilization of living costs, and a labor draft; second, mobilization of material, involving centralized allocation (rationing) of raw materials under a priorities system, checking of profiteering, requisitioning of plants, and government regulation of finance and transportation; and third, mobilization of morale, which embraced programs to obtain acceptance of social and economic rigors and deprivations and limitations on personal liberties. The plan called for the creation of a war resources administration to direct mobilization; a public relations administration to advertise and popularize the war and implement needed censorship, such as suppressing hostile publicatons; a selective service administration for drafting troops and determining occupational deferments; and special agencies for prices, transportation, power, fuel, and other major problem areas. These were to be civilian agencies, independent of peacetime government agencies and departments, and they would be created under blanket authority given the president, subject to little congressional control. The plan, then, leaned heavily on the experience of World War I and sought to profit from the problems encountered, the successes, and the failures of the previous war.[4] And its essential features were very close to the organization that emerged after the United States was drawn into the war. But if World War I provided the innovative impulse, it remained for the World War II generation to work out the practical solutions to the operating problems involved.

In total war, productive resources have to be divided between the military forces and the civilian population. In World War II, the equation was usually balanced in the interests of assigning as much as possible of national resources to military use and only those goods and services of the civilian population that were essential to maintain production of war materials were allotted to the civilian economy. It was not necessary to carry austerity as far in the United States as proved to be the case in Europe, but not even a nation as rich in natural resources and as far advanced industrially as the United States could produce the ships, planes, tanks, munitions, and all the myriad military supplies used during World War II and continue to provide civilian goods and services at peacetime levels. Therefore, various social and economic controls were imposed on the populace.

Generally, *controls* are thought of as discontinuance or withholding of many things, both material and nonmaterial, considered important or necessary by the civilian population in peacetime, or restrictions on the individual's mobility, freedom of expression, opinion, and choice. And some controls did involve direct restrictions and immediate deprivations. But controls were also operated to assure all segments of the civilian population and all the various interests represented in the populace a fair share of any goods, services, and opportunities available during the war. In other areas, they took the form of federal initiative and direction in sponsoring programs and projects, normally the province of local government and private initiative, for providing, or maintaining minimum requirements of services and facilities, in the interests of the civilian population.

The first step taken, organizationally, by the administration was the resuscitation of the Council of National Defense and its Advisory Commission that had been lying dormant since the end of the first war.[5] The commission was organized into seven divisions to deal with factors involved in industrial production and materials, employment, agricultural production, price stabilization, transportation, and consumer protection. From these, and some other important units of the council, practically all of the independent World War II emergency agencies were derived. At first, the Council of National Defense was used as a focal point for the establishment of defense agencies. Later, the Office for Emergency Management, within the Executive Office of the President, was utilized as an "umbrella agency" under which defense and war agencies were created, largely by executive order.[6] Congress, of course, provided the legislative authority, such as the Emergency Price Control and Emergency Stabilization Acts of 1942, and the War Labor Disputes Act of 1943, without which the emergency agencies could not have operated.

The emergency agencies of World War II have been defined as administrative offices set up for wartime purposes; as such, they have been considered temporary agencies created for and serving emergency ends and existing only until the government and the nation could revert to peacetime activities.[7] Volume I of the National Archives publication, *Federal Records of World War II*, lists fifty-three separate, independent emergency agencies created during the period 1939 to 1948. If one broadens the definition to include administrative units created for wartime emergency purposes within the permanent peacetime agencies and departments and within the Judiciary and the Executive Office of the President, and also includes special congressional committees, units actually established during the war or administering wartime control functions or programs, not just peacetime offices performing wartime chores, the number of emergency agencies more than trebles the fifty-three listed in the World War II guide as independent. In this discussion, I have adopted the broadened definition since "old line" agencies and departments exercised civilian controls programs during the war that were discontinued at the end of the war.

Civilian controls were administered by a complex system of interlocking functions and coordinating agreements among the emergency agencies. About halfway through the war, relations among regulatory and contracting agencies became somewhat acrimonious. Consequently, it was found necessary to establish an agency to formulate policy regarding control of the civilian economy and a separate office to adjudicate competing claims at a high enough level to enforce harmony in production operations. The Office of Economic Stabilization was established to accomplish the first objective, and the Office of War Mobilization, headed by Jimmy Byrnes as virtually associate president, for the second. Later, the Office of War Mobilization and Reconversion combined the two agencies. Administrative changes that occurred both between and within the agencies were very complicated. In the following survey of some of the more important controls, reference will be made only to those agencies that were in existence at the end of the shooting war. It will be understood that, in so doing, I will be referring to predecessor agencies as well.

At the center of all of the economic action during the war was the War Production Board, which, through its "Controlled Materials Plan," analyzed requirements and scheduled production by controlling the allocation of raw materials and various components to industry under a system of priorities based on policy, or need for the product, and available supplies of materials. In a sense, the WPB was the central supply agency, a general or department store. The agencies that contracted with industry for military and civilian goods (which included units of WPB itself) were, in this sense, the customers of WPB. They were referred to as "claimant" agencies. The claimant agencies, in turn, allocated and fixed priorities on materials and goods that WPB had allotted to them. Other agencies involved with the civilian sector operated labor or public relations programs or other controls that contributed to the war effort, but all more or less necessitated by or contributing to operations set in motion by the War Production Board.

Competing demands for military and civilian goods resulted, inevitably, in shortages that led to controls on production. As shortages threatened inflation, controls were forced on the civilian as consumer. Production of many types of consumer goods was discontinued for the duration of the war, and production of others was curtailed drastically. Civilian automobiles were "cut-back" during the defense period and discontinued entirely during the war. Items such as refrigerators, washing machines, vacuum cleaners, electric stoves, and radios disappeared from the stores. When this occurred, prices, even of second hand items, shot up. To prevent inflation and to assure reasonably equitable distribution of scarce commodities, price and rent stabilization and rationing were authorized. Ration currency was issued for food products, meat, shoes, automobile tires, gasoline, and other items. Not only was the quantity of consumer goods affected by wartime controls but style and quality as well. Substitutions were made in materials and, in some instances, this had a lasting effect on tastes, as consumers came to prefer the substitutes.

The WPB's Office of Civilian Requirements and the War Food Administration's Civilian Foods Requirements Branch were the principal agencies involved in determining the amounts of supplies to be allotted to the civilian market. The Office of Price Administration operated price and rent stabilization and rationing control programs. Concurrently with controls on price and distribution of consumer goods and services, wage and salary stabilization controls were applied by the National War Labor Board and the Salary Stabilization Unit of the Bureau of Internal Revenue, respectively. The Federal Reserve System administered controls curbing consumer buying, and the Treasury Department was authorized to collect taxes at the source. Thus, payroll deduction of income taxes was instituted.

Regulations of the Office of Defense Transportation affected operation

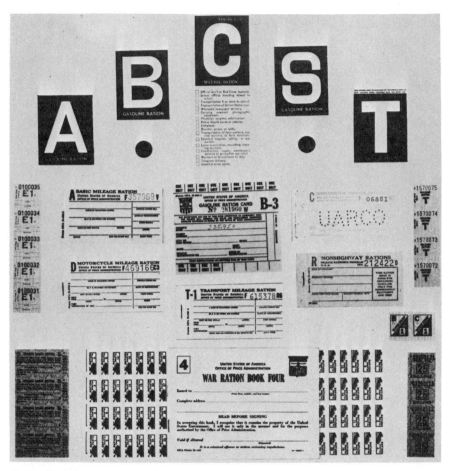

Examples of the variety of ration currency used during the Second World War.
(RG 188, Office of Price Administration, National Archives.)

of private automobiles and civilian travel by air, rail, bus, and taxi. The Bureau of Human Nutrition and Home Economics of the Agriculture Department and the National Academy of Sciences conducted research on wartime nutrition and health needs that were geared to civilian requirements.

The Consumer Protection Division of the Advisory Commission to the Council of National Defense actively promoted programs in the interest of consumers during its brief existence in the defense period. Its functions with regard to health and welfare were distributed to other agencies, and the remainder relegated to the OPA's Information Division, which illuminates the relative importance of the civilian during the war. However, late in the war, with planning for reconversion anticipated, the OPA created an Office of Consumer Relations Advisor to coordinate a program of the local Consumer Advisory Committee, which attempted to influence consumer groups and keep in touch with consumer opinions and needs. OPA's enforcement programs also provided protection to the consumer through efforts to cope with profiteering, black market operations, mislabeling, and other abuses and evasions of regulations which sought to keep the cost of living down.

Controls that affected the civilian as consumer also affected the civilian as supplier of consumer goods and services. Primarily, these controls were directed at the businessman who engaged in production and distribution for the civilian market, but the small businessman who sought to engage in war production was reached also. The principal controls on the producer, as on the consumer, were operated by the WPB and OPA. The Office of Civilian Requirements and various industry units of the WPB, particularly those such as the Consumer Goods Bureau, acted as claimants before WPB for raw materials and components for the production of civilian goods that the WPB had determined could, or should be allocated to the civilian market.[8] WPB also encouraged production of standardized war models of certain types of civilian goods and substitution of materials. Curtailment of civilian production also had the effect of forcing producers to convert to production of war materials, which they had been reluctant to do during the defense period.

OPA administered and enforced price controls on raw materials and finished products. Rent controls also affected the businessman. The agency licensed businesses selling materials or goods subject to price controls. The Enforcement Division of OPA was empowered to deny materials to, and suspend licenses of, or bring legal action against businessmen who engaged in profiteering, hoarding, black market operations, false advertising, and other violations of wartime regulations. Geared to the OPA program, the United States Emergency Court of Appeals was created for the sole purpose of hearing complaints against OPA price and rent regulations.

Wage and salary stabilization also restricted the producer by discouraging him from making offers of higher wages to induce workers to change jobs (a practice termed "labor piracy" and much frowned upon during the war). The Justice Department worked with OPA in criminal prosecutions of violators of price regulations, and the department's Anti-Trust Division cooperated with WPB, OPA, and the War and Navy Departments to work out exemptions from prosecution to businesses represented on the Industry Advisory Committee. The Federal Trade Commission and the Labor Department made checks and surveys to detect business violations of production, price, and rationing regulations.

The Office of Defense Transportation regulated domestic transportation facilities and thus affected the distribution of goods to both producer and consumer. Regulations on the operations of motor vehicles particularly affected the small businessman. The War Food Administration's regulation of production and distribution of agricultural products placed controls on the farmer. The WFA also administered the price stabilization program for farm produce. The Petroleum Administration for War regulated production and distribution of petroleum products. Within the Interior Department, the Solid Fuels Administration for War operated similar controls affecting coal, and the Office of Fishery Coordination performed like services on the fishery products industry. These agencies were also the claimant agencies before WPB for the equipment needs of the industries they regulated.

The Federal Security Agency, Tennessee Valley Authority, Federal Works Agency, and National Housing Agency exercised controls over the construction industry through housing and community facilities development in areas that experienced great influxes of population to man expanding war industries.

During the war, production generally, and military production particularly, tended to gravitate toward the nation's larger producers. The Smaller War Plants Corporation was created to help small businessmen get a share of war contracts. The corporation arranged loans, made equipment available, and found contracts for small businesses. The agency also channeled government surplus to small businessmen and to veterans starting out in business.

The Defense Supplies Corporation of the Reconstruction Finance Corporation administered subsidy controls in the production of meat, butter, flour, woodpulp, and petroleum. And special wartime tax programs administered by the Treasury Department afflicted the civilian producer during the war; but they reduced inflationary pressures, and rebate provisions built into these programs cushioned many businesses in the reconversion period after the war.

Controls also affected the civilian engaged in production at the opposite pole to the businessman—the worker. Immediately after the United States entered the war as an active participant, the president negotiated an agreement with labor and management for peaceful settlement of labor disputes. The National War Labor Board was created to enforce this "no strike pledge," and later in the war, received statutory authority to settle labor disputes. The wage stabilization controls administered by this agency further reduced workers' leverage against employers. The National Railway Labor Panel was created to settle labor disputes in the railroad industry, and the Wage Adjustment Board operated within the Labor Department to effect wage stabilization in the construction industry.

The Selective Service System made decisions on the deferment of essential workers for industry and cooperated with regulatory agencies such as ODT, PAW, WFA, Solid Fuels Administration for War, Office of Fishery Coordination, Federal Communications Commission and Board of War Communications, War Shipping Administration, War Manpower Commission, and other agencies in determining criteria for deferments.

The War Manpower Commission directed its efforts toward recruiting and training workers for war industry (including special programs reaching women, members of minority groups, and professional and specialized personnel) and labor-management relations. This agency negotiated employment stabilization agreements in localized areas to prevent labor piracy and supervised the activities of the United States Employment Service. After state employment services had been "federalized," the United States Employment Service was the principal agent for directing workers into areas and war industries where the need for their services was greatest.

The War Food Administration operated programs for the recruitment, placement and utilization of farm labor, and wage stabilization controls for the agricultural industry. WFA also operated programs for feeding workers in war plants. The Division of Transport Personnel of the ODT administered recruitment and training programs for workers in the transportation industry, and similar programs were operated by the War Shipping Administration, the Civil Service Commission, the Railroad Retirement Board, and the Office of Education.

The WPB sought to achieve increased production with available manpower. During the war, this agency also had jurisdiction over the Shipbuilding Stabilization Committee, which acted to stabilize wages, hours, and working conditions in shipyards. Labor-management relations programs were also administered by WSA and the Maritime Commission, and ODT.

The Fair Employment Practices Committee sought to overcome employment discrimination against minority groups and to have them accepted as workers in war industries.

Another category of controls placed restrictions on, and sought to enlist the cooperation of, influence, and to provide services for the civilian in his role as citizen. Here, the Office of Civilian Defense endeavored to get the citizen involved in war programs such as buying war bonds, donating blood, cultivating victory gardens, and participating in drives to salvage critical materials. The agency also recruited volunteer workers for price, rent, and ration boards, and protection against air raids and sabotage of war plants.

Civilians were assailed on all sides by radio, newspapers, posters, and motion pictures to cooperate with the programs of the emergency agencies. Many were urged to take war jobs by such slogans as, "Mine America's coal, we'll make it hot for the enemy," "The more women at work the sooner we'll win," and "Take a war job to help him fight."[9] They were told by other slogans that, "Food fights for freedom," "Keep the home front pledge," and to "Share and play square," by observing price and rent ceilings and cooperating with ration programs, "Don't feed black market greed," slogans and posters warned, otherwise, "An overcharge is the same as a pay-cut," or "You help the enemy if you buy black market", or "Take care of your tires or you'll walk," and "When you ride alone, you ride with Hitler—join a car-sharing club today!"[10] The War Finance Division of the Treasury Department and the Federal Reserve System promoted sales of war bonds through payroll savings plans, and the Office of Education urged school children to buy savings stamps.

The Office of War Information was organized early in the war period to coordinate all of the government's information and publicity programs. On the domestic front, the government, through control of the media of communications, endeavored to develop and maintain enthusiasm for the war effort. The charge has been made that, as the war progressed, dissemination of information seemed to develop more and more into public relations and that it proved difficult to prevent these programs from shading off into propaganda.[11] During the war, the domestic press and radio agreed to censor news and information that might aid the enemy. This program was directed by the Office of Censorship, and the Federal Trade

Commission cooperated by checking compliance of the communications media with the voluntary censorship controls. In this area, also, the Post Office Department administered laws denying second-class mailing privileges to publications considered subversive.

Social services, day care centers for children of working mothers, and health, recreational, housing, and community facilities programs were administered by agencies such as the Committee for Congested Production Areas, the Office of Community War Services, Public Health Service, Office of Education, Women's Bureau, Children's Bureau, Federal Works Agency, National Housing Agency, and the National Capital Housing Agency. Control here was exercised through the ability of the government to determine where programs were to be operated and what programs operated, or what facilities were developed or constructed in a given area and the extent of the programs. For the most part, these programs were operated to induce workers to take jobs in areas where war industries and military installations were developed and expanded to a point where living conditions in surrounding areas became substandard. But the programs also operated to the benefit of consumer and citizen.

And, finally, we must consider the situation of selected groups of civilians upon whom total controls were imposed when it was deemed necessary in the interests of the war effort. The most prominent of such was the group, approximately one hundred thousand strong, evacuated from Pacific Coast areas because of Japanese ancestry. The army's Western Defense Command supervised the evacuation. The Federal Reserve System and the Farm Security Administration supervised disposition, storage, and wartime utilization of the property of the evacuees. The War Relocation Authority operated the "relocation centers" in which the evacuees were maintained and where housing, educational, medical, and community facilities were provided. The WRA also administered a relocation program to assist individuals or families who decided to settle in other parts of the country.

The Selective Service System's Camp Operations Division maintained civilian public service camps for conscientious objectors who refused noncombatant military duty, and the WFA, National Park Service, and Forest Fire Control Program of the Agriculture Department used the services of conscientious objectors as farm laborers and in soil conservation and forestry projects. The Immigration and Naturalization Service maintained detention camps for enemy aliens. The Post Office Department administered an alien registration program, and the Social Security Board and WRA furnished services and assistance to enemy aliens affected by government restrictions.

After this exhausting, but far from exhaustive survey of controls, it now remains to consider their documentation in federal records.

The National Archives publication, previously referred to, *Federal Records of World War II*, published in 1950 and 1951 in two volumes—the first for civilian agencies and the second for military agencies—is a compact ready reference to the administrative history, functions, and records of the federal agencies that operated programs connected with the war effort.[12] Its description of the records of those agencies and their programs is very much outdated, but it is incomparably the best starting point for anyone interested in research on the agencies and programs considered in the publication, and it is invaluable for its description of the records existing as of 1949 and 1950.

At that time, of course, some of the agencies that administered wartime functions described in the guide were still in existence and, in many instances, records of liquidated agencies were still very much in active use by successor or liquidating agencies. Now, over twenty years later, many records that in 1950 were still in the custody of operating agencies have since attained beatification in the National Archives; many, many more have suffered the fire or reincarnation that is reserved for waste paper. In some instances, the records were integrated with files being created by operating agencies in the 1950s, in which case, as is true also of some other collections we have knowledge of, they are languishing in the purgatory of the federal records centers where they still have a tenuous connection with some active agency; others have been dispersed, we know not to what limbo exactly.

Birth and death are the two most significant events in the life span of anything, and records are no exception. The terms used by archivists when referring to the terminal points marking the period of active use of files are *creation* and *disposition*. Records creation is a continuous process of day-by-day accumulation of paper through the administrative and managerial mazes where the documents and files are subjected to whatever processes result in their being in the shape they are in when dumped into the archivist's lap. Most records creation processes are fairly straightforward, even though resulting in files somewhat vague in form and bulging with excess documentation consisting, in the main, of six or seven copies of everything except what you happen to be looking for. Some agencies attempt to channel all of their records into a central filing system, or some such anomaly. The records of most agencies are usually accumulated in distinct units recognizable, even though battered and blowzy, as the files of this or that division, bureau, section, or what-have-you units. And this is the case with the records of most of the World War

II emergency agencies. The records of those agencies that are now in the National Archives, for the most part, pretty much mirror the organizational picture presented in the World War II guide.

Records disposition requires an act of will, that is, a process involving choice which determines whether or not records will be preserved for future reference by historians. Most World War II agencies had two administrative offices that wielded the major influence on the fate of their records. These were the records management and the historical units. Records management techniques were introduced and promulgated during the war under the auspices of the National Archives to effect systematic, efficient, economical, and orderly procedures for, among other things, evaluation and disposal of the, at that time, incredible amount of paper that was accumulated by federal agencies during the war.

The historical units were products of a program promoted and coordinated by the Bureau of the Budget to produce agency histories of their wartime experiences and operations. In many instances, the historical units collected documentation and created special files, which, being divorced from the operating files, were artificial creations set up solely for convenience in drafting the historical publications.

During the war period, vast quantities of records judged to have no permanent value were destroyed under records management procedures after they were no longer needed in the current operations of the agencies. At the end of the war, when the emergency programs were liquidated, further quantities of records were disposed of in the course of selection of those files to be preserved for historical and other purposes. After this, all of the remaining records of many of the World War II emergency agencies were accessioned by, that is, transferred to the custody of the National Archives. Here, the records were neatly boxed and labeled, and inventorying was begun. In fact, the inventorying is still going on. Some further trimming of the records was done, most notably, by the Archives' Accessioning Policies Review Board in the early 1960s, when that body was organized to make an overall survey of the holdings of the National Archives and dispose of any materials that, in its findings, did not have permanent value.

I want to discuss in some detail the records programs of the WMC, OPA, and WPB—the WMC because it seems fairly typical, OPA because of the enormous volume of its records and the excellent documentation of its records program, and WPB because it is in almost every respect atypical.

The War Manpower Commission had an active records management program which sought to reduce to a minimum the accumulation of records in Washington headquarters and field offices. Field units were ordered to submit lists of disposable records to the records officer in Washington.[13] The agency began disposal of its records in 1943, and the National Archives disposal records show authorization for destruction of routine housekeeping, administrative, and public information files as well as some statistical data, such as forms containing data regarding employment in firms during the reconversion period, destruction of which was authorized on the grounds that the data had been used in statistical compilations. In one communication to field directors, the chief of administrative services reported disposal of two tons of occupational questionnaires.[14] These were forms filled out by draft registrants. Later jobs show authorization for disposal of all files of some offices. Finally, the records of all WMC regional offices, with the exception of specific items that were to be preserved, were authorized for disposal.

The WMC historical unit accumulated considerable documentation of the agency's programs and arranged these documents in an arbitrary system. It is a valuable file, including documents of interest on a variety of subjects regarding the manpower programs, and I recommend it as a starting point for research. The agency's historical program did not result in any publication. The file includes a few drafts of chapters for the projected history, but the program did not even get through the first draft stage. Consequently, there is no history of the War Manpower Commission.

The records of the WMC in the National Archives now total over one thousand cubic feet and comprise practically all of the known extant records of the agency. Since the records were accessioned by the National Archives, some further weeding of duplicate materials and routine administrative files has been made, the last of which was effected by the Accessioning Policies Review Board in 1962. The files of the WMC 4th regional office have been sent from the National Archives to the newly established Archives Branch of GSA's Federal Records Center in Atlanta, Georgia. A few files of a statistical nature are listed as being in the Washington National Records Center, and a small amount of material is in the GSA Region 9 Federal Records Center. Files of the World War II National Roster of Scientific and Specialized Personnel, which was administered by the WMC during the war, were transferred to the custody of the National Science Foundation. Files of the local USES offices were transferred to the custody of the states when the local offices were returned to the state employment services at the end of the war. The National Archives has recently published an inventory of WMC records.

Early in its existence, the OPA instituted a central filing system; but by the middle of 1942, the agency had grown so large and complex that the centralized system broke down and each office or other unit set up its own filing system.[15] An OPA records management program was set up and administered by the late T. R. Schellenberg of the National Archives. During the war period, he was records officer of OPA. Under his direction, surveys were made of all records, including OPA field office records, and disposition programs were worked out after the records had been analyzed. The records program is well documented.

The major problem presented by the OPA records was the sheer bulk of the files. By the end of the war, in spite of the fact that vast quantities of records had been disposed of during the war, over a million cubic feet of the agency's records were in existence. In 1945, the National Archives presented a plan for the evaluation and disposal of OPA records.[16] The proposal received strong criticism from Dr. Robert E. Stone, chief of the OPA Historical Branch, who said, in effect that the Archives proposed to save only about 7.5 percent of the OPA records, consisting of files of top-level executives, but, he said, this overlooked the fact that most of the time, policies were formulated, worked out, and implemented all up and down the chain of policy making, and that if someone wanted to know what facts policies were based on, or what the results of policy decisions were, he would have to consult files of people operating at lower levels. He said further, that he would rather have OPA records evaluated by economists and business specialists and the like, who would be better prepared to know what records were significant, whereas the sampling techniques advocated by the archivists would result in the destruction of much valuable material, and, as he also noted, such procedure was, " . . . clearly contra to the best advice of archivists generally."[17] It is to be hoped that much of Dr. Stone's sage advice was heeded, but the process of liquidation of war programs closed out the OPA before long, and the amount of OPA records remaining is very close to Stone's estimate of what would be preserved under the archivist's recommendations.

Several agencies, among them the Bureau of the Budget, took a strong interest in the economic data collected by OPA, and the agency brought together a panel of experts in statistical and economic data to make recommendations as to the value of the data in OPA files for preservation or disposal of the records.[18] Another proposal regarding OPA records was the transfer of records of local boards to state and local institutions. This had to be abandoned, however, because the general counsel of OPA ruled that this would violate the confidentiality of OPA's data.[19]

It can be seen from this that serious efforts were made to try to preserve, as far as possible, any records and data that had any lasting value.

Disposal of OPA records began in 1943. I will mention some of the most important developments. Routine administrative and housekeeping records and files of correspondence with the public of an informational character were weeded out as a matter of course; all application files were disposed of; all files of local price, rent, and ration boards, except for a couple saved as samples; files relating to individual cases of price determinations and adjustments; enforcement case files, except for a small sampling; and primary data gathered for various surveys undertaken by the agency, along with related working papers, were destroyed. In general, almost all of the primary economic data obtained by OPA and practically all files of the agency's contacts with individuals and businesses have been disposed of.

The National Archives began accessioning records of the OPA around 1945 and as late as 1962 was still receiving odds and ends of OPA records. The Archives now houses a little less than eight thousand cubic feet of OPA records. A small amount of material has been transferred to the Archives Branch of the Washington National Records Center and a smaller amount is in GSA's Region 9 Federal Records Center. The National Archives has so far published six inventories of its holdings of OPA records, one for each of the major operating units. An inventory of headquarters administrative files is in the drafting stage.

The OPA historical program resulted in the publication of a number of historical reports, including an extensive bibliography of significant documents. The records of the Historical Unit in the National Archives include a file of the items listed in the published bibliography.[20]

The OPA records in the National Archives include quite a bit of data furnished in confidence by business concerns about their products, processes, and operations. The confidentiality of this information was guaranteed by acts of Congress pertaining to the OPA. In 1947, the assistant general counsel of OPA rendered an opinion to the effect that the confidentiality of OPA records would extend past the life of the agency and past the life of the acts imposing the restrictions—in effect, as I read it, in perpetuity.[21] The National Archives still guards the confidentiality of the OPA records.

Beginning in 1943, the records program of the War Production Board was administered by its Policy Analysis and Records Branch, which was also the historical unit of the agency. As files were examined by the records management personnel for disposition and by the historical staff for preparation of their publications, it became the policy of the Branch to select the most significant documents and arrange them under a subject category filing scheme. The resulting file was called the "Policy Documentation File." After being subjected to this selection process, many noncurrent records were disposed of during the war period. It has been estimated that the WPB, its predecessors, and successors, together created about one hundred eighty thousand cubic feet of records, and that, by 1948, over one hundred thousand cubic feet had been disposed of.[22] During the time when WPB was being liquidated, a considerable volume of WPB records was transferred to the custody of other agencies, and this record is documented in the World War II guide. Some of these have since been brought into the National Archives. However, further disposal has been made of records described in the guide.

The chief discrepancy between the description of WPB records in the guide and the records as they exist today is with about fifty thousand cubic feet of records described as being in the custody of the Commerce Department, stored in Cameron, Virginia. These records were disposed of in 1954, with the possible exception of about five hundred cubic feet of files of the Foreign Division and Bureau of International Supply which were transferred to the custody of the Central Intelligence Agency. There are no files in the National Archives of any administrative units of WPB as such. For the most part, the almost eighteen hundred cubic feet of WPB records in the National Archives consist of the Policy Documentation File, which is approximately one thousand cubic feet in volume; a related file of approximately three hundred cubic feet, which WPB personnel had intended to integrate with the Policy Documentation File; and another special file of approximately three hundred cubic feet containing quantitative data. The National Archives published an inventory of its holdings of WPB records as of 1948, and this is now somewhat outdated. The historical program of the WPB resulted in the publication of a number of historical reports of various units and a large overall history of industrial mobilization.[23]

The remaining records of the emergency agencies discussed here are in the National Archives or in the Washington National Records Center. For example, records of the Office of War Mobilization and Reconversion, Petroleum Administration for War, Office of Defense Transportation, Committee for Congested Production Areas, Office of Community War Services, Fair Employment Practices Committee, and Smaller War Plants Corporation now constitute separate record groups in the National Archives. Administrative files of the National War Labor Board and War Relocation Authority are here, and case files of these agencies are in the Archives Branch of the Washington National Records Center. Records of the War Food Administration are included among the records of some of the administrative units of the Agriculture Department here in the National Archives. The records of the Office of War Information and of the Office of Civilian Defense are in the Archives Branch of the Washington National Records Center. Some records of the War Shipping Administration are in the National Archives. Most of the remaining records of that agency were interfiled with records of the Maritime Commission and are now in the Washington National Records Center. Security and other restrictions still apply to many of these records, but recently, some progress has been made in removing them.

Thomas Hardy said that "war makes rattling good history, but peace is poor reading." This sentiment seems also to hold true as regards the relative attention paid by historians to the military actions and the civilian experience in major wars. I started to title this paper, "Some Aspects of the Secret History of World War II," since less attention has been paid by American historians to the economic, industrial, social, and civil factors of the American experience in World War II than any other aspects of the war. In the ultimate analysis, American industrial production was the deciding factor, and the effort and organization that achieved that production should, seemingly, be of the greatest interest to scholars of World War II. Yet, over the past twenty-five years, military, diplomatic, personal, and some aspects of political developments and features of the period have been narrated in minute detail, expounded in all of their interrelationships, and interpreted and reinterpreted in the light of the past and of events of the postwar period. Military history, as far as one can tell, has been written on almost every conceivable phase of the war: from the combat history of the 894th Ordnance Heavy Automotive Maintenance Company[24] to military currency.[25] As Anatole France said of the wars of the penguins, and hence, by extension, to the military history of all wars, "It is extremely difficult to know the truth concerning these wars, not because accounts are wanting, but because there are so many of them."

This is equally true of diplomatic aspects of the prewar period, the war period, and the postwar period. We have any number of travelogues on the road to war; countless discussions of the nuances of the Atlantic, Yalta, Cairo, and Potsdam conferences; and an increasing number of authoritative treatises on the process by which we came to own the free world.

The economist, Sidney Ratner, writing in the *Journal of Economic History* in 1952, said that the military and diplomatic phases of World War II up to that time attracted the major show of attention, and he listed only seven major works on American wartime economic history, one of which was the first volume of the National Archives publication, *Federal Records of World War II,* which he included, I feel sure, in the hope that it would be consulted by historians and inspire them to use the records described therein.[26] In his 1967 bibliographical article, "Writings on World War II," Louis Morton stated that, ". . . more than any other war in history, World War II was a war of supply . . . and allied victory was due as much to industrial strength as to the operations of the armed forces," and that, "This aspect of the war has received much less attention than grand strategy or combat operations . . . . The more mundane matters of production, procurement, distribution, transportation, industrial organization, labor problems, priorities, and a large variety of service activities lack the mystery of strategic decision and the excitement of the battlefield. As a result, the writing on these matters, important as they are, is comparatively sparse." Under headings of "Mobilization," "Supply," and "Home Front," Morton lists eleven titles. For the economic history of the war, he cites just about the same titles that Ratner cited fifteen years earlier, and one which Professor Morton calls the best general account of mobilization, Ratner had relegated to a footnote as being too general.[27]

The publications resulting from the agency historical programs of World War II are often cited as histories of civilian phases of the war, and these are, in most instances, the only available publications on those phases which they treat. The official histories that I have examined, however, succeed mostly in presenting a statement of what the agency and program tried and hoped to accomplish. In most cases, the attempt was made to assess fairly their successes and failures, but when someone close to an operation undertakes to write its history, it becomes difficult to distinguish between the objective and the accomplishment.

The Library of Congress card catalog on World War II is very extensive. It must be one of their larger subject categories. Yet well over 90 percent of the entries relating to economic and social matters are either contemporaneous publications discussing approaches to wartime problems, disseminating information of current interest, and productions of wartime public relations; or immediate postwar publications produced by way of summing up the experiences of the war, such as official histories and reminiscences, most of which are journalistic, autobiographical, or polemical. These, then, are not histories, but, rather, the raw materials of history, just as are the records I have described.

From the mid-1950s, the flood of publications on the war dwindles considerably, and, on the scholarly level (with a few notable exceptions, mostly productions of younger historians), little has appeared on economic and social phases. Through the years there has been a persistent trickle of published material on the evacuation of the West Coast population of Japanese descent and the War Relocation program as though the national conscience remains uneasy over the episode. I would be almost willing to bet that more has been published on the campaign in the Aleutians.

To speak plainly, the historians of World War II have not finished the job. The full history of the war remains to be written. Perhaps the untouched phases require the methods of the economist and social scientist and the arcana of the statistician. It is true that the tools of these disciplines do not seem to include the English language, but just as historians learn to decipher thousand-year-old documents and interpret the language of diplomacy, a school of present-day historians seems to have set about to learn the languages of other disciplines and may come up with a method of translation. Archivists, too, will probably have to become conversant with these fields.

Some prime raw material for the neglected history of World War II is in the custody of the National Archives, and all archivists join me in inviting scholars to make use of it.

Notes

1. Some of the World War I agencies that administered functions equivalent to the civilian controls of World War II were as follows: the Council of National Defense and its Advisory Commission, the War Industries Board, Selective Service System, Food Administration, Fuel Administration, Railroad Administration, United States Shipping Board, Committee on Public Information, Housing Corporation, the War Labor Policies Board, Negro Economics Division, Women-in-Industry Service, and Employment Service.
2. *Industrial Mobilization Plan* (Approved jointly by Acting Secretary of War Louis Johnson and Acting Secretary of the Navy Charles Edison) (Washington, D.C.: Government Printing Office, 1939).
3. Harold J. Tobin, "War Planning," *Planning for America*, ed. George B. Galloway et al., chap. 29 (New York: Oxford University Press, 1941), pp. 561–77. The direct quotation is from p. 563. Tobin, professor of government at Dartmouth College, made an independent study of the Industrial Mobilization Plan in 1939. See *Industrial Mobilization for War*, vol. 1, of Program and Administration (Washington, D.C.: Government Printing Office, 1947), fn., p. 6.
4. The Industrial Mobilization Plan was apparently modified by Bernard Baruch, the War Resources Board, and the president. See Eliot Janeway, *The Struggle for Survival*, Chronicle of America Series, vol. 53 (New Haven: Yale University Press, 1951): 63–68; Herman Miles Somer, *Presidential Agency: The Office of War Mobilization and Reconversion* (Cambridge, Mass.: Harvard

University Press, 1950), pp. 6–9; Bruce Catton, *The War Lords of Washington* (New York: Harcourt, Brace & Co., 1948), pp. 101–2; Donald M. Nelson, *Arsenal of Democracy* (New York: Harcourt, Brace & Co., 1946), p. 88.

5. U.S., National Archives and Records Service, *Federal Records of World War II, Civilian Agencies* 1 (Washington, D.C.: Government Printing Office, 1950), p. 126.
6. Ibid., p. 142. Some of the other units of the Council of National Defense are as follows: the Office for Coordination of National Defense Purchases, Office of Small Business Activities, Office of Information, Bureau of Research and Statistics, Office of Defense Housing Coordinator, Division of State and Local Cooperation, the Health and Medical Committee, and the Office of the Coordinator of Health, Welfare and Related Activities. Of the independent emergency agencies directly engaged in the administration of civilian controls, only the Selective Service System, the Smaller War Plants Corporation, the Office of War Mobilization and Reconversion, and the Price Decontrol Board were not established by executive order.
7. Ibid., p. 123. See also, Harold Tobin, "War Planning," in *Planning for America* for a discussion of the emergency agencies envisioned by the Industrial Mobilization Plan.
8. For a discussion of various phases of controls on production of consumer goods, see Irene B. Walker, "Consumer Durable Goods, policies and programs, 1940–1945," in *Industrial Mobilization for War: A History of the War Production Board,* vol. 1 (Washington, D. C.: Defense Production Administration, 1951)
9. War Manpower Commission posters, Records of the War Manpower Commission, Record Group 211, National Archives. (Hereafter records of the National Archives are indicated by the symbol NA. The symbol RG is used for record group.)
10. Office of Price Administration posters, Records of the Office of Price Administration, RG 188, NA.
11. Catton, *The War Lords of Washington,* pp. 186–95, 221–25, 257–58, and 266–73.
12. See *Federal Records of World War II,* vol. 2, for a ready reference to the administrative history, functions, and records of military agencies. Volume 2 has a comprehensive index for both volumes.
13. Chairman McNutt to the Archivist of the United States, 7 September 1944, WMC Central File, category "Records," Records of the War Manpower Commission, RG 211, NA.
14. Chief, Administrative Services to All Regional Manpower Directors, 1 December 1944, WMC Central File, category "Records," Records of the War Manpower Commission, RG 211, NA.
15. Report on inventory of OPA National Office files, 6 January 1945, T. R. Schellenberg File, "Disposition Instructions," Records Branch, Records of the Office of Price Administration, RG 188, NA.
16. "Proposed Records Retirement Program for the Office of Price Administration," prepared by the National Archives, January 1945, Records Branch, Records of the Office of Price Administration, RG 188, NA.
17. "An Appraisal of the National Archives Report Entitled, 'Proposed Records Retirement Program for the Office of Price Administration,' " 1945, 87 pp.,

Program Plans, FY 1945, Records Branch, Records of Price Administration, RG 188, NA.

18. Chester Bowles to the Archivist of the United States, 15 October 1943, Records Branch, Records of the Office of Price Administration, RG 188, NA.
19. Records Branch, Records of the Office of Price Administration, RG 188, NA.
20. William Jerome Wilson et al., *OPA Bibliography, 1940–1947*, Office of Price Administration and its predecessor agencies, Miscellaneous Publication no. 3 (Washington, D.C.: Government Printing Office, 1948).
21. Memorandum, 22 January 1947, T. R. Shellenberg File, Records Branch, Records of the Office of Price Administration, RG 188, NA.
22. From documentation in National Archives disposal job II-NNA-658.
23. Civilian Production Administration, *Industrial Mobilization for War*. See fn. 8.
24. U.S., Department of the Army, *History of the 894th Ordnance Heavy Automotive Maintenance Company, June 1941 to May 1945* (n.p. 1945).
25. Albert I. Dorn, *World War II Prisoner of War Scrip of the United States* (Iola, Wisconsin, 1970); Walter Rundell, Jr., *Black Market Money: The Collapse of U.S. Military Currency Control in World War II* (Baton Rouge: Louisiana State University Press, 1964).
26. Sidney Ratner, "The Economic Historian of the Second World War," *Journal of Economic History* 12, no. 3 (Summer 1952): 263–70.
27. Louis Morton, *Writings on World War II*, Service Center for Teachers of History, American Historical Association Publication no. 66 (Washington, D.C., 1967).

Discussion Summary

Joseph Howerton was asked whether all records of wartime emergency agencies were now accessible and whether there was any plan to include them, and especially the unpublished historical studies prepared by some of them, in the National Archives microfilm program. He replied that records of the agencies described in his paper were open for research; the only possible exception was information furnished to the government (e.g. OPA and WPB) in confidence, which was still not releasable. The National Archives had no plans at present to microfilm the records.

Responding to a request to comment further on the role of Bernard Baruch, Blum said that although Baruch was commonly thought of as an important figure in prewar economic mobilization planning, his significance was greatly exaggerated. Baruch often expressed publicly and to Roosevelt his views about what ought to be done, but Roosevelt tended to ignore his advice. The myth of Baruch's importance resulted largely from his skill at public relations. He was a financier and philanthropist and although he refrained from entering politics openly, he let it be understood that he had much influence behind the scenes and thus developed a popular reputation of greater magnitude than was warranted. Roosevelt's refusal to appoint him chairman of the War Production Board ultimately impressed upon him the realities of his position. In contrast to the Baruch myth, Blum emphasized that many people of outstanding importance emerged from the World War II emergency agencies, among them a future secretary of labor, James Mitchell, and a Supreme Court justice, William J. Brennan. Although they were still relatively obscure figures, everyone knew of Baruch.

Another questioner felt that the actions of the wartime emergency agencies did not really seem to have been accepted and recognized as precedents, for we were now re-debating essentially the same problems and the ideology that underlay them. To this observation Blum responded that the thinking that went into prewar economic and mobilization planning exemplified the same basic shortcoming—a failure to recognize that America was constantly changing, that new ideas and attitudes were always evolving. The military, for example, was willing to deal with civic organizations and the American Federation of Labor but was reluctant to work with labor organizations when they became more powerful in the late 1930s. Similarly in the early seventies, in discussing the draft, we sometimes failed to take into consideration the new forces and attitudes that were evolving in the country. Nor did we study as much as we should what other countries were doing to deal with similar problems.

IX

Research for Official
Second World War
Historical Programs

Herbert E. Angel, deputy archivist of the United States, served as chairman for the final session of the conference on the afternoon of June 15. The writing of "official" history involves special opportunities for the historian but presents special problems as well. The papers, presented by writers of American and British "official" history, respectively, were designed to explore those special characteristics.

STETSON CONN

Preparing the Army's History
of the Second World War

When I joined the army's Historical Division twenty-five years ago, it and several other army historical offices were just beginning the preparation of the comprehensive narrative history of the army's role in the Second World War, to be published in the series, *The United States Army in World War II*, and in the associated series, *The Army Air Forces in World War II*. The first volume of what we came to call the "big history," when it went to press in the fall of 1946, contained a forecast that ninety-nine volumes eventually would be published in these series, a forecast that compares rather satisfactorily with the actual appearance to date of seventy-seven of them, including those of the United States Air Force, which with about eight more to come will make an achieved total of eighty-five. Privately, in the early days, the founding fathers of the project agreed that the army would do well to get out fifty volumes. Actual performance has therefore considerably exceeded immediate postwar expectations as to numbers, and I think it has at least matched them in terms of quality. My purpose is to suggest some of the reasons for this altogether favorable outcome of the most ambitious narrative historical project ever undertaken in the United States.

Of course this undertaking would never have come to pass if the army had not really wanted to know the truth about its recent past, and if history had not received strong backing within the army from a number of civilian and military leaders, most notably perhaps of Assistant Secretary of War John J. McCloy during the war and of Chief of Staff Dwight D. Eisenhower in the immediate postwar years. Naturally it helped that their superiors, Presidents Roosevelt and Truman, had a genuine interest in history and in encouraging federal historical work. Further, historical work in the army was nothing new, having been carried on almost continuously since the closing months of the Civil War. The preparation of the operational records of the Union army for publication that began then grew into a project that took nearly forty years to complete and produced 128 documentary volumes. A new central historical office established by the War Department in the midst of the First World War laid plans for a

215

The first volume of the "United States Army in World War II" being presented to President Eisenhower in 1954. With the president are Kent Roberts Greenfield, Forrest C. Pogue, and Maj. Gen. Albert C. Smith. (National Park Service; Dwight D. Eisenhower Library, no. 72-853-2.)

multi-volume narrative history of that war of a scope considerably broader than that of the World War II project; but the army's actual printed historical products about World War I were to consist of seventeen documentary volumes containing the principal papers of the American Expeditionary Forces, not published until 1948, several useful but innocuous order of battle books, and a few narrative accounts of particular operations that remained almost unknown even to military historians.

The army's older historical office remained active throughout the Second World War, but its preference for publishing documents instead of narratives and for using officers rather than civilian professionals as historians made it unacceptable as a vehicle for undertaking a narrative history of the new great war. Instead, counseled by the Historical Advisory Committee that included three eminent civilian scholars, the army in 1943 established a new historical shop that devoted itself exclusively to World

War II and to paving the way toward writing a definitive history of the army's role in the war. This new office, the ancestor of the present Office of the Chief of Military History, has always been located within the military hierarchy of army headquarters and thus headed by a military chief. However, from the beginning, the chief has had as his principal adviser a civilian chief historian with delegated responsibility for judging the historical and literary quality of all historical works to be published by the army—an arrangement described quite accurately by my predecessor as a so-called happy marriage of the military and civilian professions. Further, while the successive military chiefs assigned to direction of the office were all able and interested men—and general officers from November 1945 on—the continuity in leadership during the first fifteen years came from the first two chief historians, Walter Livingston Wright and Kent Roberts Greenfield, both eminent scholars. The latter in particular was an outstanding scholastic leader who for twelve years before the war served as history department chairman at Johns Hopkins University and who as chief historian for twelve years after it exerted almost a paramount influence over the army's great history. For its research and writing staff, the World War II office also came to rely principally upon well-trained civilian historians, many of them men brought into the army as historians during the war and then persuaded to stay with it thereafter to work on the big history. Most of them were relatively young men, full of vigor and enthusiasm for the tasks they undertook. A minority of professional women were also enlisted, some of whom turned out to be topnotchers, especially in technical fields. At one time the best historians the army had on quartermaster, ordnance, and signal matters, among others, were women. By and large, the office chose the right man or woman for the right job, recognizing that historians were not freely interchangeable parts. The successful authors of campaign histories, for example, were usually professionally trained historians who had served during the war in the theater about which they wrote. Some of the volumes planned for the army series were never undertaken because the office could not get the right person to prepare them.

As a preliminary to preparing the comprehensive history—one might say as a tune-up for it—the newly established historical office edited or prepared and published between 1943 and 1947 fourteen pamphlets on particular overseas operations in an *American Forces in Action* series. Over a similar time span and also as a backdrop, the quartermaster historical shop turned out and published twenty-one monographs on aspects of its support to army operations, and army historical offices in all major agencies and commands at home and overseas prepared literally thousands of historical monographs that remained unpublished but available as guidance to authors of the World War II series.

Although from the outset the protagonists of the World War II history preferred a narrative to a documentary approach, they really had no choice, on two counts. First, the sheer volume of army records related to the war—said to amount to more than seventeen thousand tons at its close —made impossible any meaningful selection for a manageable documentary series. And second, most of the war records dealing with matters of historical interest were classified, and today the army is still struggling to get them declassified. It was far simpler to grant responsible scholars free access to the records, and then review and clear for publication the narrative histories they produced rather than the original records.

Before Dr. Greenfield accepted the post of chief historian in 1946, in a lengthy interview with Chief of Staff Eisenhower, he obtained assurances that collectively meant preparation of the army's World War II history under a mantle of academic freedom. Each author would be responsible for his own handiwork, with a signed preface asserting this responsibility and name credit on title page and spine. Nothing has been published in the army series that has not received an author's entire approval. Further, the authors, to use Greenfield's phrase, were to "call the shots as they saw them." This did not mean license to present a prejudiced or inadequately researched story; it did mean that within the series there was room for differing interpretations—indeed, the discerning reader could find them within the multi-authored first volume of the series to be published. And, while manuscripts were circulated widely for comment to participants, including high-ranking generals, an author's text remained unchanged unless reliable and contemporary written evidence was forthcoming. These points emphasize that the army's histories are official in a restricted sense only; they are prepared on company time and primarily for company use, and generally they have been published by the company printer—the Government Printing Office. But they are not in any sense official doctrine or an official version of factual information.

Full action on the final assurance that Greenfield received from General Eisenhower, access to all relevant records, was not achieved without a struggle. But a War Department order of July 1946, in due course, opened up all the army records that were really pertinent, and in 1947, army and other service historians were granted at first authority to see and use, and later on to cite, records of the Joint and Combined Chiefs of Staff. In the same year General Eisenhower had to be talked out of a wholesale declassification of army records, but he did insist on publishing a directive in November 1947 that established a firm foundation for a liberal policy of clearance and that bristled with admonitions against official publication of anything less than the truth. I quote portions of it: "The Army possesses no inherent right to conceal the history of its affairs behind a cloak of secrecy. . . . The history of the Army in World War II, now in preparation, must, without reservation, tell the complete story of the Army's participation, fully documented. . . . The maximum downgrading of all information on military subjects will be accomplished, except only when to do so would in fact endanger the security of the nation. . . . The foregoing directive will be interpreted in the most liberal sense with no reservations as to whether or not the evidence of history places the Army in a favorable light." I might add that soon after Eisenhower became president, he directed that steps be taken to allow qualified unofficial researchers to use more generally executive files that were still classified.

Since the army in its narrative histories followed standard American scholarly historical practice on documentation, it needed no directive on that score. From the beginning, footnotes in the army's series were designed not only to assure the reader of the authenticity of the text but also to provide other scholars with a guide to the records. In each volume a bibliographical note, describing the several types of record sources used, supplemented the footnotes.

Throughout the history of the series, army historians have resisted all proposals for publishing a censored or an expurgated version of an author's work. Sometimes it has taken a long while and much argument to get a manuscript cleared for publication without censorious change—one book that I worked on was held up for more than four years—but on censorship we have followed the precept of Dr. Greenfield: "If we publish books that conceal the truth in any degree not required by loyal respect for the requirements of security, and are found out—as we will be, in time—all that we have published will be discredited." In the army's view, it would be an equal act of heresy to circulate a classified version of a major work for internal use and at the same time publish a sanitized version for public consumption.

As a general rule, research for the army's World War II histories has been held to the records and views of the agencies and individuals in the chain of command, on up as necessary to the president as commander-in-chief. But army historians have also turned when they needed to the records of the other services, the United States Navy, Marine Corps, and Air Force. Among the groups of army records, two of the largest needed for the series, those of the War Department staff agencies and those of army units, large and small, were gathered from late 1945 into a historical records section of the army's adjutant general, and until 1949 located close to the army's historical office. This section, with its holdings greatly expanded and broadened, went on to become the National Archives' Modern Military Records Division; and its most able and always helpful supervisor, Sherrod East, with whom I worked from 1946, went on with the section and beyond to become before his retirement the assistant archivist for military Archives. I wish I could mention all of the other archivists whom I and the other army historians found outstandingly helpful to our World War II work over the years, people like Alice Miller who presided over the records of the army's Operations Division (more familiarly known as OPD), Sherrod's assistant Bill Nigh, Lois Aldridge and Hazel Ward who are still with the National Archives, and many others. Consistently, whether the records have been under army or National Archives control, we have experienced only the best of cooperation from the archivists, and in a very true sense, the army's World War II series has been their venture as well as ours. Incidentally, the archivists would have been the first to know if we historians had not told the whole truth as best we could, and I have never heard of such a criticism.

Access to records of combined commands presented some problems, particularly to those of Eisenhower's SHAEF, the Supreme Headquarters Allied Expeditionary Force, and of the Mediterranean's Allied Force Headquarters, or AFHQ. By agreement, originals of the SHAEF records were deposited in the United States, with microfilm copies in Great Britain, and for AFHQ records, just the opposite arrangement was made, the United States receiving the microfilm. Britain and the United States also captured most of the surviving German records, and the United States held most of the German army and higher command records for many years. We also brought a large volume of records from Japan, although army historians never made as much use of them before their return as they did of the German records—in part because we had no one in the shop who could read Japanese fluently. The availability of enemy records, an incidental fruit of the policy of unconditional surrender, of course made it possible for both the British and American official histories to start telling both sides of the war story soon after the event. In due course about two thousand five hundred German and one hundred eighty Japanese reports or monographs by enemy officers were obtained to supplement these records. Aside from their use in the general series, the availability of these records and reports has enabled the United States Army to publish twenty-three separate historical works on German and Japanese military operations.

Voluminous as the American and enemy record holdings were, army historians both during and after the war were about the foremost practitioners of oral history in the nation. S.L.A. Marshall in the Pacific and Europe developed his technique of the group combat interview with members of small units as soon after an action as possible, a technique that contributed considerably to dispersing the traditional fog of war. Army historians everywhere did whatever interviewing they could to supplement the written record, and the methods of oral history they developed were to be used extensively in the later Korean and Vietnam conflicts. It really is no coincidence that Forrest Pogue, biographer of General Marshall, but before that, author of the army's *Supreme Command* volume, is now the president of the Oral History Association.

The respect that Forrest Pogue commands in the historical profession today illustrates how far army historians have come from the normal suspicion of court historians that existed in the academic profession generally in the United States at the close of the last great war. Looking back two years later, one army official recalled this suspicion as the greatest disadvantage in enlisting a professional staff to work on the army series. Too many outsiders, he wrote, considered that "as kept historians we were expected to be producers of excuses for the army's mistakes, not bona fide historians working to expose those mistakes in order that they could be corrected." To overcome such distrust the army tried to attract not only the best but the most independent-minded historians that it could, and in the beginning offered salaries that represented a favorable differential over those in the teaching world. Under the aegis of the chief historian, all that they wrote was subjected to intensive review, both during its preparation and after an author thought he had completed his manuscript. Before publication the manuscripts also received a solid literary editing. Of course not every volume in the army series could be outstanding, but it was essential that every one of them should be reasonably good. The private scholar who lays a bad egg injures only himself, for a federal historian to do so would risk the whole crate.

I can do no more than summarize some of the other principles, practices, and developments that in my judgment contributed to the favorable outcome of the army's World War II history project. At the outset, the army decided to address its big history to a selected rather than a general reading public. After all, it would be rather difficult to write a popular history in a hundred volumes! Instead it was visualized that the audience for the series would be a professional military public, a professional scholarly public, and a general but limited public of thoughtful citizens. Basically, the volumes in the army series were designed to be works of reference, "not bedtime reading for anybody," as Dr. Greenfield once remarked; but it was important to have them written in clear and common

English, not in federal prose. Originally the army planned to produce a one or two-volume popular history of the war to parallel the major series, and work on it actually began in 1945. But after the author's untimely death this project, though much talked about, was never revived. As for volumes in the big series, although they were aimed at a restricted audience, it was felt they should have army-wide appeal, and not significance chiefly to one part of the army. Thus, a general volume on training would have been acceptable for the series, although we were not able to produce one; but a volume on training in a particular branch would have been too parochial. It was also understood that no work should be undertaken that would not have enduring value, and as a rough rule of thumb it was hoped to produce works that would be useful to a thoughtful military and civilian public for at least half a century. Finally, the professional leaders of the project wisely recognized that the large staff of writing historians employed (about fifty at the peak) faced almost as many different problems in their work as army historians as would a similar number of historical writers in any other sector of the profession—they were not cogs in a machine.

Only one of the army volumes on the Second World War was written entirely under contract. While we have generally found it convenient to contract for indexes, it has been our experience that in-house production by full-time professional employees is the most efficient and in the long run the most economical way to produce army history. On another front, we owe a deep debt to a son of Mother Russia, Wsevolod Aglaimoff, for the excellence of the maps in the series. He was not only an imaginative and meticulous cartographer, he was also a careful and well-trained scholar who never hesitated to check on the sources when there was any shadow of doubt about the accuracy of an author's text. We also became very materially indebted on another score. It is axiomatic that a war's history cannot be written in final and complete form until the war is over and the records are available. In an overseas war the latter process takes up to three years. But in the military establishment postwar demobilization is apt to strike all elements impartially. With preparation of the series beginning to roll, manpower people levied a 50 percent reduction on the historical staff in the summer of 1947. In the nick of time, the historical office obtained a nonappropriated fund of $4,000,000 from surplus wartime Army Post Exchange profits, and this extra money made it possible to free the series from financial threat until work on it was substantially completed.

My predecessor as chief historian saw the army's World War II project as an adventure in contemporary history on a scale never before attempted in the United States. Indeed in this country, if not in Europe, the majority of historical scholars in 1945 viewed contemporary history with almost as much suspicion as they felt toward official history. But the army and the other services could not afford to wait a quarter or a half a century for an objective record of their wartime experiences. Further, despite the mass of records, there were many significant gaps in them generated by telephonic and radio communication, gaps that could be filled only by systematic interrogation of surviving participants as soon as possible after the event. On the other hand, as Dr. Greenfield has pointed out, the mass of written records was so enormous that he doubted whether history could be successfully written from them except by the generation that created the records and knew how to use them selectively. He was convinced that, in modern times unless the history of large events was tackled promptly, it would never be written either correctly or adequately. We have of course been aware that writing about the recent past sacrifices perspective and of the other perils of recent history, such as our own emotional involvement; but working with disadvantages as well as advantages in mind, I think we in the army have done as much as anyone to give respectability in this country to scholarly contemporary history.

It is altogether fitting that I should be followed in this discussion by Dr. Frankland who worked so valiantly on the parallel British history of the war. From the inception of the army project its staff worked most harmoniously not only with the historians of the other American services but also with the historical organizations of the British Commonwealth of Nations. With so many record groups shared, it was inevitable that we should collaborate with the British, but it is a pleasure to testify that doing so has always been both fruitful and pleasant as well.

May I end with the observation, based upon my twenty-five years of service with the army just concluded, that the United States Army since World War II has consistently wanted and continues to want to know the truth about its past, instead of using historical evidence selectively to support established positions. I believe also that the army's World War II series has gone far to satisfy the want for knowledge about our nation's biggest war.

WAR DEPARTMENT
CLASSIFIED MESSAGE CENTER
OUTGOING CLASSIFIED MESSAGE

1 AC/S, OPD
2-3 CH. THEATRE GP.
4 CH. EUROPEAN
5-6 CH. STR. & POL. GP.
7 M/C FILE
8 LIAISON

Combined Chiefs of Staff
W.D. Ext. 77500
Col. C. R. Peck

25 April 1945

26 APR 45 AM

Supreme Headquarters,
Allied Expeditionary Forces,
Forward Echelon,
Rheims, France

British Joint Staff Mission,
Washington, D.C.

Number: WARX 73140

TOPSEC Book Message to SHAEF Rheims for Eisenhower for
action, to AMSSO pass to British Chiefs of Staff for
information, FACS 200 from the Combined Chiefs of Staff

Your SCAF 230 refers.

1. You have no responsibility relative to seizure
of German archives, records, properties or establishments
in neutral countries. For your information the Department
of State and Foreign Office are inquiring of their respective diplomatic representatives as to chances of obtaining
prior agreement from neutral Governments which, on defeat
or surrender of Germany, would authorize seizure of such
archives, records, properties or establishments by forceful
efforts of U.S./U.K. authorities or by neutral forces when
requested by the Allies.

2. However, the Combined Chiefs of Staff will be glad
to have an outline of the plans referred to in your cable.
End

SCAF 230 is CM IN 13097 (13 Mar 45)

ORIGINATOR: CC/S

INFORMATION: Adm Leahy; Gen Arnold; Gen Hull; Gen Bissell;
Adm King; C of S
CM-OUT-73140   (Apr 45)   DTG: 2601562   rrm

DECLASSIFIED
E.O. 11652, Sec. 3(D) and 5(D) or (E)
OSD letter 3 Nov 1972
BY CLL   NARS, Date 5/20/74

TOP SECRET

7

COPY NO.
255

THE MAKING OF AN EXACT COPY OF THIS MESSAGE IS FORBIDDEN
16—89609-1   GPO

An official record on Allied concern for German records, 1945. (RG 165, War
Department General and Special Staffs, National Archives.)

Historical Research and Archival Policies

The purpose of this paper is to gain a better understanding of the interest and research needs between archivists and historians. This objective is implicit in the title, "Historical Research and Archival Policies." I am mainly concerned about the lack of understanding between these two factions and about the lack of common purpose between what the historian is aiming to achieve and what the archivist is offering.

In my view, the principal purpose of an archivist is to serve a historian. I know there are other purposes that an archivist has in mind; there are other perfectly legitimate consultants of archives other than historians, but I do suggest that the main purpose of an archivist is to serve historical research.

This anxiety of mine is not purely a theoretical product—I have indeed occupied both sides, historian and archivist. And it seems appropriate to mention briefly my own experience of these two sides so that one can draw conclusions based on my observations in these areas.

From soon after the end of the Second World War until fairly recently, I was an official military historian employed by the Cabinet Office in London, and in that capacity, I was the joint author of the *Official History of the Strategic Air Offensive Against Germany.* That experience, of course, gave me several opportunities to observe archivists and the services that they had to offer, since the research for that work was almost entirely primary research. I was concerned almost entirely with documentary sources, both in the United Kingdom and in the United States.

At the beginning of that experience, I was also a part-time member of the staff of the Bodleian Library in Oxford where I had the specific task of arranging the Clarendon Papers, which had been received in the library. These were the papers, not of the famous Lord Clarendon of the Restoration period, but of the third Earl of Clarendon of the second creation, the Earl of Clarendon who was foreign secretary of Great Britian in 1870.

Since 1960, I have been director of the Imperial War Museum in London which, among other great collections, contains three major archives. These archives are the collections of basically private papers of military and civilian leaders who have been concerned with the conduct of war in this century, a huge photographic archive consisting of more than three million photographs, and a film archive which is one of the greatest film archives in the world consisting of over thirty million feet of ciné-film. The above experience will verify that I have had some experience in trying to use archives for historical purposes.

What indeed is the issue between the historian and the archivist? The issue on the archival side may be expressed under three main headings: (1) the *arrangement* of the collections; (2) the *summarization* or calendaring, or indexing, or whatever the policy of that particular archive is with regard to, not only the collections but also the individual items in the collections; and (3) the *finding aids* which the archivist will devise for the benefit of those who use the archive, and this would, of course, be primarily the historian. That is one side of the issue—the archival side.

The other side is the historian's side, and I suggest that his point of view is best expressed by the wish to read freely or to view freely if the archive is visual, among the material which, very broadly—and I emphasize very broadly—is relevant to his field of study.

Now I know that there may well be historians who disagree with me about this definition; they would perhaps seem to lean more in the direction of what I expressed as the archival point of view. They would perhaps stress the importance of being led to the strictly relevant material, and they would no doubt observe that, especially in the twentieth century —and after all, it is the twentieth century with which we are concerned— the sheer volume of material which confronts the historian makes it necessary to devise scientific means of leading him to those parts of huge quantities of records that are relevant to his study.

This is one aspect of the problem that is solved in other people's minds by appointing teams of historians to work together on projects, and by that means, tending to overcome the volume of material which confronts the individual historian, or indeed, any group of historians. Perhaps we need not particularly concern ourselves with the second of those two solutions, namely, the team approach to the writing of history, although this does raise issues that are of great importance. It leaves us with the question of how far the historian can, or even should, be directed to the relevant areas of his research by the archivist.

The Clarendon project, which I mentioned earlier, is an example of what I have in mind. These papers consist of a collection which had been, more or less, sealed up by Clarendon's wife at the time of his death, and subsequently, they had been examined by Sir Herbert Maxwell who wrote an excellent two-volume work on the basis of them. Other than that, no use had been made of the papers. They were very much in the condition in which they had been left by their creator or inheritor, because some of the papers belonged to earlier periods than the life of Lord

Clarendon himself, or they had been rearranged by his wife after his death and perhaps, to a minor extent, by Sir Herbert Maxwell. However, they were essentially in what one might describe as a "working condition."

What was the archivist to do about making these papers available in terms of immediate relevance to the various fields of study that are embraced in that particular collection? Lord Clarendon was a professional diplomat. He was ambassador in Spain during a period of internal upheaval, he was viceroy of Ireland, he was a cabinet minister, he was foreign secretary on several occasions, he was also an aristocrat with interesting society connections, he married a rich heiress who had connections with West Indian sugar planters, and he was at the centre of affairs at times of great international crisis for his country. For example, the period of the Crimea War found him as foreign secretary; the eve of the Franco-Prussian War found him as foreign secretary; he was viceroy of Ireland during the period of mass immigration, or just before the period of mass immigration to the United States; and he was ambassador in Spain during a terrible civil war.

Nevertheless, his papers would throw light on aspects of history far removed from international affairs, war and diplomacy. They would throw considerable light upon the social development of Britain. For example, Clarendon's use of the word "democracy" and his use of the word "liberal" as opposed to "whig," his use of the word "public opinion"—all these phrases and many others in his papers throw light upon the social developments of Britain in those years. His wife's papers, which are also included in the collection, throw considerable light upon the commercial development of the West Indies in the years just before the period covered by the Clarendon Collection proper. The Irish papers are extraordinarily interesting to any student of any aspect of Irish affairs at the middle of the nineteenth century.

What operative factors should the archivist consider in arranging a collection? This was the question that confronted me in looking through the papers and trying to arrange them in a form that would make them readily accessible to scholars. In arranging the papers, one must bear in mind the need for them to be well arranged for all types of historians, or at least, to be arranged in such a way as not unduly to prejudice the interests of historians and others.

In my view, what one is left with is the working arrangement of the papers. In other words, the best way to arrange an archive is to keep it in its working position. A *working position* is simply the position in which the papers were deposited by their creator.

The next aspect that confronted me in the Clarendon Collection was the question of summarizing the papers as a shortcut for historians who wished to see what they contained. Again, the problem is what aspects of the papers would one concentrate upon? Would one choose the papers one considered of the greatest public importance, or of the greatest social importance? In the end one gets perilously close in attempting to summarize the paper to the original length of the paper, which, of course, makes the exercise a self-defeating one.

But description of the character of the papers is a different aspect, namely: was the letter a memorandum, was it a Cabinet paper, a private paper, was it a draft, was it written in Clarendon's own handwriting, was it written in his wife's hand, or was it a copy in an out-letter book? All these questions should be answered very carefully. If it was a letter, its description should consist of the date, sender, addressee, and postmark. All these details should be very carefully recorded and listed.

And on the last question that I mentioned on the archival side, the question of the finding aids, there are, of course, very sophisticated methods now being introduced, of locating items in collections, and it may well be that these methods will, in the future, produce useful results. Today, however, or to use the American expression, "as of now," I do not see great hopes from the historian's point of view concerning these sophisticated methods. Simpler methods than computerized indices seem to be more immediately productive. In the case of a collection of papers, such as the Clarendon Collection, the historian should be shown simply the listing of the papers, their character, and a consolidated description of the work that I described under the second heading, namely, a description of the papers.

Some people will feel that such a policy is a reactionary one, but I should like to consider it now from the other side of the fence and mention a few further arguments pointing in the same direction from my experience as a historian. Working on the *Strategic Air Offensive Against Germany in the Second World War*, one was necessarily, to a very great extent, working in very well accommodated, carefully filed, official papers. But one, of course, was also working with private papers and other sources which were somewhat chaotic in their organization, filing, and description. One was working with former enemy material that was in a yet more chaotic condition because it had been seized by victorious armies and transported to London or Washington or elsewhere in packing cases and often without listing of any description or even without a note as to its provenance. One's experience of using documents was, in these senses, very wide indeed.

One might describe the range as between the British Chiefs of Staff Papers, which were very highly organized numbered papers, each one with a title, and for which complete lists existed of the titles and dates of the papers. That would be one end of the scale.

At the other end of the scale, there were certain parts of the Speer Collection of archives that I discovered in Cadogan Gardens in London, in packing cases in a basement. The chief finding aid one needed for these particular papers was a powerful screwdriver with which to lever off the top of the packing cases. What one found inside could be almost anything.

The questions that I was seeking to resolve by consulting these collections, and I stick to the two examples I have given—the Chiefs of Staff Papers and the Speer Collection—were how far was the policy concerning the strategic air offensive coordinated between the various services? What strategic expectation was there from the bombing offensive? Were the Chiefs of Staff consistent in upholding a steady policy, or did they shift their aims to a marked extent? How far did the British Chiefs of Staff present a united or a divided view to their American counterparts? Were the bombing directives imposed by higher decisions from the Chiefs of Staff or were they rubber-stamped by the Chiefs of Staff on the advice of lower echelons? Those were the sort of questions that one was looking to see the evidence about in those particular areas of one's research.

In the Speer archives, I was looking to try to discover how far the bombing had been effective in terms of, for example, reducing industrial production in Germany, or perhaps affecting the morale of the country, or perhaps in indirect ways such as diverting materials which might have been used on the Russian front to protect Germany from the bombing. Those were the sort of questions that I was examining in the Speer Collection.

I have indicated enough to show the difficulties of leading one to the exact relevant area of operation because the ideas which one is examining are, broadly speaking, philosophical ideas, and philosophical ideas are, broadly speaking, subjective ideas in the sense that they proceed from the consideration in the mind of the particular individual who is coining them, trying to establish them, or disprove them. They are unlikely in their inception, or even in their conception, to be shared by other historians. Still less likely are they to be shared between historians and archivists.

One finds, especially in the field of military studies in the twentieth century, great differences in interpretation simply of the meanings of words, and I do not mean only the classic cases of different interpretations on different sides of the Atlantic. I mean actual obscurity on both sides of the Atlantic with regard to the same words. For example, the word "strategic" is one which commands no very great unanimity of opinion. Then there are other words—like "Point-blank" the code word used during the strategic air offensive—which mean quite different things to different people. So that in terms of finding aids, or archival summaries, these sorts of obscurities would not be merely concealed but rendered more obscure by the attempt to be helpful.

My thesis, which should now be becoming clear, is dependent upon the belief that the pursuit of history from the point of view of the historian is a very personal and subjective problem. I do not believe that the art of history is scientific in the sense of being exact. I believe that the bulk of evidence about the past perishes as it is deposited. I believe that it is as impossible to recreate the past as it is to bring a dead man back to life. I believe that all that is possible for the historian is the discovery of a small amount of the evidence about the past, most of which has perished forever. I think that historical interpretations are more likely to be right because the instinct of the historian is right, rather than because he has assembled and proved his case in the scientific meaning of those words. I believe that in the discovery of what can be discovered about the past, there is always an enormous element of chance, and that this chance concerns not only coming across evidence but also being in the right frame of mind to see its significance. One knows from what one has heard about great scientific discovery how true this thought is in that relationship. I believe it is true also in this one.

Much work of historical genius and many historical inventions are due, not to direct information or evidence or inspiration, but to indirect factors. I believe that apparently irrelevant information may be as useful to a historian as apparently relevant information. It may in some cases be even more useful. So that the chances of discovery and historical progress are very great indeed and should not be underestimated as I believe they frequently are.

The archivist will aspire to be more than a mere storekeeper, and rightly so. But the question is, what should he aspire to be?

Now there are, of course, in the archival profession very important aspects embracing the actual preservation and safekeeping of the material, and these are complex questions which concern an enormous range of issues from, in the case of documentary records, such questions as, should they be mounted or should they be kept loose? Should they be laminated or should they be kept preserved by methods which leave open access to the actual paper? And, in the case of ciné-films, should they be copied onto acetate-based film and, if so, how is one to guard against the risk of shrinkage? In the case of still photographs, should they be microfilmed? Should they be preserved as ordinary negatives? All these questions raise complex and testing problems. But it would perhaps be inappropriate for me to dwell upon those aspects of the problem.

I prefer to stick to what one might broadly describe as the historical aspect of the archivist's problem.

It is easy to express what the solution is and difficult to achieve it. The solution, in my view, is that the archivist should seek to enable the historian to get good browsing access to his collections. The archivist should be able to discuss with the historian the means of best achieving that access. This means the archivist must know a good deal about the collections in his care, and this in turn may be a formidable problem which is, of course, proportionate to the bulk of the material concerned. It is an argument in favor of specialized archives, no doubt an unfashionable view, but one which does argue in favor of a certain degree of subdivision of archival collections. It is also an argument in favor of the archivist going through the collection systematically, noting what its components amount to in terms of the character of the papers as opposed to their actual contents.

In this connection I should like to refer briefly to a great collection of private papers—the collection of the late Sir Basil Liddell Hart. Not surprisingly, there has been a good deal of discussion and, in some of the discussions, I have been consulted about how this important collection of private papers should be dealt with archivally. I do not know what solution has been decided upon; I do not know if the solution has yet been decided upon, but here is the case of a huge collection of papers dealing with an enormous variety of subjects ranging from armoured warfare to women's fashions and religion.

My hope is that the collection will be dealt with by listing and describing each item. This should give browsing access to the historian and provide the archivist with that degree of stocklist which he requires, if only for the security of the collection. I take the view that the historian or philosopher approaching the Liddell Hart Collection will know enough of his subject from having read the secondary sources beforehand—and that, incidentally, is a course of action that I strongly recommend to all historians, and which some of them do not seem to undertake—and will have read his secondary sources sufficiently to know enough about the subject to be able to interpret this straight item list describing the character of the paper to see whether it is likely to be helpful to him or not.

I think that if I may conclude by referring to the even more complex problems confronting the film archivist, that the same principle exactly applies, namely, that one should try to offer the historian or film produ-cer, or television producer, browsing access to the sort of material which is likely to be helpful in providing direct evidence on an issue that concerns him. And this perhaps is best done by using the reel as the unit rather than the scene or sequence in the reel, if only to keep the bulk within manageable proportion. And it is best done, in my view, by fairly general observations about the character of the unit, for example, is it a newsreel item? What year was it made? Is it a reconstructed scene or a genuine action scene? Has it been edited or is it still unedited? Is its quality reasonably clear so that it could be used for various purposes? Can the reel be reproduced perhaps in the form of a still in a book, or shown on a television screen?

Those are the sort of questions which should be recorded about the reel, and they should be sufficient to give the historian, the television producer, or the other users of the film archive the sort of access that is required.

In my view, the historian's requirements are so obscure that it is impos-sible for archivists to meet them in advance. The best that can be done for the historian is to offer him good browsing material. Open the fields to him and see what benefit he will get from grazing in them. I suggest that the archivist's best policy is first to get his collection into the order it was in when it was deposited, and second, to list the items in it describing their *character* but leaving their *contents* as a matter for the historian's decision.

Discussion Summary

In the general discussion Frankland was asked about the British government's policy respecting declassification of World War II records. It was his understanding, he replied, that this called for opening for public use all such records, with a few exceptions, on January 1, 1972. The view of the British government was that the war as a whole should be regarded as a single unit of study and that strict application of the thirty-year rule, opening the records progressively year by year until 1975, would hamper rather than facilitate historical research.

If the archivist should look to the historian as his master, Dean Allard (Division of Naval History) asked, whom then should the historian regard as *his* master? Frankland responded that it must unquestionably be the man of action. One should have sympathy, he thought, for men who exercise great responsibilities, especially in wartime, and strive to make the best decisions they can under the circumstances prevailing and in the light of the information available, only to be descended upon later, when all is over, by well-informed experts bent upon demonstrating where their decisions went wrong. The historian, he believed, should serve the man of action not by antagonizing him but by trying to show the significance of what he had achieved, which perhaps he might not be the most competent person to judge.

Contributors

Selig Adler

Samuel P. Capen Professor of American History at the State University of New York at Buffalo, Dr. Selig Adler graduated from the University of Buffalo and received his doctorate from the University of Illinois. In addition to numerous contributions to historical journals, Dr. Adler is the author of *The Isolationist Impulse,* published in 1957, and *The Uncertain Giant: American Foreign Policy between the Wars,* published in 1965. He is now at work on a volume tentatively entitled *Franklin D. Roosevelt and the Near East.* A contributing editor of the periodical *Judaism,* Dr. Adler is also an honorary life member of the Executive Council of the American Jewish Historical Society.

Albert A. Blum

A graduate of City College of New York, with a doctorate from Columbia University, Prof. Albert A. Blum served briefly with the Office of the Chief of Military History and since 1960 has been on the faculty of Michigan State University, where he is currently professor of Labor History in the School of Labor and Industrial Relations. He has published numerous studies in the fields of labor history and manpower mobilization and a number of articles on the Selective Service System during World War II. His book, *Drafted or Deferred: Practices Past and Present,* was published in 1967 by the University of Michigan's Bureau of Industrial Relations.

Stetson Conn

A graduate of George Washington University, where he earned his M.A. in 1934. Stetson Conn served on the faculties of Yale University and Amherst College before joining the Office of the Chief of Military History in 1946. In 1958 he became chief historian of OCMH, a post he occupied until shortly before his retirement in 1971. Mr. Conn is coauthor of two volumes in the *U. S. Army in World War II* series, *The Framework of Hemisphere Defense* (1960) and *Guarding the United States and Its Outposts* (1964).

Russell H. Fifield

Educated at Bates College and Clark University, Dr. Fifield has been a member of the faculty of the University of Michigan since 1947, serving as professor of political science since 1954. He has been associated in a research or advisory capacity with the Department of State and the East Asian Research Center, Harvard University. His publications include *Woodrow Wilson and the Far East* (1952), *Diplomacy of Southeast Asia, 1945–58* (1958), and *Southeast Asia in U. S. Policy* (1963).

MEYER H. FISHBEIN

Meyer H. Fishbein received his B.S. and M.A. degrees from American University. Joining the staff of the National Archives in 1940, he became chief of its Business and Economics Branch in 1957 and since 1968 has been successively deputy director and director of its Records Appraisal Division. In 1968 he served as director of the Conference on the National Archives and Statistical Research, and he is also editor of the volume *The National Archives and Statistical Research*. His publications include articles in *Social Forces, Business History Review, Labor History,* and the *American Archivist.*

NOBLE FRANKLAND

Educated at Trinity College, Oxford, Dr. Frankland served in the Royal Air Force during World War II. He joined the Air Historical Branch of the Air Ministry in 1948 and became official military historian, Cabinet Office, in 1951. From 1956 to 1960, he was deputy director of studies, Royal Institute of International Affairs, and since 1960 he has been director of the Imperial War Museum. He is author (with Sir Charles Webster) of the four-volume *Strategic Air Offensive against Germany, 1939–1945* and was editor of the *Documents on International Affairs* for 1955, 1956, and 1957.

LLOYD C. GARDNER

A graduate of Ohio Wesleyan University, Lloyd C. Gardner received his Ph.D. from the University of Wisconsin in 1960. Following service in the United States Air Force, 1960–63, he joined the faculty of Rutgers University, where he became full professor in 1968 and chairman of the Department of History in 1970. His publications include *Economic Aspects of New Deal Diplomacy* (1964); *A Different Frontier: Selected Readings in the Foundations of American Economic Expansion* (1966); *Architects of Illusion* (1970); *The Creation of the American Empire,* with Walter LaFeber and Thomas McCormick (1973); and *Looking Backwards: A Reintroduction to American History,* with William O'Neill (1974).

JOSEPH HOWERTON

Joseph Howerton did his undergraduate work at the University of Richmond and George Washington University and has done graduate work at American University. Upon joining the staff of the National Archives, he worked initially with records of the Navy Department and more recently has specialized in the records of agencies and departments concerned with labor, transportation, social services, business, and economics.

D. CLAYTON JAMES

D. Clayton James received his M.A. and Ph.D. degrees from the University of Texas and since 1965 has been a member of the faculty of Mississippi State University, where he is professor of history. He has contributed articles and reviews to various historical journals, including the *American Historical Review, Journal of American History, Journal of Southern History,* and *Military Affairs.* He is the author of *Antebellum Natchez* (1968) and *The Years of MacArthur, 1880-1941,* Vol. 1, (1970), and he edited *South to Bataan, North to Mukden: The Prison Diary of Brigadier General W. E. Brougher* (1971). *The Years of MacArthur, 1941–1945,* Vol. 2, is in press, and he is working on the third volume of that biography. He has been a visiting lecturer at the Army War College and various universities.

ROBERT W. KRAUSKOPF

A graduate of Indiana University with an M.A. and Ph.D. from Georgetown University, Robert Krauskopf joined the staff of the National Archives in 1948, serving successively in the War Records Division and the Records Appraisal Division. In 1966 he was appointed director of the Modern Military Records Division and in 1971 became director of the Old Military Records Division. He has contributed articles and reviews to the *American Archivist* and *Military Affairs.*

HENRI MICHEL

Henri Michel, director of research at the National Center for Scientific Research, Paris, for more than twenty years has been secretary-general of the *Comité d'Histoire de la 2ème guerre mondiale,* serving as editor of the well-known *Revue d'Histoire de la 2ème guerre mondiale.* Since 1970 he has been president of the *Comité International d'Histoire de la 2ème guerre mondiale,* whose membership extends to thirty countries. He has contributed to numerous French and foreign journals, and his publications include *Les courants de pensée de la Résistance* (1962), *Biblio-graphie critique de la Résistance* (1964), *Jean Moulin, l'unificateur* (1964), *La guerre de l'ombre* (1970), and *La drôle de guerre* (1972). His two-volume work *La Seconde guerre mondiale* (1968–69) received the grand prize for history of the Académie française.

LOUIS MORTON

Daniel Webster Professor and professor of history at Dartmouth College, Louis Morton was educated in New York City and received his doctorate from Duke University. He began his teaching career at City College of New York, then served as research associate in history at Colonial Williamsburg before entering the military service in 1941. That year his first volume, *Robert Carter of Nomini Hall: A Tobacco Planter of the 18th Century,* was published by the Princeton Press. After service with the United States Army in the Pacific Theater, he joined the army's military history office where he served first as chief of the Pacific Section and then as deputy chief historian, Department of the Army. During this period, he supervised the preparation of the twelve-volume series of the official army history of World War II, *The War in the Pacific.* Two of these volumes, *The Fall of the Philippines* and *Strategy and Command,* he wrote himself. He is also author or coauthor of a number of other works, including *Command Decisions in World War II, Total War and Cold War, Schools for Strategy, The Historian and the Diplomat,* as well as numerous articles and reviews. He is also general editor of the seventeen-volume Macmillan series, *Wars and Military Institutions of the United States,* nine volumes of which have been published to date. In 1959, he was awarded the coveted Rockefeller Public Service Award and the following year joined the faculty of Dartmouth College, where he has served as provost and is currently chairman of its Department of History.

JAMES E. O'NEILL

James E. O'Neill graduated from the University of Detroit and received his Ph.D. in history from the University of Chicago. He served on the faculties of the University of Notre Dame and Loyola University and was a specialist in the Library of Congress, 1963–65. In 1969 he became director of the Franklin D. Roosevelt Library and in 1972 deputy archivist of the United States. He has published articles in a number of journals, including the *Journal of American History, Victorian Studies, Catholic Historical Review, South Atlantic Quarterly,* and the *American Archivist.*

CARROLL PURSELL

A graduate of the University of California, Carroll Pursell received his M.A. at the University of Delaware and his Ph.D. at Berkeley. He taught first at Case Institute of Technology and, since 1966, has been on the faculty of the University of California, Santa Barbara. He is the author of *Early Stationary Steam Engines in America* and coeditor of *Technology in Western Civilization* and *The Politics of American Science* and has published articles in *Isis, Technology and Culture, Agricultural History,* the *Smithsonian Journal of History,* and *Proceedings of the American Philosophical Society.*

BARBARA W. TUCHMAN

Barbara Wertheim Tuchman received her B.A. from Radcliffe College in 1933. She served as a research assistant for the Institute of Pacific Relations in New York and Tokyo, 1934–35, and was an editorial assistant and staff writer for the *Nation,* 1936–38. She became American correspondent for the *New Statesman and Nation* in 1939 and served with the Office of War Information, 1944–45. Her books include The *Zimmerman Telegram* (1958), *The Guns of August* (1962) (Pulitzer Prize, 1963), *The Proud Tower* (1966), and *Stilwell and the American Experience in China* (1971) (Pulitzer Prize, 1972). She is a contributor to *Harper's,* the *Atlantic, New York Times Magazine, Saturday Review,* and other journals. She was elected to the American Academy of Arts and Letters in 1972 and has received honorary degrees from numerous colleges and universities.

RUDOLPH A. WINNACKER

A native of Germany, Dr. Winnacker graduated from the University of Wisconsin and received his doctorate from Harvard University in 1933. After serving on the faculties of the University of Michigan and the University of Nebraska, he joined the O.S.S. in 1941, working in its Research and Analysis Branch in Washington and overseas. In 1945 he became a historian in the War Department's Historical Division and, since 1949, has been chief historian of the Office of the Secretary of Defense. He is a member of the National Historical Publications Commission and has contributed articles and reviews to numerous historical journals.

PAVEL ANDREYEVICH ZHILIN

Director of the Institute of Military History, Ministry of Defense,

USSR, since 1966, and a corresponding member of the USSR Academy of Sciences, General Zhilin is well known as a writer, lecturer, and military historian. His degrees include that of Doctor of Historical Sciences, and he has received the Order of the Red Banner of Labor. He has served as deputy chief editor of the *Military Historical Journal* (*Voyenno-Istoricheskiy Zhurnal*). In addition to numerous articles, he is the author of *Kutuzov's Counter-Offensive, 1812* (1951), which was awarded the Stalin Prize. He also has edited a volume entitled *Fateful Decisions* (*Rokovyye Resheniya*), concerning significant events in World War II.

BENEDICT K. ZOBRIST

Dr. Zobrist earned his M.A. and Ph.D. degrees in history at Northwestern University and has carried out postdoctoral study at the East Asian Institute of Columbia University, the University of Illinois, and Tunghai University, Taiwan. After serving with the Manuscript Division of the Library of Congress, the Newberry Library of Chicago, and Augustana College, where he was professor of history, associate dean of the faculty, and director of graduate studies, Dr. Zobrist joined the Harry S. Truman Library in 1969. He became director of the library in 1971.

Bibliography

For many years the National Archives and Records Service has produced descriptive and other types of finding aids to facilitate the use of its record holdings by both staff members and the general public. Some of these finding aids have been issued as National Archives publications; others remain in an unpublished state pending refinement or other revision. Those published finding aids currently available relating wholly or in part to official records and other materials on the Second World War period, are listed below. In addition to these materials, the National Archives and Records Service since 1969 has published *Prologue: The Journal of the National Archives,* which includes in each issue useful references to new accessions and new publications and to the progress of the records declassification program initiated in 1971.

National Archives Guides and Reference Information Papers

GUIDES

Guide to the Records in the National Archives. 1948. 684 p. (New edition in press.)
Federal Records of World War II. Civilian Agencies, Vol. 1. 1950. 1073 p. *Military Agencies,* Vol. 2. 1951. 1,061 p.

RIPs (Reference Information Papers)

The Historical Programs of the Civilian Government Agencies during World War II. RIP no. 43. 1952. 117 p.
The Middle East. Compiled by Elizabeth H. Buck. RIP no. 44. 1955. 96 p.
Rumania. Compiled by James S. Vivian. RIP no. 46. 1970. 18 p.
The Russian Empire and the Soviet Union. Compiled by Elizabeth H. Buck. RIP no. 41. 77 p.

NATIONAL ARCHIVES INVENTORIES AND SPECIAL LISTS

RECORDS OF THE LEGISLATIVE BRANCH

UNITED STATES SENATE (RG [RECORD GROUP] 46)

Preliminary Inventory of the Records of Certain Committees of the Senate Investigating the Disposal of Surplus Property. 1945–48. Compiled by George P. Perros and Toussaint L. Prince. PI no. 59. 1953. 24 p.

Preliminary Inventory of the Records of the Senate Committee on Education and Labor: Subcommittee on Wartime Health and Education, 1943–46. Compiled by George P. Perros. PI no. 42. 1952. 11 p.

Preliminary Inventory of the Records of the Special Committee of the Senate on Atomic Energy, 1945–46. Compiled by George P. Perros. PI no. 62. 1953. 8 p.

Preliminary Inventory of the Records of the Special Committee of the Senate to Investigate the National Defense Program, 1941–48. Compiled by Harold E. Hufford and Toussaint L. Prince. PI no. 48. 1952. 227 p.

Preliminary Inventory of the Records of the Special Committee of the Senate to Investigate Petroleum Resources, 1944–46. Compiled by George P. Perros. PI no. 61. 1953. 19 p.

Preliminary Inventory of the Records of the United States Senate. Compiled by Harold E. Hufford and Watson G. Caudill. PI no. 23. 1950. 284 p.

UNITED STATES HOUSE OF REPRESENTATIVES (RG 233)

Preliminary Inventory of the Records of Certain Committees of the House of Representatives Investigating the Disposal of Surplus Property, 1946–48. Compiled by George P. Perros. PI no. 65. 1954. 21 p.

Preliminary Inventory of the Records of the Select Committee of the House of Representatives Investigating National Defense Migration, 1940–43. Compiled by George P. Perros. PI no. 71. 1954. 30 p.

Preliminary Inventory of the Records of the Select Committee of the House of Representatives on Post-War Military Policy, 1944–46. Compiled by George P. Perros. PI no. 70. 1954. 6 p.

Preliminary Inventory of the Records of the United States House of Representatives, 1789-1946. Compiled by Buford Rowland, Handy B. Fant, and Harold E. Hufford. PI no. 113. 2 vols. 1959. 587 p.

RECORDS OF THE EXECUTIVE BRANCH, PRESIDENTIAL AGENCIES

PRESIDENTIAL COMMITTEES, COMMISSION, AND BOARDS (RG 220)
Preliminary Inventory of the Records of the American War Production Mission in China. Compiled by John E. Maddox. PI no. 88. 1955. 10 p.
Preliminary Inventory of the Records of the War Refugee Board. Compiled by Henry T. Ulasek and Ira N. Kellogg, Jr. PI no. 43. 1952. 6 p.

OFFICE OF GOVERNMENT REPORTS (RG 44)
Preliminary Inventory of the Records of the Office of Government Reports. Compiled by H. Stephen Helton. PI no. 35. 1951. 106 p.

RECORDS OF THE EXECUTIVE BRANCH, DEPARTMENT OF STATE

GENERAL RECORDS OF THE DEPARTMENT OF STATE (RG 59)
Preliminary Inventory of the General Records of the Department of State. Compiled by Daniel T. Goggin and H. Stephen Helton. PI no. 157. 1963. 311 p.

FOREIGN SERVICE POSTS, STATE DEPARTMENT (RG 84)
List of Foreign Service Post Records in the National Archives. Compiled by Mark G. Eckhoff and Alexander P. Marvo. Revised by Mario Fenyo and John Highbarger. SL no. 9. Revised 1967. 35 p.

RECORDS OF THE EXECUTIVE BRANCH, DEPARTMENT OF DEFENSE
DEPARTMENT OF THE ARMY: Staff Offices

OFFICE OF THE CHIEF OF FINANCE (RG 203)
Preliminary Inventory of the Records of the Office of the Chief of Finance (Army). Compiled by Richard W. Giroux. Revised by Maizie H. Johnson. PI no. 142. 1962. 17 p.

OFFICE OF THE CHIEF SIGNAL OFFICER (RG 111)
Preliminary Inventory of the Records of the Office of the Chief Signal Officer. Compiled by Mabel Deutrich. PI no. 155. 1963. 26 p.

CHEMICAL WARFARE SERVICE (RG 175)
Preliminary Inventory of the Records of the Chemical Warfare Service. Compiled by Raymond P. Flynn. PI no. 8. 1948. 5 p.

DEPARTMENT OF THE NAVY: Staff Offices and Bureaus

OFFICE OF THE CHIEF OF NAVAL OPERATIONS (RG 38)
Preliminary Inventory of the Cartographic Records of the Office of the Chief of Naval Operations. Compiled by Charlotte M. Ashby. PI no. 85. 1955. 17 p.

U. S. MARINE CORPS (RG 127)
Records of the U. S. Marine Corps. National Archives Inventory No. 2. Compiled by Maizie Johnson. 1970. 90 p.

BUREAU OF MEDICINE AND SURGERY (RG 52)
Preliminary Inventory of the Records of the Bureau of Medicine and Surgery. Compiled by Kenneth F. Bartlett. PI no. 6. 1948. 18 p.

BUREAU OF ORDNANCE (RG 74)
Preliminary Inventory of the Records of the Bureau of Ordnance. Compiled by William F. Shonkwiler. PI no. 33. 1951. 33 p.

BUREAU OF SHIPS (RG 19)
Preliminary Inventory of the Records of the Bureau of Ships. Compiled by Elizabeth Bethel et al. PI no. 133. 1961. 241 p.

BUREAU OF YARDS AND DOCKS (RG 71)
Preliminary Inventory of the Records of the Bureau of Yards and Docks. Compiled by Richard G. Wood. PI no. 10. 1948. 28 p.

BUREAU OF NAVAL PERSONNEL (RG 24)
Preliminary Inventory of the Records of the Bureau of Naval Personnel. Compiled by Virgil E. Baugh. PI no. 123. 1960. 135 p.

HYDROGRAPHIC OFFICE (RG 37)
Inventory of the Records of the Hydrographic Office. National Archives Inventory No. 4. Compiled by Maizie Johnson and William J. Heynen. 1971. 28 p.

BUREAU OF AERONAUTICS (RG 72)
Preliminary Inventory of the Records of the Bureau of Aeronautics. Compiled by William F. Shonkwiler. PI no. 26. 1951. 9 p.

Commands and Installations
NAVAL DISTRICTS AND SHORE ESTABLISHMENTS (RG 181)

Preliminary Inventory of the Records of Naval Establishments Created Overseas during World War II. Compiled by Richard G. Wood. PI no. 13. 1948. 8 p.

RECORDS OF THE EXECUTIVE BRANCH, DEPARTMENT OF THE INTERIOR

OFFICE OF THE TERRITORIES (RG 126)
Preliminary Inventory of the Records of the Office of Territories. Compiled by Richard S. Maxwell and Evans Walker. PI no. 154. 1963. 117 p.
Preliminary Inventory of the Records of the Office of the U. S. High Commissioner to the Philippine Islands. Compiled by Richard S. Maxwell. PI no. 151. 1963. 24 p.

Discontinued Agencies
SOLID FUELS ADMINISTRATION FOR WAR (RG 245)
Preliminary Inventory of the Records of the Solid Fuels Administration for War. Compiled by Edward F. Martin. PI no. 34. 1951. 31 p.

RECORDS OF THE EXECUTIVE BRANCH, POST OFFICE DEPARTMENT

RECORDS OF THE POST OFFICE DEPARTMENT (RG 28)
Preliminary Inventory of the Records of the Post Office Department. Compiled by Arthur Hecht et al. Revised by Forrest R. Holdcamper. PI no. 168. 1967. 54 p.

RECORDS OF THE EXECUTIVE BRANCH, DEPARTMENT OF AGRICULTURE

OFFICE OF THE SECRETARY OF AGRICULTURE (RG 16)
Preliminary Inventory of the Records of the Office for Agricultural War Relations. Compiled by Harold T. Pinkett. PI no. 37. 1952. 19 p.

Discontinued Agencies
OFFICE OF LABOR (WAR FOOD ADMINISTRATION) (RG 224)
Preliminary Inventory of the Records of the Office of Labor of the War Food Administration. Compiled by Harold T. Pinkett. PI no. 51. 1953. 18 p.

RECORDS OF THE EXECUTIVE BRANCH, DEPARTMENT OF LABOR

WAGE ADJUSTMENT BOARD (RG 236)
Preliminary Inventory of the Records of the Wage Adjustment Board.
Compiled by Leonard Rapport. PI no. 72. 1954. 9 p.

RECORDS OF THE EXECUTIVE BRANCH, DEPARTMENT OF HOUSING AND URBAN DEVELOPMENT

GENERAL RECORDS OF THE DEPARTMENT OF HOUSING AND URBAN DEVELOPMENT (RG 207)
Preliminary Inventory of the General Records of the Housing and Home Finance Agency. Compiled by Katherine H. Davidson. PI no. 164. 1965. 28 p.

RECORDS OF THE EXECUTIVE BRANCH, INDEPENDENT AGENCIES

FEDERAL COMMUNICATIONS COMMISSION (RG 173)
Preliminary Inventory of the Records of the Federal Communications Commission. Compiled by Albert W. Winthrop. PI no. 93. 1948. 21 p.
FEDERAL TRADE COMMISSION (RG 122)
Preliminary Inventory of the Records of the Federal Trade Commission. Compiled by Estelle Rebec. PI no. 7. 1948. 7 p.
SELECTIVE SERVICE SYSTEM, 1940–(RG 147)
Preliminary Inventory of the Records of the Selective Service Systems, 1940–1947. Compiled by Richard G. Wood. PI no. 27. 1951. 53 p.

Discontinued Agencies—1933–50

COMMITTEE FOR CONGESTED PRODUCTION AREAS (RG 212)
Calendar of Negro-Related Documents in the Records of the Committee for Congested Production Areas in the National Archives. Compiled by Elaine C. Bennett for the Committee on Negro Studies of the American Council of Learned Societies. 1949. 100 p.
Preliminary Inventory of the Records of the Committee for Congested Production Areas. Compiled by Leo Pascal and Jeanne McDonald. PI no. 128. 1960. 16 p.

COMMITTEE ON FAIR EMPLOYMENT PRACTICE (RG 228)

Preliminary Inventory of the Records of the Committee on Fair Employment Practice. Compiled by Charles Zaid. PI no. 147. 1962. 50 p.
FOREIGN BROADCAST INTELLIGENCE SERVICE (RG 262)
Preliminary Inventory of the Records of the Foreign Broadcast Intelligence Service. Compiled by Walter W. Weinstein. PI no. 115. 1959. 53 p.

FOREIGN ECONOMIC ADMINISTRATION (RG 169)
Preliminary Inventory of the Records of the Foreign Economic Administration. Compiled by H. Stephen Helton. PI no. 29. 1951. 180 p.

NATIONAL WAR LABOR BOARD (WW II) (RG 202)
List of Wage Stabilization Cases Acted on by the Headquarters Office of the National War Labor Board, 1942–45. Pt. 1: Cases Arranged by Issue Involved, Pt. 2: *Cases Arranged by Industry Involved.* Compiled by Estelle Rebec, Arthur Hecht, and Paul Flynn. SL no. 10. 1953. 162 p.
Preliminary Inventory of the Records of the National War Labor Board (World War II). Compiled by Estelle Rebec. PI no. 78. 1955. 188 p.

OFFICE OF CENSORSHIP (RG 216)
Preliminary Inventory of the Records of the Office of Censorship. Compiled by Henry T. Ulasek. PI no. 54. 1953. 16 p.

OFFICE OF COMMUNITY WAR SERVICES (RG 215)
Preliminary Inventory of the Records of the Office of Community War Services. Compiled by Estelle Rebec. PI no. 132. 1960. 28 p.

OFFICE OF EMERGENCY MANAGEMENT (RG 214)
Preliminary Inventory of the Records of the Office for Emergency Management. Compiled by Henry T. Ulasek. PI no. 92. 1956. 20 p.

OFFICE OF INTER-AMERICAN AFFAIRS (RG 229)
Preliminary Inventory of the Records of the Office of Inter-American Affairs. Compiled by H. Stephen Helton. PI no. 41. 1952. 138 p.

OFFICE OF PRICE ADMINISTRATION (RG 188)

Preliminary Inventory of the Records of the Accounting Department of the Office of Price Administration. Compiled by Meyer H. Fishbein and Elaine C. Bennett. PI no. 32. 1951. 108 p.

Preliminary Inventory of the Records of the Enforcement Department of the Office of Price Administration. Compiled by Meyer H. Fishbein and Betty R. Bucher. PI no. 120. 1959. 65 p.

Preliminary Inventory of the Records of the Information Department of the Office of Price Administration. Compiled by Betty R. Bucher, PI no. 119. 1959. 53 p.

Preliminary Inventory of the Records of the Price Department of the Office of Price Administration. Compiled by Meyer H. Fishbein, Walter W. Weinstein, and Albert W. Winthrop. PI no. 95. 1956. 272 p.

Preliminary Inventory of the Records of the Rationing Department of the Office of Price Administration. Compiled by Meyer H. Fishbein et al. PI no. 102. 1958. 175 p.

OFFICE OF WAR INFORMATION (RG 208)

Preliminary Inventory of the Records of the Office of War Information. Compiled by H. Stephen Helton. PI no. 56. 1953. 149 p.

Special List of Photographs Made by the Office of War Information at the United Nations Conference on International Organization, San Francisco, 1945. Compiled by Emma B. Haas, Anne Harris, and Thomas W. Ray. SL no. 11. 1953. 40 p.

OFFICE OF WAR MOBILIZATION AND RECONVERSION (RG 250)

Preliminary Inventory of the Records of the Office of War Mobilization and Reconversion. Compiled by Homer L. Calkin. PI no. 25. 1951. 156 p.

PETROLEUM ADMINISTRATION FOR WAR (RG 253)

Preliminary Inventory of the Records of the Petroleum Administration for War. Compiled by James R. Fuchs and Albert Whimpey. PI no. 31. 1951. 152 p.

PRICE DECONTROL BOARD (RG 251)

Preliminary Inventory of the Records of the Price Decontrol Board. Compiled by James J. Fleischmann and Victor Gondos, Jr. PI no. 46. 1952. 4 p.

R<small>ETRAINING AND</small> R<small>EEMPLOYMENT</small> A<small>DMINISTRATION</small> (RG 244)
Preliminary Inventory of the Records of the Retraining and Reemployment Administration. Compiled by Thayer M. Boardman. PI no. 28. 1951. 17 p.
S<small>HIPBUILDING</small> S<small>TABILIZATION</small> C<small>OMMITTEE</small> (RG 254)
Preliminary Inventory of the Records of the Shipbuilding Stabilization Committee. Compiled by Leo Pascal. PI no. 121. 1958. 40 p.
S<small>MALLER</small> W<small>AR</small> P<small>LANTS</small> C<small>ORPORATION</small> (RG 240)
Preliminary Inventory of the Records of the Smaller War Plants Corporation. Compiled by Katherine H. Davidson. PI no. 160. 1964. 87 p.
U. S. W<small>AR</small> B<small>ALLOT</small> C<small>OMMISSION</small> (RG 230)
Preliminary Inventory of the Records of the United States War Ballot Commission. Compiled by Robert W. Krauskopf. PI no. 24. 1951. 4 p.

W<small>AR</small> P<small>RODUCTION</small> B<small>OARD</small> (RG 179)
Preliminary Inventory of the Records of the War Production Board. Compiled by Fred G. Halley and Josef C. James. PI no. 15. 1948. 59 p.

W<small>AR</small> R<small>ELOCATION</small> A<small>UTHORITY</small> (RG 210)
Preliminary Inventory of the Records of the War Relocation Authority. Compiled by Estelle Rebec and Martin Rogin. PI no. 77. 1955. 45 p.

W<small>AR</small> S<small>HIPPING</small> A<small>DMINISTRATION</small> (RG 248)
Preliminary Inventory of the Records of the War Shipping Administration. Compiled by Allen M. Ross. PI no. 30. 1951. 35 p.

W<small>ORLD</small> W<small>AR</small> II W<small>AR</small> C<small>RIMES</small> R<small>ECORDS</small> (RG 238)
Preliminary Inventory of the Records of the United Counsel for the Prosecution of Axis Criminality. Compiled by Fred G. Halley. PI no. 21. 1949. 182 p.

R<small>ECORDS OF OR</small> R<small>ELATING TO</small> O<small>THER</small> G<small>OVERNMENTS</small>

N<small>ATIONAL</small> A<small>RCHIVES</small> C<small>OLLECTION OF</small> F<small>OREIGN</small> R<small>ECORDS</small>
S<small>EIZED</small>, 1941–(RG 242)
Index of Microfilmed Records of the German Foreign Ministry and the Reich's Chancellery Covering the Weimar Period. 1958. 95 p. Available on Microfilm Publication T407, $5.

Supplement to the Guide to Captured German Documents,1959, 69 p. Original prepared by Gerhard L. Weinberg and the War Documentation Project Staff. Published by the Air University. 1952.

Guides to German Records Microfilmed at Alexandria, Va. (Distribution restricted to institutions, but Guides 1–56 are available as Microfilm Publication T733.

  1. *Records of the Reich Ministry of Economics.* 1958. 75 p.
  2. *Office of the Reich Commissioner for the Strengthening of Germandom.* 1958. 15 p.
  3. *Records of the National Socialist German Labor Party.* 1958. 141 p.
  4. *Records of the Organization Todt.* 1958. 2 p.
  5. *Miscellaneous German Records Collection, Pt. 1.* 1958. 15 p.
  6. *Records of Nazi Cultural and Research Institutions and Records pertaining to Axis Relations and Interests in the Far East.* 1959. 161 p.
  7. *Records of Headquarters, German Armed Forces High Command, Pt. 1.* 1959. 222 p.
  8. *Miscellaneous German Records Collection, Pt. 2.* 1959. 203 p.
  9. *Records of Private German Individuals.* 1959. 23 p.
 10. *Records of the Reich Ministry for Armaments and War Production.* 1959. 109 p.
 11. *Fragmentary Records of Miscellaneous Reich Ministries and Offices.* 1959. 19 p.
 12. *Records of Headquarters of the German Army High Command, Pt. 1.* 1959. 19 p.
 13. *Records of the Reich Air Ministry.* 1959. 34 p.
 14. *Records of the German Field Commands: Armies, Pt. 1.* 1959. 61 p.
 15. *Records of Former German and Japanese Embassies and Consulates, 1890–1945.* 1960. 63 p.
 16. *Records of the Deutsches Ausland-Institut, Stuttgart, Pt. 1: Records on Resettlement.* 1960. 105 p.
 17. *Records of Headquarters, German Armed Forces High Command, Pt. 2.* 1960. 213 p.
 18. *Records of Headquarters, German Armed Forces High Command, Pt. 3.* 1960. 118 p.
 19. *Records of Headquarters, German Armed Forces High Command, Pt. 4.* 1960. 76 p.
 20. *Records of the National Socialist German Labor Party, Pt. 2.* 1960. 45 p.

21. *Records of the Deutsches Ausland-Institut. Stuttgart, Pt. 2: The General Records.* 1961. 180 p.
22. *Records of the Reich Ministry for Public Enlightenment and Propaganda.* 1961. 41 p.
23. *Records of Private Austrian, Dutch, and German Enterprises, 1917–46.* 1961. 119 p.
24. *Records of Headquarters of the German Air Force High Command.* 1961. 59 p.
25. *German Air Force Records: Luftgaukommandos, Flak, Deutsche Luftwaffenmission in Rumanien.* 1961. 34 p.
26. *Records of Reich Office for Soil Exploration.* 1961. 11 p.
27. *Miscellaneous SS Records: Einwandererzentralstelle, Waffen-SS, and SS-Oberabschnitte.* 1961. 34 p.
28. *Records of the Reich Ministry for the Occupied Eastern Territories, 1941–45.* 1961. 60 p.
29. *Records of Headquarters, German Army High Command, Pt. 2.* 1961. 154 p.
30. *Records of Headquarters, German Army High Command, Pt. 3.* 1961. 212 p.
31. *Records of the Office of the Reich Commissioner for the Baltic States, 1941–45.* 1961. 19 p.
32. *Records of the Reich Leader of the SS and Chief of the German Police, Pt. 1.* 1961. 165 p.
33. *Records of the Reich Leader of the SS and Chief of the German Police, Pt. 2.* 1961. 89 p.
34. *Records of German Army Areas.* 1962. 234 p.
35. *Records of the National Socialist German Labor Party, Pt. 3.* 1962. 29 p.
36. *Miscellaneous German Records Collection, Pt. 3.* 1962. 61 p.
37. *Records of Headquarters, German Navy High Command (OKM).* 1962. 5 p.
38. *Records of German Field Commands: Rear Areas, Occupied Territories, and Others.* 1963. 200 p.
39. *Records of the Reich Leader of the SS and Chief of the German Police, Pt. 3.* 1963. 198 p.
40–66. Records of German Field Commands:
40. *Army Groups, Pt. 1.* 1964. 126 p.
41. *Divisions, Pt. 1.* 1964. 160 p.
42. *Armies, Pt. 2.* 1964. 110 p.
43. *Armies Pt. 3.* 1964. 108 p.
44. *Armies Pt. 4.* 1964. 96 p.

45. *Divisions, Pt. 2.* 1964. 118 p.
46. *Corps, Pt. 1.* 1965. 156 p.
47. *Armies, Pt. 5.* 1965. 162 p.
48. *Armies, Pt. 6.* 1965. 85 p.
49. *Armies, Pt. 7.* 1965. 124 p.
50. *Armee-Abteilungen.* 1966. 45 p.
51. *Panzer Armies, Pt. 1.* 1966. 112 p.
52. *Army Groups, Pt. 2.* 1966. 139 p.
53. *Panzer Armies, Pt. 2.* 1967. 160 p.
54. *Armies, Pt. 8.* 1967. 132 p.
55. *Corps, Pt. 2.* 1967. 150 p.
56. *Armies, Pt. 9.* 1968. 166 p.
57. *Rear Areas, Occupied Territories, and Others, Pt. 2.* 1968. 25 p.
58. *Corps, Pt. 3.* 1968. 84 p.
59. *Corps, Pt. 4.* 1968. 144 p.
60. *Corps, Pt. 5.* 1968. 124 p.
61. *Corps, Pt. 6.* 1969. 186 p.
62. *Corps, Pt. 7.* 1970. 233 p.
63. *Divisions, Pt. 3.* 1970. 143 p.
64. *Divisions, Pt. 4.* 1970. 141 p.
65. *Divisions, Pt. 5.* 1970. 143 p.
66. *Divisions, Pt. 6.* 1972. 177 p.

Guide to Records of the Italian Armed Forces: Pt. 1, 1967. 146 p. *Pt. 2*, 1967, 133 p. *Pt. 3*, 1967. 170 p.

Guide to the Collection of Hungarian Political and Military Records, 1909–45. 1972. 20 p.

Other National Archives Holdings

Audiovisual Records in the National Archives Relating to World War II. Compiled by Mayfield S. Bray and William T. Murphy. 1971. 52 p.

The Programs and Cartographic Records of United States Mapping and Charting Operations in the Second World War. Compiled by Patrick D. McLaughlin. 1971. 8p.

Select List of Sound Recordings: Voices of World War II, 1937–1945.
    1971. 15 p.
United States Navy Ships, 1775–1941. 1971. 14 p.

Publications of the Presidential Libraries

Historical Materials in the Franklin D. Roosevelt Library. 1973. 16 p.

INDEX

September 1945: Japanese representatives signing the instrument of surrender on the U.S.S. Missouri in Tokyo Bay. (U.S. Navy; National Archives, no. 80-G-700777.)